Carnival to Catwalk

Carnival to Catwalk

Global Reflections on Fancy Dress Costume

Benjamin Linley Wild

BLOOMSBURY VISUAL ARTS

LONDON • NEW YORK • OXFORD • NEW DELHI • SYDNEY

BLOOMSBURY VISUAL ARTS
Bloomsbury Publishing Plc
50 Bedford Square, London, WC1B 3DP, UK
1385 Broadway, New York, NY 10018, USA

BLOOMSBURY, BLOOMSBURY VISUAL ARTS and the Diana logo are trademarks of
Bloomsbury Publishing Plc

First published in Great Britain 2020

Cover design by Adriana Brioso
Cover image © Helen Levitt Film Documents LLC. All rights reserved.
Courtesy of Thomas Zander Gallery, Köln.

A catalogue record for this book is available from the British Library.

A catalog record for this book is available from the Library of Congress.

ISBN: HB: 978-1-3500-1499-2
          PB: 978-1-3500-2469-4
          ePDF: 978-1-3500-1500-5
          eBook: 978-1-3500-1501-2

Typeset by Integra Software Services Pvt. Ltd.
Printed and bound in India

To find out more about our authors and books visit www.bloomsbury.com
and sign up for our newsletters.

Where music flows and beauty beams,
Where myth and magic rule the hour –
Yea, myth and magic – see where pour,
Through dome, and hall, and corridor,
Kings, queens, and warriors, and sages,
That were, in dim historic ages,
The fashions too of every clime,
of every taste, and every time;
Save one – that one ye may believe,
Which Adam and our Mother Eve,
in Eden's guilty bower did weave.
Save this, most every garb is here,
from either world and hemisphere,
The wild, the warlike, and the gay,
In mix'd, bewild'ring disarray.

Comus, Grand Fancy Dress Ball, Royal Pavillion Brighton
(Brighton: Tucknott, 1871), 13.

CONTENTS

LIST OF ILLUSTRATIONS

ACKNOWLEDGEMENTS

The nature and scope of this book has meant that I have wandered far, chronologically, geographically and culturally. All long journeys rely on the support of others and in crossing new frontiers I have received the support of many people, each of whom has enriched my expedition. Of course, however clear the directions and travel guidance, rovers can still get lost or choose to navigate their own way. The muddles and omissions – wrong turns or cul-de-sacs, to perpetuate this metaphor – that do remain are therefore my fault alone (although, I might concede, worth it for the views). In particular, I want to thank Kristofer Allerfeldt, Sophie Ambler, Jeremy Angel, Bruce Asbestos, Stephen Bartley, Charles Bazalgette, Mary Beard, Beatrice Behlen, Anna Beer, Paul Bench, Matthew Bird, Andy Bruening, Tom Brimelow, Holly Bruce, Anna Buruma, Harriet Cant, Paul Carling, Amy Cartwright, Richard Cassidy, Georgina Clapham, Herbert M. Cole, Margaret Coombe, Marilyn Corrie, James Coulbault, Anja Aronowsky Cronberg, John Crouch, James Curtis, Kassia St Clair, Stefan Dickens, Emma Drake, Rachel Fallon, Ramzi Fawaz, Patrick Francis, Pipa Francis, Elisabeth Frank, Phyllis Galembo, Jacqueline Glomski, Håkan Groth, Rachel Hassall, Nick Henderson, Levi Higgs, Jamie Huckbody, Reemé Idris, Zapher Idris, Lindsay Jamieson, Jennifer Johnstone, Glynis Jones, Anders Kloster, Christian Kloster, Shayne Kopec, Marcia D.B. Levy, Timothy Long, Dominic Luckett, Ronnie Marshall, Scott McKinnon, Pamela Mitchell, Robin Muir, Sofia Nestor, Becka Noels, Elizabeth Owen, Tom Payne, Rebecca de Pelet, Helen Przibilla, Deagal Remyr, Giles Reynolds, Jamie Robinson, Philip Rogerson, Ruth Rogerson, Lindsay Schober, Nina Schönig, Lee Self, Sophie Stewart, Ben Street, George Tatham, Annette Timm, Frank Trentmann, Anne-Marie Van de Ven, Vivian Vassar, Alex Watson, Björn Weiler, Clayton Whisnaut, Andrew Wilkie, Martin Williams, James Winter and Frank Wittendorfer. The support and sagacity of Lucy Clayton, 'Queen of Fancy Dress' and co-host of Dress: Fancy Podcast, has helped me to clarify ideas. At Bloomsbury, Pari Thomson was a reliable source of help in the early stages of the project; Yvonne Thouroude in the latter stages. Throughout, my editor Frances Arnold has been a much-needed source of kindness and encouragement. Amy de la Haye was kind enough to read parts of the book in draft form. The anonymous reviewers provided divergent but helpful insights. Thank you, all.

Introduction - From Carnival …

There is something compelling about dressing up. Two thousand years ago, the Emperor Commodus wore a lion skin, carried a club and called himself Hercules.[1] In January 2017, women dressed as vulvas to protest the inauguration of Donald Trump as president of the United States of America.[2] As with today, people of the past wore costumes for amusement and fun, the more arresting and inventive the better; incorporating bold colours, unusual materials and adapting conventional articles of clothing to appear extreme. But the longevity of this sartorial phenomenon has not been sustained on laughter alone. If people in fancy dress have predominantly been pleasure seekers, it is too frequently forgotten that they have also been protesters and promoters, the petrified and self-possessed, the peripheral and the powerful. And they remain so. Fancy dress costume, which I define as *a performative form of dress, imaginative and incongruous, worn for a discrete occasion and limited time that disrupts the place of the individual within the social and political relationships of a specific community*, is probably the only form of clothing that all people alive today have worn, or will wear, at some point in their lives, regardless of sex, status and society, however briefly and creatively.[3] Few forms of clothing are simultaneously so universal and exceptional.

This book aims to understand the enduring global appeal of dressing up from the Middle Ages to modernity.[4] In the process, it seeks to explain how an ephemeral, idiosyncratic and polyvalent form of clothing and appearance has enabled disparate groups and individuals to communicate through what they wear. Shedding light on a long-standing and popular form of cultural expression, this book makes no claim to be comprehensive. It seeks, first and foremost, to contribute to debates about the communicative qualities of dress in accord with Barbara Babcock's observation that the 'socially peripheral is often symbolically central, and if we ignore or minimize inversion and other forms of cultural negation we often fail to understand the dynamics of social process generally'.[5] A main reason this cannot be a comprehensive study is because in seeking to provide a focused account of fancy dress costume, and to promote enquiry about it, the sartorial form is considered apart from other types of dress. Through four thematic chapters that analyse specific examples of fancy dress costume, rather like case studies, this book adopts a diachronic approach. The rationale is to understand, through comparison and juxtaposition, how fancy dress has changed in conjunction with social and political developments. This method, which deliberately collapses chronologies to identify themes across global cultures, is conceived to facilitate a more critical consideration of why this unique form of clothing remains significant, in both senses of the word, today.

Unmasking fancy dress

Definitions seek to clarify, but they can also confound analysis. There is, perhaps, a heightened risk of this for fancy dress costume. Writing this book has made me even more aware of the prevalence of dressing up, but it has also taught me that people's experience of fancy dress tends to engender a 'love' or 'loathe' response. This strong reaction, which leaves little room for equivocation, appears to have dissuaded scholars from investigating further. Consequently, whilst recent academic work has recovered the 'criticality' of costume, and new analytic terms have been coined to identify subcategories – including the 'carnivalesque', 'grotesque', 'critical fashion', 'experimental fashion' and 'costume of conflict' – fancy dress remains peripheral.[6] I suspect three common (mis)perceptions about this sartorial form account for this marginalization; namely, that fancy dress is inherently frivolous, it requires minimal skill to create, and it is genuinely popular and culturally purportless.[7] Where scholars have considered fancy dress, it is typically within other categories of costume. The definition that I offer above and the examples that I discuss in this book assert fancy dress as a distinctive form of costume that requires specific acknowledgement and understanding.[8]

Advancing my definition, I assume that any complete fancy dress costume will include all of the stated constituents and contain most, if not all, of the following characteristics: it will be worn for a short period of time, typically on only one occasion; the circumstances in which it is worn are usually set apart (chronologically, physically, psychologically) from the conventional routines of its wearer's community; it will display limited, or no, conformity to the social, political or dramatic expectations of its wearer's community; it will heighten the agency of its wearer by clarifying aspects of their character; it may appear frivolous but this characteristic is not inherent; physical comfort is often less important to its wearer than the perceived psychological contentment the costume provides them. Most importantly, I assume that fancy dress costume is always affective – it will have an impact on how the wearer and their audience feel and behave – even if this is not readily apparent.

The term fancy dress is first recorded in England during the sixteenth century, but it was not until the eighteenth century, when masquerades were at the height of their popularity, that it was used frequently.[9] Initially, the term described women's clothing that incorporated decorative elements from contemporary fashions. Minimal attempt was made to alter one's appearance.[10] After the decline of masquerades in the 1790s, the term fancy dress became widespread, probably on account of its fuzziness, and referred to any public occasion where dress-up, worn by men and women, was involved.[11] This usage continues today. In colloquial American, the term 'costume' is occasionally substituted – fancy dress can refer to (men's) smart or formal attire – although 'fancy dress' is conventionally used by American museums, scholars and the Merriam Webster dictionary.[12] Across continental Europe, linguistic variation masks a shared conceptual understanding. In France and Spain, fancy dress is referred to as 'disguise' (*le déguisement* and *la disfraz*, respectively) and in Germany and Italy as 'costume' (*das Kostüm* and *il costume*, respectively). Fancy dress is not prevalent in Asia, where cultural traditions emphasize social congruence and harmony over individuality – a fact reflected by examples in this book. This has started to change, notably through *kosupure* (コスプレ), or cosplay, a portmanteau of the English words 'costume' and 'play', in which people dress and perform as fictional characters, typically from manga and anime.

To clarify fancy dress costume, it is necessary to state what it is not. Fancy dress is not disguise, worn for the purpose of camouflaging a person's conventional identity to gain acceptance, temporarily or permanently, into another community.[13] When Emperor Nero dressed as a plebian, apparently to rough up Romans; when King Alfred dressed as a mime and juggler to infiltrate a Danish camp; and when Heinrich Himmler shaved his moustache, wore an eye patch and the uniform of a discharged Gestapo agent to avoid identification in 1945, the costumes worn by these men were imaginative and incongruous on a personal level, but congruent with the society they sought to join.[14] Fancy dress is not religious or ceremonial clothing. The garments worn by spiritual and social leaders on important public occasions can appear unusual and highly creative – for example, ecclesiastical vestments and shamanistic dress accessories – but these items of clothing tend to possess fixed meanings that do not appreciably change over time, chiefly because they are symbolic of the entrenched beliefs of the society in which they appear. A final category excluded from this study is clothing worn for re-enactment. The adoption of period-specific clothing and comportment may appear incongruent, but the desire for authenticity and accuracy restricts personal imagination and agency. Typically confined to members-only societies, re-enactment has little impact on social and political relationships.[15]

The semantic and conceptual fluidity of fancy dress costume is understandable considering its incongruity, transience and specific geographical and cultural presence. Fundamentally, the lack of definition is a consequence of academic marginalization. If scholars have generally eschewed study of clothing and the body because of its perceived 'frivolity', fancy dress, which is more patently comic, has received scant attention.[16] The sporadic commentary that does consider fancy dress costume is characterized by picture-orientated studies and lifestyle articles for general audiences.[17] This work has most likely galvanized academic prejudice against the topic because it tends to place an uncritical emphasis on the determinism of dress – long since a *bête noire* among scholars – through the recurrent insistence that a person's choice of costume reflects their character more clearly than that of their daily wardrobe. In 1959, for example, author Lawrence Langner opined:

> The selection of the fancy dress costume is never an accident when there is full freedom of choice; but an expression of a conscious or unconscious desire of the wearer.[18]

Along with many other commentators, Langner also thought fancy dress costume affected behaviour:

> The man who goes to a fancy dress ball attired as a sheik is more apt to believe himself to be irresistible and to make a fool of himself with the woman he encounters than if he wore a sober black dinner jacket and tie. The young woman who makes a point of dressing as Cleopatra to emphasize her sexual attractions is more apt to misbehave than if she dressed more conservatively, since she invites the complementary misbehavior on the part of the men to whom she obviously conveys her feelings by her clothes.[19]

To an extent, Langner's comments reflect social attitudes of the 1950s. His suggestion that infant girls who dress as boys could 'in extreme cases' become homosexual, and vice versa for boys, was borne of what Ramzi Fawaz has called the 'homophobic and sexist logic of anti-communist political rhetoric'.[20] Nonetheless, his point is representative of an abiding belief that fancy dress costume is adept at conveying a wearer's true character. Contemporary media perpetuates this idea. In March 2017, a Spanish priest apologized after dressing as Playboy founder Hugh Heffner and dancing with two men, dressed as Playboy bunnies, on a carnival float. It was reported that the priest, who vowed never to dress up again, was advised to attend a spiritual retreat to repent his 'unacceptable' behaviour.[21]

The marginalization of fancy dress costume is also a consequence of academic practice. Increasingly, studies of clothing incline towards a synchronic approach. This method facilitates in-depth analysis, but it encourages a focus on specific time periods, locations and groups, which will likely as not include people with broadly similar attitudes to society and dress.[22] As a polyvalent form of clothing that bestrides cultures and short chronologies, fancy dress costume is ill-suited to this mode of research. Whilst academic study of fancy dress costume has been undertaken, it is generally limited to three main chronological periods: pre-Reformation carnival, eighteenth-century masquerade and elite balls of the nineteenth and twentieth centuries. Much of the work has been undertaken by cultural historians, anthropologists and sociologists, who have made 'carnival/esque' an analytical concept and who consider the mask's metaphorical significance over its material value.[23] More recently, literary scholars have used the descriptions of masquerades in novels, plays and poetry to explore gender.[24] Studies by dress historians are conspicuous for being few in number although curators have long been aware of the cultural importance of fancy dress costume.[25]

This discontinuous approach does much to explain scholars' hesitant conclusions about the role and meaning of fancy dress costume. Some claim the sartorial phenomenon and the circumstances in which it is worn are too heterodox to explain sufficiently. It has been remarked that festive participants are 'often unreflective and unanalytical about what they are doing'.[26] The eighteenth-century masquerade can be 'overwhelming' to a modern analyst for it 'holds out too many messages, too much potential significance'.[27] It has also been observed that '[t]he activities of … festival[s] do not endure beyond the time given to them; the expectations satisfied within it do not continue in the period that follows. There is no tomorrow: the evidence of an exuberant squandering of time, of energy and of goods reveals the festival's lack of concern with an afterward.'[28]

These uncertain observations highlight the problem of studying fancy dress costume synchronically; singling out disparate periods for analysis creates distortion by removing events from their cultural and chronological frame. To utilize existing studies of fancy dress in this study, to 'ground' the book's thematic chapters, and to establish a clear background for the anthropological, sociological and historical theories that I use, and introduce later in this chapter, it is necessary to provide a genealogy of fancy dress from the Middle Ages to modernity. A diachronic summary is all the more necessary because this is the first book-length study of fancy dress costume.

Fancy dress through history

Between the Middle Ages and modernity, the role and meaning of fancy dress costume changed by degree, rather than by kind. Shifts in signification are more apparent in the West than the East, where fancy dress has long been prevalent. Serving as chronological markers rather than rigid classificatory stages, notable changes are discernible in the use and meaning of fancy dress costume from the twelfth century, from the middle of the eighteenth century and from the beginning of the twentieth century. These periods of transition are analogous to those noted by Samuel Kinser in his important studies of carnival.[29] The connection between fancy dress costume and carnival is strong because carnivalesque festivities almost invariably involve dress-up.

From the twelfth century to the seventeenth century

The public wearing of costume can be traced to pre-Christian seasonal festivals. The most important of these was known, by the fifteenth century, as carnival. As James Scott avers, carnival was 'the ritual site of various forms of social conflict and symbolic manipulation' that varied with 'culture and historic circumstances ... serving many functions for its participants'.[30] In the Catholic Church, carnival became a period of feasting and frivolity that began after Epiphany and culminated on Shrove Tuesday, or *Mardi Gras* (Fat Tuesday), which marked the beginning of Lent. Where carnival could be ribald and riotous, Lent was a forty-day period of self-reflection and abstinence, commencing on Ash Wednesday and concluding before Easter Sunday, which celebrated the resurrection of Jesus Christ. The festivities and dramatic performances that occurred during carnival used fancy dress costume to emphasize the symbiotic relationship between play and productivity. Analogous events occurred in China and Japan at the beginning of New Year.[31]

Carnival was not an isolated event. Kinser explains, 'it now seems ... likely that Carnival-time, beginning as an urban and courtly reaction to Lenten rules, gradually attracted to itself a variety of agricultural and social practices which were originally celebrated at different points in late winter and early springtime.'[32] In the West and East ludic activities were conceived 'to promote and increase fertility of new crops, and animals ... to cure illnesses, to avert plague ... to turn boys into men and girls into women, to make chiefs out of commoners'.[33] Many of these recreations, which involved boys acting and dressing as bishops and clothes being worn inside out, inverted traditional meanings to demonstrate their transformational and rejuvenating force.[34] Simultaneously entertaining and edifying, these events were staged at transitional moments in the seasonal calendar to enhance their effect. In pre-industrial, 'orally-centred' societies, to use Kinser's term, where the authority of religion was strong and largely unchallenged, the wearing of fancy dress costume was typically a manifestation of people's desire to celebrate and affirm political and religious cohesion.[35]

Participation in dramatic and transformational acts, whether overtly religious or more secular, was generally appealing at a time when life was short, harsh, and enlivened by few distractions.[36] Contemporaries, and subsequently many historians, regarded these festivities as a social safety valve that enabled individual and group frustrations to be vented. This is true to an extent, but the fun was never entirely pacifying. The opportunity to temporarily transgress social roles meant that festive occasions could be used to challenge social and political authority. Carnival could stoke tensions as much as sate them.[37] For example, the men and women who held Kenilworth Castle against Henry III of England in 1266 appear to have taken inspiration from carnivalesque behaviour and costume to signal their repudiation of royal authority and to galvanize their impossible stand against the king's army (Chapter 2). Fears about misrule continuing beyond festive periods go some way to explain the frequency of legislation that prohibited the public wearing of face coverings.[38] The inversion of conventional symbols during festive periods could equally provide an opportunity to bolster social structures.

The *charivari* is a specific example of a festive entertainment that promoted cohesion and stability. A carnivalesque permutation presided over by adolescent males, it involved a comic form of public humiliation being meted out to men and women who had transgressed social mores, by forcing them to ride backwards on a donkey. Natalie Zemon Davis suggests this ritual transferred a temporary authority to the future leaders of a locality – its young men – by 'socializing them to the conscience of [that] community by making them the raucous voice of that conscience'.[39] In Japan, the participation of young men in 'comically obscene' hunting and fertility dances may have served a similar function.[40] Davis's study, along with those of Michael Bristol and Anu Mänd, provides an important corrective to Mikhail Bakhtin's argument that carnival was primarily an opportunity for the lowly to challenge the lofty. As Mänd has shown in her forensic analysis of carnival in the eastern Baltic, it was frequently the social and political leaders of a community who funded the festivities.[41] In this sense, fancy dress costume and the occasions when it was worn are examples of the ridiculous helping to substantiate the sublime.

The religious wrangles that occurred within sixteenth-century Europe permanently affected the place of seasonal festivities and carnival. Protestant reformers, who believed in salvation through faith alone, dismissed these recreations as superstitious and sought to remove them. Consequently, carnival lost its 'mortal and moral' counterpart, Lent, which Protestants beyond England did not acknowledge.[42] The social and economic consequences of this change are apparent within Pieter Bruegel's painting 'The Combat of Carnival and Lent' of 1559. In the foreground of the painting, the gluttonous and brightly dressed figure of a man, representing carnival, is engaged in a mock tourney with an emaciated representation of Lent, depicted as a nun.[43] The duelling figures fight with meat and fish, respectively, the supply of which was heavily affected by the dietary stipulations of the fasting period.[44] Behind them, Bruegel depicts social activities and traditions that attained meaning because of their place within the doctrinally influenced chronology of carnival and Lent, including a 'hunt of the wildman' and a burning bonfire.[45] These and other activities were displaced, if not eradicated, by the advent of Protestantism (Figure 1).

FIGURE 1 'The Wildman, or The Masquerade of Orson and Valentine', after Pieter Bruegel The Elder, engraving, 1566. Courtesy of Boston Museum of Fine Arts.

The Protestant doctrine of salvation through faith alone privileged the individual over the community and weakened the public spirit that fuelled carnival, but other factors contributed to annul festive traditions. Equally important – and quite possibly linked if we accept Max Weber's notion of the Protestant work ethic – were the consequences of commercial expansion, technological innovation and population growth that became more apparent during the sixteenth century.[46] The cumulative impact of these developments was first to dilute, finally to dissolve, traditional dependencies and hierarchical bonds.[47] The impact of the printing press and the ending of an orally centred society were equally important in widening social fissures. Developing ideas from Claude Lévi-Strauss, Kinser suggests the establishment of a 'letter-centred society' created a culture 'obsessed with universals' and 'well-arranged perfection' that lacked the flexibility, personality and polyvalence of its orally centred antecedent.[48] The effect of these changes was, at least, twofold. First, public drama became representative, where formerly it had been performative. Second, the transmission of ideas was more effectively handled by people who exercised authority over the printed word.

Changes to festive entertainments became quickly apparent across Europe. In Britain, the religious see-sawing that occurred between Henry VIII's death in 1547 and the Glorious Revolution of 1688, as Protestant and Catholic monarchs attempted to enforce religious settlements that reflected their personal faith, caused the decline of many popular entertainments.[49] The rate at which these events waned was often directly proportional to the efforts of religious leaders who pressed them into service as propaganda, although there was regional variation.[50] For example, around 1539, a Protestant in the service of Henry VIII suggested that summer 'playes of Robyn hoode, mayde Marian [and] freer Tuck', which encourage 'lewdenes', 'rebawdry' and 'disobedience', could be 'deleted and others dyvysed to set forthe and declare lyvely before the peoples eies the abhomynation and wickednes of the bisshop of Rome, monkes, ffreers, nonnes, and suche like.'[51] According to David Cressy, the politicization of the seasonal calendar after the Reformation and Restoration of 1660, which included the veneration of monarchs on the day of their accession and the curtailment of saints' days, increased social tensions as it seemed that a privileged few were imposing their preferred culture on everybody else.[52]

Cressy's thesis can be questioned because support for accession day bonfires and bell ringing is equivocal, but his comments on the politicization of culture in the sixteenth and seventeenth centuries are compelling.[53] They chime with points made by Kinser about 'shifts in consciousness' with regards to the celebration of carnival in Nuremberg, one of Germany's largest cities. During this period, the nature of Nuremberg's annual carnival changed from a ritual into a spectacle as a modern 'mode of representation', again to borrow Kinser's terminology, came to replace a medieval one.[54] Where carnival had been *performative*, enjoining audience participation, and referencing the present by harnessing fear, glory and satire, it came to be *representative* by reducing the role of the audience to that of onlooker and alluding to the past through symbols that had a fixed meaning, akin to the tenets of Protestantism, which the city's council endorsed.[55] As in England, religious and political upheaval, exacerbated by the spread of Lutheran, later Calvinist, thought, began to change the festive calendar by censoring the more raucous elements of carnival as participants were straight-jacketed into officially sanctioned roles, or silenced altogether.

If this seems removed from the subject of fancy dress costume, changes in people's outlook at the beginning of the seventeenth century are essential to grasp if the shifting role and meaning of this sartorial form is to be understood. When ritual – which is all encompassing for actors and audience – becomes spectacle – where the role of actor and audience is distinct – a once immersive experience is fragmented into a series of connected moments, which can be individually scrutinized and, if desired, altered. In Germany, this gave Luther and his adherents an opportunity to press the imagery associated with carnival into Protestant propaganda. They printed satiric verses and engravings that presented the pope in carnivalesque guise as an 'apparition of the devil'.[56] In much the same way, popular summer plays were being deconstructed in England to portray the pope's 'abhomynation and wickednes'.[57] In short, Kinser's 'aesthetic evolution' undermined the 'sociable reconciliation' that carnival had provided and, he argues, set high and low culture on diverging paths. Carnival became 'an odd necessity', 'a crazy streak in people's lives'.[58] Simultaneously, the separation initiated between festivity and faith, leisure and labour, facilitated adaptation and experimentation in fancy dress costume because it was no longer aligned so closely with Catholic belief. This flexibility enabled dressing up to become a more nuanced, and effective, means of conveying the zeitgeist.

The development of the masque is one example of how shifting social and political relationships altered the role and meaning of fancy dress. An allegorical drama accompanied by music in which the performers wore elaborate masked costumes, the masque was avowedly secular, based within the princely court and conceived to celebrate the institution of monarchy. Masques are documented in sixteenth-century Europe, and include descriptions of Francis I of France dressing variously as a sphinx, hermit and crayfish, but the entertainment achieved its greatest artistic expression between 1605 and 1631 in England, a result of the tense partnership between poet Ben Jonson and architect Inigo Jones.[59] The masque was possibly inspired by popular folk entertainments that were performed at the change of season (i.e. sword dances, morris dances, mummers' plays) or the city pageants that marked a ruler's ceremonial *adventus* into their cities. A more direct influence was the elaborate court-based performances, akin to the *Commedia dell'Arte*, which had been staged in fifteenth-century Italy.[60] The elision between fancy dress and choreographed dramatic performances was notable during the fifteenth and seventeenth centuries. As religious upheavals curtailed more popular and raucous forms of festivity that involved dress up, the continuing centralization of royal and aristocratic authority encouraged the proliferation of court-based entertainments.[61] Noteworthy, in light of the points raised above, is the suggestion that England's masque developed because of a specific need to explain and sate a 'mental unrest' during a period of noticeable and rapid change.[62]

From the eighteenth century to the nineteenth century

Social upheavals caused by political revolution, continued technological advancement and Europe's global expansion made fancy dress a truly popular and global phenomenon during the eighteenth and nineteenth centuries. Carnivals, street parades and masked balls were staged in the United States of America and Canada, if not for the first time, certainly on a regular basis. Under British rule, fancy dress events are recorded in India and the West Indies during the late nineteenth century. In the same century, Western intervention in China and Japan increased, although it is difficult to determine the impact on traditional festivities. In the sixteenth century, fascination with Portuguese styles of dress had led to the incorporation of European headwear in carnivalesque entertainments in Japan, so it is likely that sustained contact stimulated further exchanges, as it did in literature and painting.[63] As fancy dress spread and fused with different cultures, its role and meaning changed. Where costumed events had tended to celebrate and enforce societal structures, in the eighteenth century there was a greater likelihood that costume wearers would be self-reflective and more inclined to challenge social conventions through parody. There is no clear point of demarcation. Elements of social criticism can be identified in earlier costumed entertainments; for example, John Milton's *A Masque Presented at Ludlow Castle 1634*.[64] However, the instance of people wishing to escape the woes engendered by the pace of commercial and technological change by donning costumes is more apparent only after 1700.

At a time when the relationship between self and society was being critically scrutinized, most notably within the arts, by writers – Rousseau, Goethe, Lemontov – and painters – the pre-Raphaelites – fancy dress costume, no longer bound to seasonal festivities, became something of a cultural conduit, enabling people of different sex, sexual orientation, status and society to mediate the pressures they perceived to be upon them.[65] In her study of Victorian costumed entertainments, Rebecca Mitchell suggests fancy dress enabled people to 'negotiate' rather than 'escape' their self-presentation.[66] The compulsion for (bourgeois) people to regulate – to civilize – their public behaviour became acute during the seventeenth and eighteenth centuries. This was a consequence of Enlightenment moralizing and the increasing complexity of social and political relationships. In search for respite, Terry Eagleton has shown how people created 'discursive spaces' as they struggled to disengage from their denigrated cultural habits.[67] One manifestation of the desire for space and privacy was the wearing of anonymizing clothing. Initially, this was apparent in the wardrobes of women, who wore face masks publicly, but the popularity of such concealment rapidly encouraged the proliferation of fancy dress entertainments in London, later Paris. As Christoph Heyl opines, 'The masquerade gave a new chance of satisfying the still existing desire for social contact and communication while at the same time it satisfied the new desire for privacy'.[68]

Consequently, it was during the eighteenth century that social commentators became convinced of a connection between a person's choice of costume and their character. A conventional view, which echoed earlier fears about masks and disguises, was that people wore costumes to conceal their identity and to act nefariously. Whilst lacking credible evidence, a major concern was that the behaviour of masked people was somehow more reflective of their character than their socially prescribed daily attire. In March 1732, an article on masquerades in London's conservative *Gentleman's Magazine* inveighed that 'people in disguise do things which their characters would not suffer them to do publickly.'[69] Another contributor to the magazine, writing nearly 150 years later in April 1880, adopted a similar, albeit less critical, stance:

> The character of the dress of a person stands so near to the character of the person who is the wearer of it, it is difficult to touch on one without the other.[70]

By the end of the nineteenth century, the wearing of fancy dress costume had become more socially acceptable. There were two main reasons for this. First, restrictions placed on masquerade attendance meant fancy dress entertainments tended to become private affairs, hosted by the social elite and involving European royalty. This provided a veneer of respectability, which contributed to their spread.[71] In Russia, Peter the Great endorsed fancy dress entertainments, ostensibly as part of his programme of 'Westernization'.[72] Across the Atlantic, English women who settled in British North America commissioned portraits that depicted them holding masks, apparently to provide a cultural link to London, as much to explore their gendered role in a 'savage' environment.[73] Second, the wide appeal of fancy dress, and the correlative commercial opportunities this offered, meant that it was pressed to serve civic-centred initiatives.[74]

'Modernism's emergent individualism' shifted attitudes towards fancy dress events and affected the costumes people wore.[75] If garments that disguised people's conventional identities had been prevalent at masked balls during the eighteenth and nineteenth centuries, costumes that maintained them were prevalent by the late nineteenth century.[76] Colleen McQuillen identifies two distinct types of fancy dress costume – 'conceptual' and 'synecdochic' – that became increasingly popular. Conceptual costumes depict allegorical subjects and themes. Characterized by a 'non-literal and non-lineal construction', they are an 'artistic arrangement' of materials, animated by the wearer, that spectators need to interpret.[77] Consequently, they can be highly creative and personal. Synecdochic costumes are more literal and use 'objects to convey "thingness".'[78] They are 'incommunicative of anything beyond their self-contained object status' and often depict specific commodities or occasions.[79] If these costumes are relatively easy to interpret, they show creative skill through a wearer's ability to use a limited number of items to represent the chosen subject. McQuillen considers conceptual and synecdochic costumes to be distinct from character costumes.[80]

The changing role and meaning of fancy dress can be comprehended through the rise and decline of the masquerade. The masquerade was a largely eighteenth-century phenomenon although, like the masque, there were Italian, possibly eastern, antecedents.[81] Like the masque, the masquerade seems to have provided something of a social coping mechanism. The sartorial and social licence that masquerade permitted – other than attendance at church, it was the only occasion when women could be unchaperoned in public – seemed to offer respite from the disorientation induced by the period's seemingly ceaseless expansion (Figure 2).[82] It is telling that masqueraders were the first fancy dress revellers to look to the past for costume inspiration.

FIGURE 2 *'Mascarade', Paul Gavarni, lithograph, 1832. Courtesy of Yale University Art Gallery.*

Masques had invoked gods, Christian saints and labourers, but there had never been an appreciable desire for direct historical mimicry.[83] By contrast, eighteenth-century masqueraders drew inspiration from a variety of historic sources. Sixteenth and seventeenth portraiture, particularly paintings by Sir Anthony Van Dyck and Jean-Antoine Watteau, gave rise to a specific form of faux-historic 'Van Dyck' and 'Watteau' costume. The desire for *tableaux vivants*, where costumed sitters staged portraits with the newly available daguerreotype camera, is a curious example, although by no means atypical, of how fancy dress participants embraced the present to escape into the past.[84] Within aristocratic circles, there was a particular fascination to imitate members of the ill-fated, and thus romantically compelling, Stuart and Bourbon dynasties.[85] The Grand Tour, which took place in Italy, later Constantinople (Istanbul), provided further stimulus for (aristocratic) people's historical costume.

Masquerade was not entertainment for the elite alone. As Aileen Ribeiro has argued, it facilitated social equality, enabling the wealthy and the rest to cohabitate, if only for a few hours.[86] Author and politician Horace Walpole described one masquerade in which George II delighted at his anonymity: '[The king] was well disguised in an old-fashioned English habit, and [was] much pleased with somebody who desired him to hold their cup as they were drinking.'[87] Masquerade enabled women to participate in fancy dress entertainments, although the extent to which their attendance challenged or confirmed their gendered roles remains debated.[88] In Berlin, masquerade afforded opportunities for homosexual men to socialize; initially in private, but the opening of gay bars by the end of the nineteenth century provided venues for masked balls.[89] Masquerade presented the means to enjoy, or critique, the latest fashions; from the Macaronis who were conspicuous for their body-hugging garb, to the height of women's hairstyles.[90] Masquerade also reflected the preoccupations of the eighteenth century. Improved relations with the Ottoman Empire inspired oriental costumes; visits of American chiefs to London in 1734 and 1762 inspired Indian costumes; and British support for Austria in its war against Prussia inspired hussar dress.[91] The entertainment seemed so relevant and necessary that many (aristocratic) people commissioned portraits in which they were arrayed in masquerade costumes, both real and imagined.[92]

The emphasis that wearers of fancy dress, drawn from all sectors of society, came to put on their individual and escapist desires marks the eighteenth century as a turning point in the development of the sartorial phenomenon. Whilst fancy dress events would continue to celebrate and sustain social cohesion, there was now a marked focus on personal gratification. In his study of queer identities in nineteenth- and twentieth-century Germany, Clayton Whisnaut observes that 'escape from the routine and social conventions of civilization allows new pleasures to be discovered, new forms to be explored, and new kinds of relationships to be established. Sometimes the escape into nature might also be presented as a passage through time into a long-lost past.'[93] Contemporaries perceived this change and expressed concern that fancy dress costume, and the behaviour it appeared to encourage, was socially harmful.

A desire for sartorial escapism and concealment certainly contrasts starkly with the 'realness' of the eighteenth century, which is documented in the quantity of printed material that discussed politics and people's lives in immense detail. The eager consumption of this information spurred the chastisements of social critics, who provided frequent reminders that too much knowledge had precipitated Original Sin. More forthright faultfinders linked Eden and fancy dress entertainments directly. It was suggested that Adam and Eve had provided the first example of dress-up when they donned fig leaves to conceal their nakedness.[94] As masquerade became increasingly popular, contemporary critics lambasted it as a pernicious demonstration of the period's overweening pride. Some even saw it as a harbinger of a social crisis that seemed close at hand.

An earthquake at Livorno on the western coast of Tuscany in January 1742 prompted the Grand Duke to decree that 'masquerades at the theatre there might be for ever abolished'. A similar, and 'laudable', effort was made by politicians in Westminster, to suppress the 'mock carnivals at Ranelah-House', but the zeal to abolish these entertainments existed among the magistrates alone. In London, masquerades therefore continued, albeit with the presence of guards.[95] The belief that masquerades triggered earthquakes, which some people reckoned to be 'under divine management', died hard.[96] On 1 November 1775 – ominously, All Saint's Day – much of Lisbon was destroyed by an earthquake. Across Europe, masquerades were banned for most of the following year. Thereafter, subscription masquerades became commonplace, as a means of limiting numbers and vetting attendees.[97] It was not until the state visit of Christian VII of Denmark in 1768 that England's enthusiasm for masquerade was revived.[98]

Historians have been inclined to see the decline of masquerades at the end of the eighteenth century as 'the last brilliant, even brittle eruption of an impulse inexorably on its ways to extinction'.[99] This is a consequence of adopting a synchronic approach and looking at the eighteenth century in isolation. First, masquerades continued into the nineteenth century.[100] Second, the format of the eighteenth-century subscription masquerade provided the basis for many later fancy dress events, including the *Bal du Rat mort* in Belgium, the *Bals des Quat'z-Arts* in Paris, the balls of St Petersburg's Imperial Academy of Arts and the Chelsea

FIGURE 3 *Photograph of Wimbledon students crossing the road in London to attend the Chelsea Arts Club Ball, 1951. CACB/51/P004. © Chelsea Arts Club.*

Arts Club balls in London, which became equally disreputable (Figure 3).[101] The decline of the eighteenth-century masquerade needs to be placed in a broader social frame.

Masquerade fed off reality, but in its distortion and romanticism of it, the entertainment rendered contemporary happenings harmless, even trivial. In a period of pronounced economic, technological and social transformation, there was a strong likelihood that this flight from fact would at some point seem a dispensable distraction. Newspapers, and the reports they carried at the century's end about the overthrow of French monarchy; literature, which had generally been critical about masquerade (notably novels by Daniel Defoe and Henry Fielding)[102]; and printed satire by William Hogarth reveal that reality was triumphing over romanticism and ribaldry. If confirmation were needed, the fatal shooting of Sweden's Gustaf III at a masquerade ball in 1792 seemed to show that grim reality would always trump gay fantasy (Chapter 2). These changes had a deep impact on people's outlook, and this was reflected in the fancy dress entertainments they attended and the costumes they wore.

By the time Venice celebrated its last carnival in 1797 (it was prohibited by Napoleon I and not revived until 1979), a different form of fancy dress entertainment had begun to take its place, which seemed to reflect a desire for cohesion and stability: the mock tournament. Mock tournaments had been held on the accession days of Elizabeth I and James I of England during the sixteenth and seventeenth centuries, but they became a global phenomenon by the end of the eighteenth century.[103] Frederick II hosted a tournament in Berlin in 1750. Similar events followed in Parma (1769), Stockholm (1777), Copenhagen and Dresden (1791), Laxenburg and Pisa (1800), Malta (1828), Barcelona (1833) and Turin (1839). In 1778, a tournament was organized in Philadelphia to honour General Sir William Howe, commander of British forces during America's War of Independence. In June 1839, another tournament was held in New Orleans.[104] One of the largest tournaments – and disappointing on account of torrential rain – occurred at Eglinton on 30 August 1839 in south-west Scotland.[105] The tournament was conceived because Queen Victoria and her government had dispensed with the traditional coronation banquet and tournament in 1838 because of concerns it would appear extravagant at a time of financial stringency.[106] Aristocrats, who lost the opportunity to fulfil their ceremonial duties, were peeved. The performance of a mock tournament provided a symbolic opportunity to demarcate social positions and the importance of tradition.

The tournament was no less escapist than the masquerade, for it harked back to a misremembered past when the code of chivalry was considered omnipresent.[107] This invention of tradition, accompanied as it was by a short-lived revival of archery, suggests a desire to return to a time associated with constancy and certainty. As David Cannadine has shown, the nineteenth century was characterized by the creation and revival of pseudo-historic ideas and activities, including many folk traditions.[108] Refracting contemporary events through (supposedly) similar incidents of the past, however accurately, presumably provided people with a reassurance that was otherwise obfuscated by the pace of their lives. The point is easier to raise than refine, although a rhyming poem that commemorates the Grand Fancy Dress Ball held at Brighton's Royal Pavilion in 1865 suggests some fancy dress events were conceived to diminish the unsettling consequences of modernization. The following extract describes the end of the ball, when costumed revellers began their journeys home in the early hours of the morning:

Yet still bright fancy's eye recalls,
The bygone days when courts were gay,
When higher morals held their sway,

And bench, and pulpit, vied with lay;
Dim mediaeval ages, when,
Right bowed to might, and lordly men,
Might hold their own and of their store,
Contended not, dared take them more,
We linger still, believing fain,
Without, is many a gallant train,
Of mail-clad knights, and cavaliers,
Beefeaters, jesters, halberdiers,
Of vassals, pages, squires, and bowmen,
Of bill, and spear, and sturdy yeoman.
Thus fancy wanders, and 'tis sweet,
To follow where her step doth lead,
For poets say that 'neath her feet,
Bright flowers will spring but never weed,
And yet, alas, for all her power!
No more she rules the giddy hour –
The spell is broken – hark! Without,
The rush, the rumble, and the rout,
The din of harsh discordant cries,
The villain cabs, the vulgar flys,
All – and it irks us much to say,
Too mindful of the modern day, –
We're done, in sheer regard we're done,
Lest passion, reason should outrun,
As fancy halts, tho' by the way,
'Tis lightly told, that Hotspur bold,
Mail'd, helm'd, and plum'd, in fiery need,
Bestrode a new velocipede.
Took the express – not to the moon;
But Warkworth – and arrived at noon.[109]

Two further elaborations in the role of fancy dress costume during the nineteenth century indicate a similar desire to (re-)establish stability; first, the organization of children's fancy dress balls and, second, fancy dress balls conceived specifically to raise money for charities and public works. The association between children and fancy dress was not entirely new. Britain's royal princes, the future George IV and his brother Frederick, enjoyed dressing up, and many eighteenth-century portraits depict aristocratic children in fancy dress costume.[110] Of course, a painting does not prove participation in fancy dress events; the English women who commissioned masquerade portraits in British North America did so without participating in such festivities.[111] Nineteenth-century juvenile balls, however, were popular entertainments, borne of changing attitudes about the nature and role of children.

Between the seventeenth and nineteenth centuries, and influenced however imperceptibly by the writings of John Locke and Jean-Jacques Rousseau, people came to believe that children were born innocent.[112] Society, parents not least, therefore had a duty to guide the development of the young. According to Daniel Thomas Cook, greater awareness of the needs of boys and girls provided the necessary 'groundwork for a children's material, commercial culture'.[113] It is certainly no coincidence that as ideas on child nurturing crystallized during the late nineteenth century, the production of children's amusements and the publication of children's literature increased. A.N. Wilson observes that the second half of the century witnessed 'a special flowering of children's literature' when the now-famous titles of Lewis Carroll and Rudyard Kipling were published: *Alice's Adventures in Wonderland* appeared in 1865, and *The Jungle Book* was originally published as a collection of short stories between 1893 and 1894.[114] Placed within this social frame, fancy dress events for juveniles seem to have been another example of the widespread recognition of children's unique status.

The British monarchy was among the earliest organizers of Children's fancy dress balls and a juvenile ball was held at Buckingham Palace on 7 April 1859. Successive balls were held at Mansion House, the official residence of London's Lord Mayor, where they became annual events. The costumes worn by children on these occasions were inspired by the characters they encountered in their new stories. A white cotton dress printed with pale blue stripes and pink roses in the style of Kate Greenaway illustrations is now in the Museum of London.[115] Another of the Museum's costumes, a shepherdess, with a white satin bodice, long gaiters and poke bonnet, was based on the clothing of Violet Grey, a character played by stage actress Edna May in 'Belle of New York', which opened in London in 1898.[116]

Whilst the proliferation of juvenile activities and literature reflects society's awareness of children's specific needs, it highlights the desire for escapism among adults. Wilson notes that some of the books favoured by children were not originally written for them.[117] Adult literature that provided access to a more welcoming alternative reality had appeared earlier in the nineteenth century. The poems and books of Sir Walter Scott, whom George IV declared to favour more than 'every Bard past and present', were bestsellers.[118] Set within an idealized medieval world, Scott's writing captured the imagination of readers – young gentlemen particularly – because 'it was presented so vividly, was so different from the life they themselves lived, and yet seemed to express certain virtues and characteristics which they felt their own age was in need of.'[119]

Fancy dress that provided entertainment and, from the perspective of its hosts, cultural edification, became more apparent with the expansion of the British Empire.[120] For example, Ralph Strachey, a civil engineer who spent much of his life in India working for Britain's East Indian Railway Company, attended several fancy dress parties, which he described in letters to his sister Philippa, who lived in London. Strachey's brother, Lytton, also delighted in fancy dress as a member of the Bloomsbury Group with fellow author Virginia Woolf.[121] Today, Strachey's irreverent correspondence appears condescending and casually racist, but it shows how colonial subjects – in these examples, material beneficiaries of British rule – participated voluntarily, perhaps joyfully, always unequally, in fancy dress entertainments. In December 1892, Strachey attended a fancy dress ball in Barakar, West Bengal, to raise money for a construction project at the Asansol Convent. The ball opened with '[a] fairly tableau!':

[Dr] Barthe and 19 fairies!! Such fairies. None of your flimsy delicate feathery whippersnappers but good honest robust heavy weights from whom no genii need be afraid to fly. Perhaps it would have been more appropriate to call them brownies or even darkies but that is a slight matter.

The chorus was equally impressive. Here, Strachey's erroneous reference to *Iolanthe* is noteworthy for showing how contemporary live performance could influence the costumes and choreography of fancy dress; in this case, Gilbert and Sullivan:

Barthe looked very elegant as a mixture of Watteau shepherd and light opera villager and brought down the house in his duet with Phoebe(?) (out of Iolanthe).[122]

In January 1899, Strachey attended a ball where 'H.B. ... called himself a negative and had everything white that ought to be black and everything black that ought to be white, including his face'.[123] As in England, fancy dress events in India were organized for children. One such event occurred in January 1900. In his letter home, Strachey mentions a 'huge tent for tea, a "high flier" swing and a merry go round' that was acquired for the children to play on.[124]

Strachey's letters are useful for describing how fancy dress entertainments spread from Europe. They also show how fancy dress could assert cultural hegemony, however subconsciously. In the case of Strachey's letters, the fancy dress events appear to have fostered constructive relationships between the rulers and the ruled. This was not always the case. In December 1988, a Guyanan newspaper, *Stabroek News*, published a story on the origins of masquerading in the Caribbean. According to the report, slaves took advantage of the carnival season between Christmas and Ash Wednesday that had been established by the Western 'plantocracy'. During the period of festivity, 'slaves had what amounted to official sanction for street parades, celebrations and revelry ... [T]he people of African descent took advantage of this "license" to openly perform some religious rites which they had been forced to suppress and which had gone underground'.[125] In the southern states of America, the Reconstruction-era Ku-Klux Klan provides a very different example of how fancy dress, adapted from Western traditions of *charivari* and used in a purposefully frightening form, openly and violently asserted domination (Chapter 2). As it became globally prevalent, the accessibility and polyvalence of fancy dress costume meant people found ways to use it to challenge social conventions and to serve themselves and the causes they championed.

The factors that encouraged the proliferation of fancy dress in the West go some way to explain its scarcity in the East. The democratic ideas and institutions that facilitated the public expression of critical (self) reflection through the arts and an incipient media were, on the whole, largely absent in Asia. Within China and Japan, social and religious conventions were more rigid than in Europe, communication between regions was more limited and access to cultural stimulus – particularly drama, poetry and literature – restricted until the nineteenth century.[126]

From the twentieth century to today

The role and meaning of fancy dress costume shifted again during the twentieth century as it became a regular form of entertainment in people's lives and 'reached near epidemic proportions' prior to the First World War.[127] In his discussion of carnival in the United States of America, Samuel Kinser writes of a 'symbolic flatness' and 'poverty of imagination' to describe the recycling within carnival performance of the twentieth century. The same is broadly true of dressing up, which became a routine ritual for many families. For example, the diaries of Londoner Vera Verena Pennefeather record her family's participation in fancy dress events alongside mundane notes about the weather and a broken car. On Saturday 6 January 1923, her sons attended a 'fancy dress party at Gatlands. Returned 7pm. Others stayed till 11pm'.[128] On Friday 1 January 1926, another prosaic entry reads:

Boyo and baby went to fancy dress party at Elmgrove given by the Bullocks. He and baby went as the knave of hearts and baby as butterfly.[129]

The inclusion of fancy dress into people's daily rhythms is conveyed dynamically in the photography of Helen Levitt, whose candid New York street scenes feature masked children at Halloween.[130]

The advent of department stores and television acted as a catalyst for the continued commercialization of fancy dress, but whilst this facilitated and encouraged the wearing of costume, it tended to stymy inventiveness. In contemporary photographs, certain costumes become recurrent: bandits, shepherdesses, kings, queens and guardsmen. Children, in particular, were frequently dressed as domestic products as companies and cooperatives recognized the advertising potential that fancy dress parties provided (Chapter 1). This is not to suggest that fancy dress costume became a cultural 'white noise', prevalent but purportless. The wide appeal of fancy dress costume made it a valuable means of determining taste and status, and it was used frequently to demarcate patrician and plebian spheres. For the social elite, the twentieth century was punctuated by fancy dress balls, as the newly minted and blue-blooded tried to enhance their social prestige through creative, frequently quixotic, entertainments (Chapter 1). To navigate the dos and don'ts, guide books written by 'experts' advised people on appropriate dress and comportment. The proliferation of fancy dress occasions in the twentieth century had two, more important, consequences. First, it emphasized the creative role and domestic authority of women, who typically designed and made outfits for their family and local communities. Second, the widespread adoption of fancy dress costume, and the correlative recognition of its ability to invert convention, saw it used with increasing frequency to champion a variety of social and political causes.

The diverse contexts in which fancy dress costume appeared during the twentieth century were a consequence of its commercialization. Fancy dress 'warehouses', pattern books and guides had existed in the eighteenth century, but the development of department stores and urban centres with 'commercial spaces dedicated to fun' did much to increase interest in fancy dress in the late nineteenth century.[131] Popular though it was, dressing up was a serious matter. Periodicals regularly reviewed the latest and most arresting designs, and large sums of money were available to people who dressed with unusual creativity. In 1894, George J. Nicholls, author of the apparently authoritative *Bacons and Hams*, won first prize and forty guineas at the annual Covent Garden Fancy Dress Party for dressing as a side of bacon (Figure 4).[132] The prize money was equivalent to the annual salary of a semi-skilled worker.[133]

To ensure accuracy, people were encouraged to choose a character that suited their physiognomy and psychology. In London, Debenham & Freebody and Liberty & Co. partnered with 'experts' to publish fancy dress guides that provided costume guidance and details of local suppliers. In 1887, Debenham & Freebody published *Fancy Dresses Described; or What to Wear at Fancy Dress Balls* with Ardern Holt, a columnist in Queen magazine (now Harper's Bazaar).[134] The preface to the book's fourth edition asserted that 'The Author's name is a guarantee for the correctness of the descriptions and accuracy of details'.[135] Between 1884 and 1905, Liberty & Co. published a series of fancy dress and costume books to advertise the work of its Costume Department.[136] These elegant volumes described the exclusive services that were available from Liberty's Studio of Costume Design, 'where Artists and assistants are employed whose sole duty it is to furnish Sketches, written descriptions, and all details in connection with inquiries by post regarding Costumes'.[137] The Liberty books also relied on recognized authorities; passing reference is made to former prime minister Benjamin Disraeli, architect and archaeologist Edward William Godwin and writer and art critic John Ruskin.

Recourse to professional opinion and academia was necessary because historical authenticity was paramount; the paradox of contemporary industry and technology fuelling a consumer

The Author in Fancy Dress as a Side of Bacon,
designed by himself, which took the First Prize of
Forty Guineas at the Covent Garden Fancy Dress
Ball, April 1894.

FIGURE 4 *Photogravure of George J. Nicholls dressed as a Side of Bacon, April 1894. George J. Nicholls,*
Bacon and Hams. *London: The Institute of Certified Grocers, 1917.*

boom that largely rejected modernity is again striking. The desire for exactitude created inevitable dilemmas when sourcing appropriate materials, particularly for make-up and facial hair. Holt was prepared to admit that consistency had to yield to convenience occasionally, but she was aghast that 'Marie Stuart appears in powder; Louis XIV wears a beard; and Berengaria distended drapery'.[138] So pressing was the concern for accuracy the Liberty guides stressed that partiality for a costume should not blind people to their physiognomy. Authenticity of appearance was especially great for children. It was 'wisely directed that a born Friar Tuck is not permitted to insist upon apeing Romeo, or a chubby, round-face Audrey try to disguise her bonnie comeliness in the plaintive grace of a miniature Ophelia. Let there be variety by all means. Let imagination and fancy have free play; but they must absolutely not run riot.'[139] Adults were advised to consider the 'dignity, beauty, expression, form or pose' of the person they were impersonating, especially if they were to dress as people 'idealized in pictorial art by the genius of the great masters, as they are most readily recognized, the best appreciated, and most admired'.[140] Reflecting a widely held view that history was 'a literary art' and of (moral) relevance to the present, these edicts also show that fancy dress was used to clarify social mores and hierarchies.[141]

The sense of propriety is conveyed in the Liberty guides, which include prices in guineas. The guinea, a gold coin equivalent to twenty-one shillings, had been replaced in 1816, at least sixty years before the earliest of the fancy dress guides discussed here appeared, but the specie continued to be invoked in aristocratic circles. The variety of accessories that Liberty supplied also hints at how fancy dress costume was, for some people, an important form of status expenditure. One of the cheapest gowns, of 'cotton-crépe stamped with a design in gold' to resemble 'Classic Greek', cost 4½ guineas (£4 4s.).[142] A gold fillet for the hair could be purchased for 7s. 6d., making a total cost of £4 11s. 6d. Ironically, the seventeenth-century-themed 'Puritan' costume was more expensive.[143] A robe of 'pale-grey cashmere; deep white lawn collar and cuffs, edged with narrow lace', cost 6 guineas (£6 6s.), or if customers preferred to use a Liberty fabric, 12 guineas (£12 12s.). A white lawn apron and cap were sold as extras and cost 15s. 6d. If all accessories were purchased, the ensemble would have cost £13 7s. 6d. This was a considerable sum. In 1891, the average annual wage of a manufacturing worker in Britain was a little over £34; in 1911 it was just over £37.[144]

For the period's plutocrats – Thorstein Veblen's Leisure Class – the ostentatious expense of fancy dress added to its allure. To commemorate the opening of their Fifth Avenue mansion in New York, and to ascend further up society's gilded ladder, Cornelius Vanderbilt II and his wife Alice Claypoole Gwynne organized a fancy dress ball for the evening of 26 March 1883. The event was reported to have cost $50,000, a sum roughly equivalent to $1.2 million today.[145] Historicized costume was popular among the guests, but the garment worn by Mrs Vanderbilt, 'Electric Light', was inspired by the present. The gown of silk-satin and velvet, embroidered with silver and gold metallic thread was made by the couture house of Charles Worth in Paris and shipped to New York.[146] The price of the garment and its matching accessories is unknown, but it would have been tens of thousands of dollars; Worth was a consummate businessman and in determining prices he doubled the cost of the materials and trebled the price of labour, which is to say nothing of the delivery expenses.[147] Fancy dress parties on this scale piqued people's curiosity and newspapers described the dress of attendees in detail. However, inquisitiveness did not mean acceptance. Susan Gail Johnson has shown how the fancy dress ball of Cornelia Bradley-Martin and her husband held on 10 February 1897 attracted widespread criticism because it exposed the gulf between the wealthy and the rest. The hosts claimed their ball would stimulate local trade – they sent invitations late to prevent guests commissioning Worth – but the reported $250,000 cost of the festivities garnered censure. After the ball, and perhaps because of the negative commentary, they left New York for England.[148]

Whilst department stores like Liberty sought affluent customers, disdainful responses to more extravagant fancy dress events, not to mention the simple fact that many people had modest budgets, encouraged costume suppliers to provide accessible products and services. Liberty offered patterns for garments to be made at home. In her *Characters Suitable for Fancy Costume Balls*, Marie Schild advertised paper patterns for 6s. 6d. As the popularity of fancy dress entertainments grew, cost became a pressing concern. Magazines and newspapers offered advice on how to economize. In June 1910, 'The Ladies Page and Fashion Chat' from *The Sydney Mail* explained that 'when planning fancy dress the cost must be the first consideration. It must be remembered that a fancy dress as a rule appears on one occasion only, and that for a few hours; consequently it is not advisable to make too great an outlay'. The anonymous author, who is simply styled 'Housewife', was nonetheless on hand to provide 'hints' and reminded her readers that 'nimble fingers can do a good deal'. She advised women 'not to spend too much time over neatening seams etc., for it is really not worth while.'[149]

The author's *nom de plume* reflects contemporary attitudes about gendered roles, but her advice reveals the importance of women in the creation of fancy dress garments, for themselves, but perhaps more typically for their dependents. Preliminary studies have shown how women had a crucial role in making fancy dress costumes that were often designed by men.[150] The Kate Greenaway dress mentioned above has a very roughly stitched hem and the three press studs on the rear of the dress have each been sewn differently, so most likely the work of a relative who would have appreciated the Housewife's point about unnecessary neatness. Similarly, the stomacher of the Violet Grey-inspired dress shows evidence of being expanded, again with imperfect stitching, suggesting it was refashioned within the wearer's home. The reuse of costumes increased as fancy dress events became more frequent during the nineteenth and twentieth centuries. If it were not possible to reuse a costume, fancy dress items were given away or sold. In the eighteenth century, Horace Walpole had lent his costumes.[151] In the twentieth century, photographer and socialite Cecil Beaton repurposed his fancy dress costumes.[152] In his diary for 1942, he notes that the impoverished socialite Marchesa Luisa Casati sold off 'relics' of her fancy dress 'as the Queen of Hearts, a tarnished, theatrical necklace, or bits of worthless finery from the bottom of a trunk'.[153]

Marchesa Casati's prodigious outlay on clothing highlights the distinction between popular and privileged fancy dress entertainments in the late nineteenth and twentieth centuries. The Devonshire Ball, conceived to celebrate the Diamond Jubilee of Queen Victoria in 1897 (Chapter 1), was one of earliest fancy dress entertainments of this grand type, but there were others, some in direct imitation.[154] In July 1934, *Le Bal des Valses* was hosted by Baron Nicolas de Gunzburg, Prince and Princess Jean-Louis de Faucigny-Laucinge, at Paris's Bois de Boulogne, apparently to consume the remainder of Gunzburg's fortune.[155] Guests, including Fulco di Verdura and Coco Chanel, wore costumes inspired by the Habsburg court in Vienna. Fancy dress balls organized by Étienne de Beaumont in Paris between 1921 and 1949 were less opulent, but remained exclusive and theatrical because each had a specific theme: *Le Bal des Jeux, Le Bal de la Mer, Le Bal Colonial, Le Bal des Rois et des Reines*. On 28 November 1966, author Truman Capote hosted his Black and White Ball at New York's Plaza Hotel.[156] Proust and Surrealist balls were hosted by Guy de Rothschild and his wife Marie-Hélène in 1971 and 1972, respectively, at Château de Ferrières outside Paris.[157]

Attracting wide interest and described variously as 'legendary' and 'balls of the century', these events were certainly lavish. Occurring within the shadow of the First and Second World Wars, however, there is a sense that these festivities were responses to a world in turmoil. This point is especially relevant for the escapades of Britain's Bright Young Things, who staged various costume parties, including a Second Childhood Party, a Hermaphrodite Party and a Peter Pan Party during the 1920s.[158] In the thick of fighting during the First and Second World Wars, soldiers and sailors had turned to fancy dress, cross-dressing in particular, to provide psychological and social fortitude (Chapter 3). The need for stability was no less true for civilians, albeit for different reasons. To an extent, the lavish balls of the elite can be interpreted as a means by which younger members tried to define tottering positions within an increasingly meritocratic society that was looking for new figures to emulate and impersonate, in life and fancy dress. According to an article from *The Milwaukee Journal* of April 1933:

> Princes and cavaliers will find themselves out of jobs [at fancy dress events], their places will be taken by Mussolinis and Hitlers and girls dressed as West Point cadets or nifty bellhops ... The movies are going to have a marked influence ... The average youth who will take part in the frolics would rather impersonate Valentino as a sheik than Napoleon as a fighter, Mussolini, dictator of today, than Caesar, the emperor of the dim past ... But the girls are going out for bolder adventures. Costumers say they can hardly supply the demand of women for masculine attire and they blame Miss Dietrich for the craze among women to put on trousers.[159]

The use of fancy dress costume to convey changing social attitudes is also apparent with the twentieth century's interest in harlequin and pierrot (Chapter 3). Characters from the *Comédie-Française*, the French derivation of Italy's *Commedia dell' Arte*, the harlequin and pierrot became widely popular as fancy dress characters during the late nineteenth century and the first half of the twentieth century. Simultaneously, numerous artists, including Edgar Degas, Paul Cézanne, Pablo Picasso and André Derain, featured apparently forlorn, isolated and emaciated harlequins and pierrots in their paintings, occasionally in self-portraits. The characters, who continued to appear in contemporary circus entertainments, notably France's *fête foraine*, were also depicted in literature. The ubiquity of these enigmatic avatars, who represented (variously) death, estrangement and sorrow, is not straightforward, but at the very least it suggests social and political circumstances encouraged a critical exploration of the relationship between self and society. Fancy dress provided an immediate means to contemplate the issue of role-playing because of the parallels that exist between anonymizing layers of costume and the different identities that people construct within themselves. The presence of the harlequin and pierrot in late-nineteenth- and early-twentieth-century art is perhaps best understood as a discreet commentary on a largely subconscious theme within the zeitgeist.

Naturally, it would be a mistake to assume that all fancy dress participants sought, or recognized, deeper meaning within their dress. Current affairs and the media had more obvious influences on the wearing of fancy dress costume during the twentieth century. Between 1971 and 1972, for example, the BBC aired the cartoon *Mr Benn*. In fourteen 15-minute episodes, the eponymous hero exchanged his dour city suit for a fancy dress costume that inspired an exhilarating adventure in a parallel universe. The series proved popular and was screened twice yearly for twenty-one years.[160] In June 1982, *The Sydney Morning Herald* reported that characters from the small and silver screens, which included Darth Vader, Miss Piggy (in a gold lamé dress) and Happy Bear, were among the more popular fancy dress hires. The appeal of television and movie characters continues today, perhaps most notably during Halloween. The origins of this festivity have been traced to the Celtic festival of Samhain, but the popular, commercialized celebration of All Hallows Eve began in the early twentieth century and proceeded apace after the Second World War.[161] In 2015, annual expenditure on adult Halloween costumes was said to have reached $1.21bn in the United States of America, with a further $1bn spent on children's costumes.[162] According to research by InsideOnline, nineteen of the twenty-five most popular Halloween costumes between 1990 and 2014 were inspired by television or film.[163] In October 2016, the combination of Hollywood and Halloween persuaded officials of Mexico City to inaugurate a Day of the Dead parade akin to that which appears in the introductory sequence of the twenty-fourth James Bond film *Spectre*; the movie created 'expectations' the Tourism Board did not want to disappoint (Figure 5).[164]

Trying to explain the popular appeal of dressing up in the 1980s, one Australian supplier of costume referred to the economy: 'Times are getting a bit tougher at the moment, and I believe people turn to entertainment to escape the pressures'.[165] Enthusiasm for dress-up in the twenty-first century is also linked to escapism. According to the marketing director of Angels, a UK supplier of fancy dress costume, the economic downturn that began in 2008 'spiked' hires, as people sought distraction by wearing nostalgic costume, in the form of 1980s' cartoon characters or costumes that provided a greater sense of menace.[166] The connection between social malaise and the appeal of fancy dress became dramatically apparent at the end of 2016 in what was perhaps the first global fancy dress viral trend: the sinister clown. Beginning in South America in September, reports of a 'killer clown craze' had spread to London and Varberg, Sweden, by November.[167] In Cumbria, in the north of England, a man dressed as Batman to confront the malevolent pranksters.[168] Journalists, in their clamour to explain this phenomenon, turned to academics and scientists, who suggested the craze channelled people's deeper feelings of unease.[169]

If fancy dress events have come to prioritize the concerns of individuals, themes of community and consensus remain, perhaps because of related misgivings about disintegrating interpersonal relationships. As costumed aristocrats entertained in private during the late nineteenth and early twentieth centuries, civic authorities filled public spaces to celebrate and defend the achievements and liberties of their communities. Cologne's carnival of 1823 was conceived to rouse citizens against the encroachment of imperial bureaucracy.[170] The Sherborne pageant of 1905, ostensibly commemorating the Dorset town's foundation in 705, made news in the United States of America and Australia and sparked 'pageant fever' throughout England as people sought to proclaim their civic identity and to champion their town's commercial skill (Chapter 4). Since 1985, UNESCO has encouraged the celebration of World Book Day, which enjoins children 'to dress up to save lives'.[171] Community remains prevalent in contemporary fancy dress events as costume is used with increasing frequency to lampoon errant politicians and to champion civic-centred causes.

The organizers of London's Panama Carnival, held on 10 April 2016 following the publication of the Panama Papers, which appeared to implicate many public figures in irregular tax dealings, used social media to call for 'visuals, noise, dress up welcome'.[172] Some protesters donned pig masks to mock the former Prime Minister, David Cameron, who featured in the Papers, to remind people of the uncomfortable revelation about his Bullingdon Club initiation tasks. However unintentionally, protesters were performing a twenty-first century *charivari*. In June 2016, the result of Britain's referendum on its membership of the European Union brought more fancy dress-clad people onto London's streets. One person wore a mock crusade tunic with a red cross on a white background, blissfully unaware that Richard I's *crucesignati* had worn white crosses

FIGURE 5 *Photograph of participants in Mexico City's Day of the Dead Parade, 2016. © Maria Calls/ Getty Images.*

on a red background.[173] An accompanying 'Viking' helmet suggests historical accuracy was not a concern.[174] A more ambiguous message was expressed by the person who wore a rubber Tyrannosaurus Rex costume with the accompanying, and equally baffling, placard, 'T-Rex it not Brexit'.[175] Donning fancy dress, these people were following the lead of protest groups and social movements, which have become widespread. Global LGBT+ Mardi Gras festivals are one of the most established examples of using costume in this way (Chapter 4). Spectators at New York's annual Gay Pride in June 2016 were estimated at 2 million.[176] International women's marches are a recent example (Chapter 4). On a smaller scale, in May 2015, Cancer Research UK encouraged people to wear amusing headpieces for 'Wig Wednesday', to raise awareness and funds for their charity initiatives.

The use of fancy dress to champion social and political causes is linked to the growing popularity of urban carnival.[177] The desire for cultural expression in the face of political incapacity had been a motivation for the revival of London's Notting Hill carnival in the 1960s. Aiming to familiarize the disparate people of west London with each other's culture, the rejuvenated carnival was conceived to 'bring some colour, warmth and happiness to a grim and depressed neighbourhood'.[178] As it happened, West Indian leadership of the carnival, which became pronounced in the 1970s, was the cause of long-running tension between organizers, local government and the police. In his study of the carnival, Abner Cohen observes that 'symbolic forms have the potentialities for political articulation, serving in some situations as "rituals of rebellion" the effect of which is cathartic and ultimately a mechanism operating in the maintenance of the established order; in other situations they serve as an expression of protest, resistance and violence'.[179] Carnival continues to spark tensions in other parts of the world, including New Orleans and, more recently, in Germany.[180] In February 2017, police from the German state of North Rhine-Westphalia caused outcry when they suggested that 'carers of refugees and asylum seekers' should stay away from carnival celebrations, citing the country's 'ongoing security situation'.[181]

The ability of fancy dress to annunciate and proclaim views that would otherwise struggle to be heard has helped it to gain new adherents in the twenty-first century; so much so, it appears to be changing from an exclusively event-based phenomenon into something broader and culturally diverse. At a time when economic and political insecurity is making many people feel isolated, the ability of fancy dress to relay messages and represent the zeitgeist on account of its sartorial exceptionalism, means that many of its elements – the use of humour, cultural or chronological juxtaposition – are appearing with increasing frequency on the catwalk, as collections from Walter Van Bierendonck, Agi & Kim and Craig Green, demonstrate. This is more a difference of degree than kind because the eighteenth-century masquerade had spawned fashions as much as it had occasionally critiqued them. Scholars interested in 'critical fashion' and 'experimental fashion' have started to consider the links between fancy dress and contemporary fashion design, as have commentators who contemplate 'ugly' faces, bodies and clothes.[182]

Allusions to fancy dress in art are also becoming conspicuous, once again. Cartoonist Steve Bell often depicted Britain's former Prime Minister Theresa May in a black and white patchwork suit in *The Guardian* newspaper, perhaps to make comparisons with harlequin.[183] Artist Georgina Clapham references fancy dress in her work (Figure 6). Curator Elena Fadeeva observes:

The garb in Clapham's paintings is a melting pot of carefully curated social signifiers … combinations of historical costume, haute couture, fancy dress, vintage and contemporary fashion subcultures … and an understanding of clothing's complex layered and cultural associations through time.[184]

FIGURE 6 *'Orlando', Georgina Clapham, engraving, 2016. © Georgina Clapham.*

It may even be possible to suggest that fancy dress costume is becoming prevalent in virtual reality as online game players customize avatars with 'skins' to create distinctive identities. In *League of Legends*, the largest web-based multiplayer game, skins have sold for thousands of dollars.[185] The popularity of digital games has inspired Cosplay and, more recently, 'Genderless Kei', a sartorial and beauty trend in Japan that appears to emulate and imitate androgynous anime characters.[186] Adherents of Genderless Kei would probably not consider their look to be fancy dress, but their incongruent appearance channels key elements of this sartorial phenomenon. It is noteworthy that Asian interest in fancy dress costume is influenced by multiplayer computer games. The role of team work is important because it elides with East Asia's culture of collectivism, which emphasizes social coordination and people's interdependence, as opposed to Western individualism.[187] Empirical studies have consistently shown that East Asian people are most comfortable when their actions promote social harmony, which may explain why the incongruous attire of fancy dress has been historically absent and is emerging now in a form that promotes group identity.[188] East Asia's historic disengagement with fancy dress emphasizes how the expansion of Western rule and values made fancy dress a global phenomenon.

Fancy dress through theory

A thousand-year genealogy of fancy dress, brief though its telling has been, clarifies how the wearing of costume has been shaped by social and political fluctuations. To explain the changing role and meaning of dress up, scholars have used a variety of anthropological, historical and sociological theories. The piecemeal nature of fancy dress research means that writing on this subject is characterized by the usage of different theories, with limited attempts to establish a coherent intellectual or methodological approach. The challenge of coherence is further obfuscated by the apparent need for contemporary academics to devise their own 'isms', 'ographies' and 'ologies' and to augment or replace existing theories. The purpose of the following research summary is twofold; first, to introduce the main theories that inform the book's analysis of fancy dress costume, and second, to help readers to understand how different theories can be used conjointly to provide a more nuanced interpretation of the changing role and meaning of fancy dress costume. The book is informed by existing academic work and I have seen no virtue in devising my own concepts and paradigms.

Rachel Hann has written forcefully about the criticality of costume. 'Critical costume' encourages an interdisciplinary approach to the study of costume, which, understood in its broadest sense, includes film and theatre dress as well as fancy dress. Arguing that costume is always subversive, as an 'extra-daily performance', Hann adopts Richard Schechner's notion of 'showing doing', to focus on the slippage that occurs between character and self when it is worn.[189] 'Showing doing' is 'a deliberate scoring of an individual's awareness of their actions' and Hann contends that the 'conceptual gap between the worn and the wearer', which costume opens up, can 'reveal the process of dressing through the exposure of appearance as an act'.[190] The deliberateness of costume wearers can be challenged, but Hann's approach is virtuous for considering the physical form and psychological affect of costume concurrently. A useful supplement to the concept of critical costume is Hajo Adam and Adam Galinsky's term 'enclothed cognition', which 'designate[s] the systematic influence of clothes on the wearer's psychological processes and behavioural tendencies'.[191] Critical costume and enclothed cognition are relatively new concepts; neither is older than a decade. Consequently, they have not been fully incorporated into studies of (fancy dress) costume.

To date, academics have tended to approach the study of fancy dress by looking at human performance and play in its broadest sense, cognizant that the act of dressing up is usually conceived as part of wider and recurring social events. A common starting point is Mikhail Bakhtin's *Rabelais and His World*, which considers the inversion of social conventions through the subverting power of 'carnival laughter'. Dwelling on the physical and psychological frenzy unleashed by carnival, Bakhtin has been able to convey the excitement of this festive period far better than most analysts.[192] However, in emphasizing the subversive nature of carnival misrule through its 'grotesque realism', and by likening it to a 'second world' that was separate in time and space to 'officialdom', he minimizes its stabilizing function.[193] Strictly speaking, his study is also time-bound, a fact often overlooked. In *Problems of Dostoevsky's Politics*, published five years before *Rabelais and His World*, Bakhtin asserts that costumed entertainments from the eighteenth century onwards were far removed from those that had 'sens[ed] the world as one great communal performance' in the medieval and early modern period. Permutations of carnival in modernity were 'dogmatic and hostile to evolution and change' and reflected a tendency to 'absolutize a given condition of existence or a given social order' such that they conveyed only 'vulgar bohemian individualism'.[194]

The measured and extensive writings of anthropologist Victor Turner provide a corollary to Bakhtin's forceful thesis. Central to Turner's work is the concept of 'social drama', a four-stage process that aims to restore social rifts. An act of social aggression or breach (1) triggers a crisis (2) that necessitates redress (3). If rehabilitative attempts succeed, peace is restored (4). If negotiations falter, a new crisis can occur.[195] Necessitating reflection, the social drama is a liminal event that occurs at the 'threshold between more or less stable and harmonic periods of social process'.[196] It is often 'the scene and time for the emergence of a society's deepest values' and it typically inspires 'cultural' or 'performative' genres, including theatre, film and ritual; fancy dress could be added, although Turner never explicitly writes about dressing up.[197] The concept of social drama is useful for establishing that the appeal and relevance of human performance is frequently informed by an awareness of public responsibility. As Turner remarks, 'cognitively, nothing underlines regularity so well as absurdity or paradox. Emotionally, nothing satisfies as much as extravagant or temporarily permitted illicit behaviour'.[198] This point is reinforced by Roger Caillois in his study of human play.

Caillois sees play as aberrant. It is free, separate, uncertain, unproductive, governed by rules and make-believe, and yet maintained by the congruence of social structures and mores.[199] It is in this way that human games can 'educate, enrich and immunize the mind against [destructive and frantic instincts]. At the same time, they are made fit to continue usefully to the enrichment and the establishment of various patterns of culture'.[200] Caillois's work helps to explain the continuing appeal of dress up in complex societies where the connection between leisure and labour is weaker and where the individual assumes more importance than the group. The pairing of two categories of play, *ilinix* (vertigo) and *mimicry* (simulation), which in Caillois's formulation define the experience and impact of fancy dress, often leads 'to an inexorable, total frenzy which in its most obvious form appears to be the opposite of play, an indescribable metamorphosis in the condition of existence. The fit so provoked, being uninhibited, seems to remove the player ... far from the authority, values, and influence of the real world.'[201] This removal from society is often unwelcome in societies where people are constrained by rules. Consequently, fancy dress is likely to be at the 'periphery of public life', where it is deemed 'noisy' and 'harmless'; although Caillois notes that the wearing of masks remains 'quite menacing'.[202] The ephemeral nature of fancy dress continues to be the source of its ability to shock, awe, shame and delight. The subversive potential that Caillois attributes to *ilinix* and *mimicry* is echoed in Turner's observation that cultural genres become more critical of society as the connection between leisure and labour fades.[203]

A theme that connects the work of Bakhtin, Turner and Caillois is the creation of distinct psychological and physical spaces that empower people to contemplate, critique, and if necessary, to change the role they occupy within their respective communities. Consequently, their work can be aligned through the concept of world making, which has been enunciated particularly clearly by Ramzi Fawaz. He defines world making as any instance 'when cultural products facilitate a space of public debate where dissenting voices can reshape the production and circulation of culture and, in turn, publicize counternarratives to dominant ideologies'.[204] For minorities, in particular, world making facilitates the creation of 'forms of culture, as well as public spaces, that offer recognition to nonnormative social relations and hail audiences commonly ignored by mainstream mass-media forms'.[205] The incongruity and imagination of fancy dress costume constitutes a form of dissent even when it is of a trivial nature and 'counternarratives' are not conceived to threaten 'dominant ideologies'. However, when fancy dress costume is worn to protest, its challenge is more clamorous and the threat posed to these ideologies much greater. Throughout this study world making will be invoked, first, because of its ability to harmonize existing writing on human performance and play and, second, because of its flexibility to accommodate different forms of expression through fancy dress costume.

Academic discussions of carnival and fancy dress have made passing and profitable reference to other authors. Norbert Elias's theory of the civilizing process explains how increasing social complexity affects notions of self and, by implication, self-representation through dress.[206] Holly Bruce has employed the idea of the *gesamtkunstwerk* to describe the immersive experience of fancy dress.[207] Barbara Babcock's concept of 'symbolic inversion' is also relevant to fancy dress costume, although it has not been widely applied.[208] More recently, the relationship between fancy dress costume and contemporary clothing design has been considered in publications on 'critical' and 'experimental' fashion.[209] Therèsa Winge's study of the subcultural body offers a more specific way of analysing the connection between current fashions and fancy dress.[210]

From carnival to the catwalk

The broad nature of this book's content and methodology means that it cannot provide a complete history of fancy dress costume. This is not my intention. Consequently, there is little virtue in adopting a rigid chronological structure. The book's chapters consider four defining constituents of fancy dress; its ability to *cohere* – by encouraging individual identity and group unity (chapter one); to *challenge* – by confronting established cultural narratives and behaviour (chapter two); to *clarify* – by offering escapism from, and a space to reflect upon, uncomfortable realities (chapter three); and to *champion* – by encouraging (minority) social and political causes (chapter four). The chapters adhere to a loose chronology as the four themes follow the changing role of fancy dress costume summarized above. In the spirit of an interpretative essay, each chapter analyses three examples of fancy dress that have been selected on the basis of their cumulative ability to show the global extent of fancy dress events, the chronological extent of fancy dress events and the social diversity of fancy dress events. The examples are intentionally diverse to demonstrate the cultural prevalence of fancy dress costume. There is a certain inevitability that the majority of cases come from the West, but this reflects the development of fancy dress as much the availability of adequate sources. I have deliberately used a variety of evidence, including garments, diaries, private correspondence, paintings, interviews, photographs, published fiction and non-fiction to emphasize the importance of this sartorial phenomenon and the range of materials that exist for further research.

The diachronic and thematic approach I adopt privileges breadth over depth, although the use of specific examples does enable detailed analysis. Scholars' efforts to compartmentalize their topics for the sake of clarity can confound understanding and I am cognizant that decisions to wear fancy dress costume will span more than one of the book's themes. The rationale for my approach is threefold. First, a focused approach will reduce the methodological and intellectual confusions that have stymied investigations of fancy dress costume and limited academic engagement with the topic. Second, the ability to juxtapose dominant themes will enable the changing role and meaning of fancy dress costume to be more clearly comprehended. Third, by focusing on what might be termed the universals of fancy dress costume, I hope this study can contribute more readily to ongoing debates about the communicative qualities of clothing by providing what might, for want of a better term, be called analytical snapshots to generate questions and to encourage further investigation.

71887
Pom-Pom

71958
Spanish Costume

71906
Red Devil

Printed by the
Sun Engraving Company, Ltd.,
Watford, England,
by the new Roto Colour Process.

BUY
BRITISH
EMPIRE
GOODS

Ladies' Fancy Dress
Patterns in Bust
sizes 34, 36 and 38
inches unless other-
wise stated.

Men's Patterns in
36-inch Chest only.

74119
Persian Prince
(Man)

75627
Paint Box
Bust sizes: 36 and
38 inches only.

75624
Buy British Goods
Bust sizes: 36 and
38 inches only

FIGURE 7 *Colour supplement page ii from* Weldon's Fancy Dress for Ladies and Gentleman. *London: Weldon's Ltd., c.1926–1930. Author's copy.*

viii   SUPPLEMENT TO Weldon's Fancy Dress for Ladies and Gentlemen

77496
The Blue
Courtier
(Lady)

NIGHT

NO
MORE
STRIKE

77504
No More
Strikes
(Lady)

77490
Night

77447
The Desert
Chief

Ladies' Fancy Dress Patterns
on this page in Bust sizes 36
and 38 inches only.
Men's Patterns in 36-inch
Chest only.

77502
Mexican or
Spanish
Dancer

Fancy

the

Weldon's Fancy Dress Paper Patterns (price 1/- each, post free) include full directions for cutting out, making, and quantity of material.

FIGURE 8 *Colour supplement page viii from* Weldon's Fancy Dress for Ladies and Gentleman. *London: Weldon's Ltd., c.1926–1930. Author's copy.*

Weldons Ltd., 30–32 Southampton Street, Strand, London, W.C.2; and 231 Regent Street, W.1   39

57949
Moth or
Butterfly

75688
Elizabethan
Sea Captain
" Twelfth Night "

43918
Nigger Minstrel

62605
Gondolier

71641
Pierrot
(Lady)

69850
Caliph

69818
Modern
Harlequin

61382
Carnival
Folly

Ladies' Fancy
Dress Patterns in
Bust sizes 34, 36
and 38 inches un-
less   otherwise
        stated.
Men's   Patterns
in 36-inch Chest
        only.

68699
Ku-Klux-Klan

41618
Japanese
(Man)

Weldon's Fancy Dress Paper Patterns (price 1/- each, post free) include full directions for cutting out, making, and quantity of material.

FIGURE 9 *Page 39 from* Weldon's Fancy Dress for Ladies and Gentleman. *London: Weldon's Ltd., c.1926–1930. Author's copy.*

Weldons Ltd., 30–32 Southampton Street, Strand, London, W.C.2 ; and 231 Regent Street, W.1   45

Good Luck and the Pack

71642
Dominoes

71985
Knave of Hearts

66342
Queen of
Hearts

66345
Queen of
Spades

75651
Ace of
Spades

Ladies' Fancy
Dress Patterns
in Bust sizes
34, 36 and 38
inches unless
o t h e r w i s e
stated.
Men's Pat-
terns in 36 in.
chest only.

71902
Good Luck

66344
Queen of
Clubs

Will readers
kindly note
that Weldons
Ltd. do not
supply acces-
sories for
fancy dress.
Refer to
advertisement
pages.

71899
Ace of Clubs

66346
Queen of
Diamonds

Weldon's Fancy Dress Paper Patterns (price 1/- each, post free) include full directions for cutting out, making, and quantity of material.

FIGURE 10 *Page 43 from* Weldon's Fancy Dress for Ladies and Gentleman. *London: Weldon's Ltd.,* c.1926–1930. *Author's copy.*

1

To Cohere

Fancy dress entertainments that bring people together in celebration or recognition of an individual or institution are long-standing. Within pre-industrial societies, the edifying and galvanizing roles of costumed events is recognized. Their place within modern and contemporary societies is viewed critically, even sceptically. The case for meaningful fancy dress costume appears to have weakened in correlation to its global prevalence and connection with popular culture. It would seem that fancy dress parties, parades and pranks have become too common to warrant sustained academic reflection. Familiarity has bred contempt. Mikhail Bakhtin has been a forceful voice in suggesting that modern costumed events are essentially nihilistic and culturally trivial, reflecting only 'vulgar bohemian individualism'.[1] Superficially, his censorious assessment is compelling. In 2011, Teen Vogue's 'My Culture Is Not A Costume' campaign highlighted the 'dehumanizing' effect of fancy dress that is worn without reflection and consideration of people's feelings. A powerful video explained how costumes that appear 'funny and harmless' cause offence by perpetuating racial stereotypes through cultural appropriation.[2] Plentiful evidence exists to support Bakhtin's implicit critique that contemporary costumed and carnivalesque events frustrate serious scholarly enquiry. In 2017, New York's Annual Tompkins Square Halloween Dog Parade included canines costumed as Barbie, a barbeque and a Wall Street banker. Some of the dogs' owners wore corresponding outfits.[3] Confronted with these two examples, and many more like them, it is convenient to follow Bakhtin and denigrate acts of dressing up that involve cultural appropriation and costumed animals as 'culturally trivial', but however unusual, offensive and 'socially peripheral' these performances appear, they are not, to refer to Barbara Babcock, 'symbolically flat'. Teen Vogue's campaign highlighted the affective and long-term impact of poorly chosen costumes. The Tompkins Square Parade, which included a 'Woof of Wall Street' costume, a parody inspired by the 2014-movie The Wolf of Wall Street, shows how fancy dress is rarely as trivial as Bakhtin suggests, even when it is worn chiefly for fun. In fact, the opposite is very likely to be the case. Fancy dress that is worn for merriment and the amusement of others has the potential to be more revealing about a community's ideas and ideals. Kiera Vaclavik has shown how dressing up for World Book Day, an event that appears thoroughly innocuous, has become important for the reinforcement of community norms.[4] As Victor Turner opines, 'nothing underlines regularity so well as absurdity or paradox'.[5]

Surviving fancy dress costumes can also make clamorous, if not always eloquent, cases for their cultural importance. By way of one example, the John Bright Collection, London, includes a white cotton knee-length dress with a low-waisted and pleated shirt (Figure 11). The silhouette is similar to an evening gown with a high rounded neckline of the 1920s, which is probably when the dress was made. The costume is entirely handmade and decorated with a random pattern of duplicated symbols conventionally associated with good fortune: a cat with an arched back, a horse shoe, a frog, a four-leaf clover and a swastika. The symbols have been applied with black paint, probably by stencil because the outlines of some are blurred. Details have been added with a fine black pen. The rear of the dress is decorated with the in-filled silhouette of a large sitting black cat, its tail fashioned from a length of black tassel. This conceptual costume is a hesitant adaptation of a popular 'Good Luck' outfit from the early twentieth century (Figure 10). A more sophisticated interpretation appears in a catalogue from London fancy dress supplier Weldon's, which features a repeat design of swastikas hanging from the skirt's hem.[6] At some point, the swastikas caused the dress to be altered. The rise of National Socialism in Germany during the 1930s limited the meaning of this polyvalent symbol, which became socially repugnant. Consequently, two roughly cut white cotton panels were stitched across the problematic devices that appear on the front of the dress, at the upper right side, and the rear, along the hem. The cotton is thin and the panels are translucent. Across the centre of the front panel, 'Good Luck' has been written in thin black marker. Four rough shapes, ostensibly two horseshoes and two four-leaf clovers, have been drawn near to the corners. The rudimentary sewing of the dress, the faltering application of the symbols and its small size, suggest it was the work of a girl or young woman who lacked experience in clothes making.[7] This may explain why the costume was retained and revised. This decision demonstrates how an unexceptional costume, most likely worn for a parochial entertainment, acquired new meanings as the circumstances in which it was worn changed. Furthermore, the woman was not unreflective whilst wearing it. The impulse to censor was presumably governed by her desire to make another wearing of the costume socially acceptable and possible. The need to amend the dress was perhaps all the greater because the political charging of one of its motifs would have been untenable within the convivial environment where it was probably worn. The alterations are also suggestive of the owner's pride in their handiwork. In sum, the outfit demonstrates that fancy dress costume can be an expressive communicator of people's ideas and behaviour even when it conformed to popular trends and existed for delight alone.

The three examples in this chapter – the Devonshire Ball, the Co-operative Wholesale Society and West African fancy dress – pursue this argument and consider the meaningfulness of costumed entertainments whose avowed purpose was pleasure and playfulness. The episodes are culturally diverse but they are comparable in as much as they focus on events where fancy dress costume was conceived to demonstrate the cohesion of social networks. The chronological distance between the episodes is smaller. I intentionally begin my study in the modern period because this is when analytic comments about the unresponsiveness of festive participants emerge. I think it is important to challenge this view in the book's first chapter because subsequent arguments are predicated on the responsiveness of costumed participants and the affectiveness of what they wear. In each scenario, the temporary effacement of social hierarchies through costume, and the simultaneous desire to convey belonging, created unique opportunities for people to construct personal narratives about their place and role among their peers.

FIGURE 11 *Photograph of 'Good Fortune' costume, c.1920s. Photographed by Jon Stokes with funding from the Heritage Lottery Fund. Courtesy of Cosprop Limited.*

Demonstrating social order - The Devonshire House Ball
London, UK, 2 July 1897

On the evening of 2 July 1897 Devonshire House, in London's Piccadilly, was the setting for one of the most opulent costumed entertainments of the nineteenth century. Hosted by the Duke and Duchess of Devonshire, the event brought together approximately 700 guests, chiefly members of England's social and political elite, to celebrate the Diamond Jubilee of Queen Victoria. The queen did not attend because of illness, although she did enjoy fancy dress festivities, according to the evidence of her loquacious journals, and had hosted three costume balls at Buckingham Palace in 1842, 1845 and 1851. The monarch was represented by the family of her eldest son, the Prince of Wales. The ball is unique among nineteenth- and early-twentieth-century fancy dress entertainments because of the amount of associated evidence that survives, including letters, memoirs, newspaper reports and twelve costumes, two from the Parisian house of Charles Worth.[8] The material considered here shows the intentions and actions of participants were more complicated than may be supposed for a fancy dress event whose ostensible purpose was to bring people together in merriment around a unifying theme. If the ball did achieve cohesion, it was through the demonstration of gendered and dynastic hierarchies and, paradoxically, by facilitating rivalry between the participants, who used character, conceptual and synecdochic costumes to display their status. Some spectators, viewing the event from a different social tier, found these performances distasteful. Their response crystallized prevailing social attitudes by emphasizing inequalities of birth and income.

The format of the ball was similar to contemporary festivities of this type. Guests arrived for half past ten in the evening and lined a route on the ground floor of Devonshire House to greet the royal party, who appeared at quarter past eleven, accompanied by the national anthem.[9] The royals were welcomed by the Duke and Duchess of Devonshire, who accompanied them to a dais in the ball room. From this position the royal party reviewed the guests as they processed before them, making bows and curtsies. Hosts generally received this honour, but it would have been *lèse-majesté* to have done otherwise on this occasion.[10] The guests were organized into different costume groups, which was then fashionable. The invitation stipulated that dress should be 'allegorical or historical' before 1815. Guests were recommended to arrange themselves into historical and mythical courts.[11] The emphasis on historic characters was edifying as participants learned about their nations and ancestors. It also provided opportunities to demonstrate family associations with historical figures, or to claim them if the guests were cunning.[12] The procession that filed past the royal party included the English court of Elizabeth I, the Austrian court of Empress Maria Theresa, the Russian Court of Catherine the Great, 'Orientals' led by the Duchess, Egyptians, the French courts of Louis XV and Louis XVI, and a group of allegorical figures.[13] Fittingly for an occasion that celebrated Britain's monarchy, the procession commenced with Queen Elizabeth I and concluded with Britannia.[14] Quadrilles and dancing followed a champagne interlude. A three-course supper was served in two sittings after midnight, with the royal party eating first.[15] There was no determined departure time and guests left in early hours of the following morning.[16]

The conventional structure of the event, punctuated by jubilant displays of obeisance to Britain's monarchy, established an overarching unity. The impression of choreographed festivity is furthered by newspaper reports, which were a major source for disseminating information about the ball to contemporary audiences. Accounts of the event, which included costume descriptions, circulated around the world for at least nine weeks, until September.[17] To obtain information about the costumes some journalists made notes as guests alighted from their carriages; others relied on attendees to send descriptions of what they had worn after the event.[18] Whatever the process of compilation, reporters generally did not seek detail for accuracy or insight. First, lack of expert knowledge meant they were often unable to verify historical verisimilitude. Second, contemporaries expected guests to conform to the prevailing taste for historic dress rather than to innovate. Journalists wanted detail to astound their readers with the extraordinary. The garrulous, occasionally hyperbolic, always superficial descriptions of what was worn reveals that commentators recognized a need to conjure through words a world their readers could only temporarily inhabitant. This means the ball – like other occasions of its type – tended to be portrayed as a sophisticated *gesamtkunstwerk*, where costumed revellers blend seamlessly, certainly beautifully, into an overarching aesthetic spectacle. This was especially the case with foreign correspondents, who generally synthesized several reports to produce their own.

An example of the content and tone of contemporary newspaper accounts is provided by *The Boston Evening Transcript*, which describes the costume of Princess Daisy of Pless, who was one of three Queens of Sheba:

> No one could describe at all adequately the barbaric splendour of it, with turquoise, emerald, amethyst, and ruby, caught in a web of finest gold and spread thickly upon the dress and train of diaphanous gauze in purple and gold, its shifting light seeming to mingle with that of the jewels. Black attendants bore her train along, and among her girl attendants was her pretty sister, Miss Cornwallis West, in an Ethiopian dress of snowy crepe, gilded with jewels under a flowing robe of gold tissue.[19]

The tenor and structure of this commentary facilitates the convenient conclusion that costumed participants were typically unquestioning. This response is perhaps strengthened by the sepia photogravure taken of approximately two hundred guests by Lafayette from their tent pitched within the grounds of Devonshire House.[20] The guests in these images look resplendent and aloof as they pose in historical garments to be immortalized by the latest technology. If we consider the exposure time, it may be that their expressions convey tedium. The discordance between fiction and reality was not lost on participants. The expectation to base costumes on historical characters may have been enjoyable, but for members of the social elite it was an opportunity to appear as ancestors or legitimating luminaries to convey messages about their personal and dynastic positions in the present. This point can be explored by analysing some costumes in detail, those which survive and those that were described or photographed by Lafayette.

The women of the royal party represented the sixteenth-century court of Henri IV of France and appear to have devised a visual strategy to portray familial and gendered cohesion. Alexandra Princess of Wales dressed as Marguerite de Valois, wife of Henri IV, in a floor-length white satin gown embellished with sequins, spangles and long chains of pearls. Her costume may have cost £501 8d., or approximately £41,000 in twenty-first-century sums.[21] Alexandra's three daughters, Louise, Victoria and Maud, and daughter-in-law Mary, appeared as Marguerite's ladies-in-waiting. The choice of characters neatly suited the women's different ages and status, but they reinforced family identity and their individual roles within it. The bonds between the women were elucidated through the dresses they wore. The gowns were connected through a complementary colour scheme of white (Alexandra), turquoise (Victoria), pink (Maud) and pale blue (Mary).[22] They were also of similar design. Each interpreted sixteenth-century fashions with a stomacher, open *décolletage*, farthingale skirt (without the frame) and rigid collar. The gowns were decorated in a similar style to Alexandra's dress with sequins,

H.R.H. Princess Victoria of Wales & Princess Charles of Denmark
as Ladies of the Court of Marguerite de Valois.
H.R.H. Prince Charles of Denmark.

FIGURE 12 *Photogravure of Princess Maud, Princess Victoria and Prince Carl of Norway as members of the Court of Henri IV at the Devonshire Ball, 1897. © National Portrait Gallery.*

spangles and pearls. Kate Strasdin suggests the slashed sleeves of the surviving costumes worn by Alexandra and Maud are identical.[23] This is likely as both gowns were made by Morin-Blossier. Visual clues among the surviving photogravure, which show all five women carrying fans as a unifying prop, suggest the costumes of Victoria and Mary may have been made by the same couturier: the raised lace collars on the gowns of Maud and Mary share a comparable design. All five costumes are similarly decorated with diamante embroidery in floriate patterns.

Another indication that the women intended to present themselves as a distinct group was their decision to mimic a Valois court. The choice is curious considering their connection to Queen Victoria, whom the ball celebrated. It is all the more noteworthy because some of women's husbands, the Prince of Wales, his sons the Dukes of York, Connaught and Fife, appeared separately in an English court of Elizabeth I, with many acquiring their costumes from Alias of Soho Square.[24] According to the lists of attendees, married couples tended to appear in the same courts, which makes the division of the royal family unusual. The only daughter of Alexandra to appear within the Valois group with her husband, Prince Carl of Norway, was Maud (Figure 12). The couple's costumes survive in Oslo's National Museum and emphasize how colour bound the group together: Maud wore pink satin; Carl, plum. Carl's costume, in the style of a Danish courtier, consists of a black velvet doublet and slashed hose decorated with purple embroidery, matching purple hose, black leather boots trimmed with red, a white ruff and black plumed hat. The chromatic parity between wife and husband was closer than that between Maud, her sisters and mother, and perhaps reflected the couple's mutual affection as they were still within the first year of marriage. The connection through colour may have sought to emphasize the important role of royal women in forging dynastic links for England's monarchy. The point may be confirmed by the absence of the Duchess of Connaught, wife of Queen Victoria's youngest son, who participated in the Austrian court. If Prince Carl and Mary of Teck, as foreign-born royals, were included among the Valois group, it seems strange that Louise Margaret, daughter of Prince Friedrich Karl of Prussia, who was a similar age to the young royals, should not have been. Presumably, the determining factor was that she was not more closely related to Alexandra.

The visual synchronicity of the five costumes was noted by contemporaries. A report in Munsey's Magazine observed that 'the feature of the ball was the assemblage of princes and princesses in fancy dress. The Princess of Wales impersonated Marguerite of Valois … Her dress had been designed by an artist, who made a series of sketches for it … Her daughters … all appeared as ladies in attendance upon her.'[25] The comment is brief, but sufficient to suggest the royal women's aesthetic effect was intentional. Studies of the wardrobes of Alexandra and Maud have revealed that mother and daughter were alive to the opportunities their clothing created. Where Strasdin has shown how Alexandra, as Princess of Wales and Queen, used clothing to define her character and place within England's royal family, Anne Kjellberg and Susan North have shown how Maud, as Queen of Norway, maintained her own counsels in dress and disappointed patrons who had hoped she would adopt Norwegian styles and support the domestic fashion industry.[26]

The conspicuous visual cohesion of Alexandra and her daughters, which involved separation from their husbands, may explain the confusion with which their costumes were reported by journalists. One reporter opined that they were 'historically correct in the smallest detail'.[27] A second confused the women and stated that Princess Victoria's costume was from the 'Elizabethan period' and that the Duchess of York was Marguerite of Valois.[28] An Irish reporter, cited by Strasdin, suggested Alexandra looked 'too modern and too like herself'.[29] In truth, this assessment was correct. The costumes of the Princess of Wales and her daughters were cut according to nineteenth-century modes and stood out because of their chromatic and technical similarities. In appearing as they did, even if the meaning was not grasped by the Irish correspondent, the women questioned contemporary gender roles that were voiced in other accounts of the ball. *The Times*, for example, proclaimed, '[a]s usual on such occasions, the gentlemen, it is said, have proved far more exacting than the ladies; for the stronger sex, when once it makes up its mind to desert sobriety of plain broadcloth, knows no limit to its requirements or to its suddenly developed fastidiousness.'[30]

In a separate and foreign court the Princess of Wales and her daughters made a subtle, but no less striking, statement about their individual and collective identities. This sartorial strategy was uniquely possible at a fancy dress ball that encouraged a relatively conservative form of historically inspired dress because it ensured the princesses stood apart among the other costumes.[31] Inadvertently, however, the women's sartorial strategy confirmed the limitations of their role. Prince Carl presumably accompanied his wife because his foreign birth made him ineligible to join the royal men in the Elizabethan group. If his appearance alongside Maud elucidated the agency of woman through marriage, it surely also emphasized that effective political authority in this community was understood to reside with men who possessed closer connections to England generally, and to Queen Victoria specifically. The involvement of Grand Duke Michael Mikhailovich, a grandson of Nicholas I of Russia, as Henri IV makes this suggestion more credible (Figure 13). At the time of the ball, the Duke had been exiled from Russia for his morganatic marriage to Sophie Von Merenberg.[32] Prior to this he had courted two women within the Valois group, Mary of Teck and Princess Louise.[33] In 1897, and among the guests at Devonshire House, his position was consequently, even scandalously, insecure. This would have been emphasized by the accompaniment of his wife, who dressed as Henri's paramour. To head a costumed group that included two women whom he had considered marrying was provocative. His presence alongside the Princess of Wales likely drew attention to the group. This odd coupling may have underscored the role of royal women in dynastic networks. However, the Duke's pariah status may have meant his association was less encouraged and merely tolerated for the fact that he was not welcome elsewhere. The ambivalent position of Prince Carl and Duke Michael within the Valois court was therefore equally a reminder of the bounded positions women occupied. In sum, the experience of Princess Alexandra and her daughters was perhaps analogous to the fictitious ladies studied by Catherine Craft-Fairchild in her study of eighteenth-century women's literature. In depictions of the masquerade, Craft-Fairchild argues that there was often great 'distance between the woman's self and her representation, distance between the woman's desire and the man's'.[34] The actions of Alexandra and her daughters suggest that some women sought to close this gap.

A growing body of scholarship acknowledges how social changes during the nineteenth century provided women greater opportunities to explore their personal and collective identities. Diana Crane has shown that this was a time when women were exploring the 'non-verbal communication' facilitated by their clothing to participate more fully in a burgeoning 'commercialist culture'.[35] G.J. Barker-Benfield draws attention to rising literacy rates among British women, which enabled them to attain a greater independence through 'deep play', the pursuit of engaging in challenging activities, usually enjoyed with other women, that enabled them to explore greater freedoms; he provides examples of women participating in public lotteries and gambling, attending tea parties and dinners.[36] A form of world making, 'deep play' is analogous to Beverly Gordon's concept of 'saturated experience' in which nineteenth- and twentieth-century American women created occasions, often 'self-contained, enchanted worlds, that provided heightened sensory awareness to increase

H.I.H. The Grand Duke Michael of Russia
as Henri IV.
The Countess Torby
as Gabrielle d'Estray.

FIGURE 13 *Photogravure of Grand Duke Michael Mikhailovich and the Countess of Torby as members of the Court of Henri IV at the Devonshire Ball, 1897. © National Portrait Gallery.*

the emotional, intellectual and social satisfaction they derived from undertaking routine domestic tasks'.[37] Gordon argues that aesthetic sensitivity was greater among women than men because of the more insular lives they led, which typically involved repetitive and, on the face of it, more menial tasks that offered limited scope for interaction with adults. It is possible that women who engaged in these activities were also seeking, however imperceptibly, to advance their public roles within it.

Adhering more closely to historic styles did not prohibit guests from making a statement about where they were positioned among the hierarchy of their peers. The costume of Charles Spencer-Churchill, ninth Duke of Marlborough, was an imitation livery of a French ambassador at the court of Catherine II. The garment is not known to survive but Charles Worth, its creator, described it in his autobiography:

> We acceded to his demand after a few scandalized protestations and got to work on a Louis XV costume of straw coloured velvet embroidered in silver, pearls and diamonds. The waistcoat was made of a magnificent white and gold damask that was an exact copy of a very rare old pattern. Each pearl and diamond was sewn on by hand, and it took several girls almost a month to complete this embroidery of jewels. Had the Duke not insisted that his costume be perfection, we should never have dared put such costly work in to it. In spite of his orders about elegance, when I came to make out his bill, I was almost too afraid to begin it. But at last when I got it totalled it came to 5000 francs.[38]

An impressive sum this, and probably equivalent to £13,000 in nineteenth-century sums or over £860,000 in the twenty-first century. The Duke's dress was complemented by a costume of 'beautiful white satin' worn by his wife Consuelo Vanderbilt, which it is not known to have been made by Worth.[39] It was not uncommon for husband and wife to acquire costumes from different establishments. This is evidenced by the surviving dress of Lady Isobel Stanley, who wore a Worth gown, and her husband the Honourable Francis Gathorne-Hardy, who purchased his outfit from L. & H. Nathan of London.[40] It is nonetheless curious that Worth, who established himself dressing Princess Pauline von Metternich and Empress Eugénie, made the Duke's dress and apparently not that of his wife.[41] Like Maud and Carl, Charles and Consuelo were newly married – at the time of the ball they had exchanged vows less than eight months previously – but there was no display of matrimonial harmony. Husband and wife posed apart when they were immortalized by Lafayette, which was presumably a deliberate choice. Alone, the twenty-six-year-old Duke could demonstrate the increased horizons that his marriage provided him, without acknowledging how he was beholden to Consuelo's fortune. The Dukedom of Marlborough had been virtually bankrupt when Charles inherited the honour in 1895. His marriage to Consuelo in November 1895, who had been secretly engaged to another man, saved him from penury and affirmed his position in British society; he had been a peer in the House of Lords since 1892. His costume at the ball, made feasible through his wife's money, enabled him to demonstrate a position of belonging penury had hitherto prevented.

Other guests used sartorial sleights to demonstrate their social position. Relishing the opportunity of this being a Diamond Jubilee, one guest, described simply as 'a certain woman' by a reporter, hired '£13,000 of diamonds at a cost of £100 for the night to add to her private supply'.[42] In twenty-first-century sums, this was approximately £860,000 of diamonds being hired for a little over £6,000.[43] This was a large expense for one evening, but the projection of wealth was far in excess of the outlay. Presumably this made the transaction a shrewd investment. Not for nothing was it said that 'Golconda's mines were as a dismal swamp at midnight in the dark of the moon compared to the jewel display [at Devonshire House]'.[44] The Golkonda diamond mines were situated in South India. It was from here that the Koh-I-Noor diamond, gifted to Queen Victoria in 1849, had been found.

Discussion of some of the fancy dress costumes worn at the Devonshire ball makes it apparent that whilst the event had been conceived to bring people together in honour of Britain's monarch, the result was more complicated. Superficially, guests were united in celebration for the queen, but the costume evidence indicates that status definition was a pressing concern. The examples suggest people strategized to bolster their social position. The elaborate and expensive costumes also had the effect of demonstrating a much larger fissure that existed between the wealthy and the rest, as people beyond Devonshire House were temporarily united through the shared acknowledgement that such rarefication would not be experienced by them. The extent to which fancy dress costume balls of this grand scale demarcated prevailing social hierarchies is evident from newspaper accounts, which could wrap complimentary rhetoric around a caustic and disapproving core. If the evocative description quoted above from the *Boston Evening Transcript* suggests the journalist enjoyed and approved of the ball, his concluding remarks reveal what are likely to be truer feelings:

> The gowns were too heavy, the evening too warm and the great rooms too crowded for much dancing. To be sure the function was called a ball, but it was rather a great luxury exhibition, of the culminating barbaric sort, possible in a diamond jubilee season.[45]

The sense of separation was acknowledged by some of the ball's guests. Consuelo Vanderbilt wrote briefly about the festivity in her memoirs. The passage appears to reflect her marital strife – she separated from her husband nine years after the ball and they divorced in 1921 – as much a feeling of isolation within a society she had yet to assimilate into:

> The Ball lasted to the early hours of the morning, and the sun was rising as I walked through Green Park to Spencer House where we then lived. On the grass were the dregs of humanity. Human beings too dispirited or sunk to find work or favour, they were sprawled in sodden stupor, pitiful representatives of the submerged tenth. In my billowing period dress I must have seemed to them a vision of wealth and youth, and I thought soberly that they must hate me. But they only looked, and some even had a compliment to enliven my progress.[46]

These reflections convey Consuelo's personal feelings but her commentary is more broadly important. First, it indicates why Princess Alexandra and her daughters might have felt a desire to create a show of visual unity. The emphasis on group identity assuaged feelings of isolation and asserted the authority they possessed as (royal) women. Second, Consuelo's remarks highlight the divide between participants and spectators. They establish that messages conveyed through costume were intended chiefly for the ball's attendees. This clarifies why Alexandra's dress group generated conflicting press reports: journalists were oblivious to the social frame in which their strategy was conceived and executed. Divergent views about the meaning and value of costumes presumably explains why the Cleopatra gown of Minnie Stevens fetched £9 at auction in 1911, approximately £730 in twenty-first-century sums. This figure is much lower than those quoted above for the commission of the guests' fancy dress costumes. One account of the ball concluded by suggesting that 'the frocks which once graced a society leader will soon perhaps be found in the secondhand cloth shops of Bayswater and Whitechapel'.[47]

Instilling loyalty - The Co-operative Wholesale Society UK, *c.*1920–1940

The English Co-operative Wholesale Society (CWS), the forerunner to today's Co-operative Group, was founded in Rochdale, Greater Manchester, in 1863.[48] Advocating a new business model that provided democratic management, equitable working practices, economic incentives through the payment of a dividend to its members, and better value for its consumers, CWS was one of the more socially minded responses to Britain's 'retailing revolution'.[49] By the outbreak of the First World War, the Society had over three million members and buying depots from Sweden to Sydney.[50] If the idea of commercial co-operation was timely, the organization confronted boycotts and negative campaigning from private businesses and trade associations who thought co-operatives stymied competition.[51] Operating in these circumstances, it was necessary to establish a loyal network of co-operators who could unambiguously promote and defend the Society's interests. Fancy dress entertainments were not used extensively to promote the Society to new customers, but they did have an important role within the organization, to demonstrate adherence to co-operative principles. This was especially the case when aimed at children, whom CWS leaders looked to as future co-operators.

When the CWS was founded, welfare capitalism, the idea that businesses should facilitate the physical and psychological needs of employees to foster socially acceptable and commercially effective working environments, was well-established.[52] Nevertheless, co-operation was greeted with suspicion. The unease this generated within the Society, particularly during the first half of the twentieth century when armed conflict and economic turbulence exacerbated the difficulties of global trading, is apparent within internal publications and documents, many of which emphasize the need for loyalty. Concern about members' faithfulness to the Society is evidenced by recurring articles in *The Producer*, a monthly magazine for the employees of regional societies, that cite statistics about the buying habits of co-operative members, who purchase 'only some' of their products from Society stores and show 'apathy' about attending business meetings and Co-operative Day festivities.[53] Simultaneously, editors of *The Producer* praised the activities of co-operators that did evince commitment and engagement with the Society's ethical and enterprising ethos. A common means of demonstrating this cohesion was through fancy dress entertainments. Costumed activities were efficacious in representing co-operative values because they required commitment and cooperation to stage. The expression of Society ideas through dress also appeased members who considered conventional means of advertising dishonest.[54]

Regional co-operatives were encouraged to submit photographs of the costume activities they organized for publication. The editors of *The Producer* appear to have used these photographs, and the captions they appended to them, to instil a sense of competition between co-operative societies who were encouraged to recognize the importance of having their work publicly acknowledged. One photograph from September 1924, which shows thirteen children in fancy dress costume, is accompanied by the description, 'South Molton recently had a co-operative gala, as the accompanying photograph shows. Devon is going forward – co-operating is children, boys and girls'.[55] In an issue from October 1924, a photograph of a young boy dressed as the Society's wheatsheaf is contextualized as follows:

Devizes has a sound co-operative society that has done good work since the initial meeting attended by the late Henry Humphrey. Recently it organised a children's carnival and procession, when the C.W.S. jam lorry added to the variety of the parade, and Victor Tucker of Market Lavington won the first prize for his representation of the "wheatsheaf" – a capital, well-expressed idea worked out as shown in the accompanying picture.[56]

In these examples, the text accompanying the photographs makes a simple and not entirely convincing connection between the staging of fancy dress entertainments and co-operative development. The accuracy of the statement was presumably less important than its intended point, which was to instil in readers from different co-operative societies a desire to demonstrate their loyalty in similar fashion. Whilst fancy dress entertainments helped to advertise CWS products discreetly, it is apparent that their main utility was to act as a litmus test of co-operative dedication. This attitude to fancy dress was different to that of other British companies. Lever Brothers organized fancy dress events for children on their Founder's Day, but employees at Lyons often took the lead in organizing dress-up competitions. In both cases, fancy dress events ran alongside other activities, including boxing bouts.[57]

A belief that fancy dress was an effective means of demonstrating cohesion is shown by an example from the Middlesbrough and Burnley Co-operative Societies. The Middlesbrough Society had encountered difficulties but was revived in 1930. This provided an opportune moment to demonstrate loyalty to and affinity with CWS values. In a two-page article that appeared in *The Producer*, the author, identified as 'a special observer', describes how the cooperative had transformed its fortunes.[58] Quotations from an interview with George McEwen, who had helped to establish the Middlesbrough Society, are used judiciously to support the message of perseverance and adherence to CWS values. McEwen expressed his confidence 'that the loyalty between the Middlesbrough Society and the CWS was the mainspring of the former's recovery'.[59] He was 'full of praise for the worthy people of Middlesbrough, without whose help this phoenix-like effort would have failed. Members and employees have realized their mutual interest, and several voluntary helpers have come along in fact. The call for self-sacrificing workers is never unheeded'.[60] The article is accompanied by a black and white photograph of a juvenile fancy dress group from Burnley. The photograph is captioned, 'Young co-operators at Burnley (Figure 14). The Burnley Society has had a series of fancy dress competitions for the children and its members. Here is a group of some of the prize winners, whose appropriate characteristics were helped by materials supplied by the CWS advertising department'.[61] The image appears to be an anodyne depiction of pubescent children in costume, spontaneously assembled together. Ostensibly, it has no connection with the text, which relates to a different Society. However, in being placed together by editors, text and image emphasize a theme of loyalty. The photograph, in particular, conveys a contrived message of adherence to CWS values that belies the appearance of extemporaneity.

The photograph shows eight children in fancy dress costume, five boys and three girls. Six of the children stand before a wall, two kneel in front of them; these children appear to be younger than the rest and appear doubly distinct because their faces are blackened. For the most part, the children's costumes either depict specific CWS products or feature images of them. The blackface is curious. It may have been intended to reference the international reach of CWS and the countries of origin for its goods. At the centre of the group, among the row of standing children, a girl wears a white knee-length dress and veil, which is draped over the back of her head. Her left armed is linked through the right arm of a boy, standing to her left, who wears a black suit and top hat. The boy's bow-tie appears to be fashioned from the packaging of a CWS product. It is clear that these two children represent a newly married couple. The other children who gather around them are presumably intended to

YOUNG CO-OPERATORS AT BURNLEY.
The Burnley Society has had a series of fancy dress competitions
for the children of members.   Here is a group of some of the prize
winners, whose appropriate characterisations were helped by
materials supplied by the C.W.S. Advertising Department.

FIGURE 14 *Page from* The Producer, *xiv (April 1930), 114.*

be the wedding guests. To make it clear that this is a wedding scene, a large poster affixed
to the wall advertises CWS jewellery with the caption, 'She said yes, so he bought the ring
from the co-operative jewellers'. Superficially, the photograph announces the CWS to be
a socially responsible, family-friendly, even jovial, organization. Simultaneously, and more
subtly, it suggests the nature of the CWS organization, which could provide myriad products
and services for a family's needs, is a stabilizing force in people's lives. If children can
understand this point, it seems to suggest, anyone should. What may appear to be a mundane
and extemporaneous line-up of boys and girls in fancy dress costume, typical of the 1930s,
is therefore a contrived arrangement of children, chosen and dressed by adults linked to
Burnley's Cooperative Society, who wanted to make a specific point about their commitment
to the CWS organization. Together, text and image provide a compelling demonstration of
cooperative cohesion, commercial and social success.

The actions of the Burnley cooperative were not atypical. In February 1924, *The Producer* carried a report on a children's fancy parade that had been arranged by the Gateshead Society. The event helped to advertise CWS products, which inspired the children's costumes, but the segment's concluding remarks reveal a more pressing purpose behind the 'fearfully and wonderfully made' outfits: 'Propaganda work that interests the children is likely to be effective. At any rate, the earlier the impressions in regard to the possibilities of co-operation, the better'.[62] Another article from *The Producer* reveals a similar attitude. An anonymous author comments approvingly on a juvenile ball that was organized by the Blackpool Society for the city's Winter Gardens in December 1929. The event was considered successful because large numbers of people attended. It is noted favourably that 'many of the little people proclaimed the cooperative outlook of their parents, and Miss Eva Lawless, who lives at Ruskin House, had an alluring presentation of the Silver Seal [that formed part of the Society's margarine branding] as well as of the [Society's] wheatsheaf motto. Train up a girl in the way she should shop, that when she marries she may continue in the path of co-operation'.[63] Whilst demonstrating the loyalty of current members, the implication of this evidence is that CWS managers believed fancy dress entertainments involving children were an effective means to gain future co-operators.

The importance that CWS leadership placed on inculcating children with its ethos is evidenced by the annual International Co-operative Day festivities. Films of these events, which were convened at large open-air venues, including Crystal Palace and the Empire Stadium in London, show children engaged in a range of group activities, from dancing and sports to parading and singing. These choreographed events enabled the CWS to demonstrate the importance of its social vision to members, and possibly to other onlookers. Dancing, for example, was regarded as 'purely co-operative, because it is a form of collective activity'.[64] Fancy dress parades and competitions were similarly important in this endeavour. The extent to which the children understood their participation is uncertain. Footage from a juvenile gala in 1923 shows a group of children in fancy dress costume looking at once anxious, amused and perplexed as they pose for a photograph. As they wait for the photographer to summon their attention, a younger boy, not in costume, runs into shot in the background and turns to the camera. The boy is apprehended by an elderly man who appears momentarily as he pulls him back and out of shot.[65] In a similar way, footage from the 1934 Crystal Palace 'Festival of Co-operation' shows children, possibly in their teens, marching around the perimeter of the site in fancy dress costume. They are talking to each other, smiling and appear oblivious to their surroundings. On one occasion, they receive hasty instructions from a man who walks alongside them, perhaps a teacher or relative.[66] In this arena, and mindful of their age, the boys and girls are perhaps examples of Bristol's 'unattentive' participants.

If children were ambivalent towards CWS events, they were as likely confused by some of the costumes they wore, which often contained cultural references and humour one would not expect them to comprehend. A photograph from a 1953 CWS event in London shows twenty-three young girls standing in three rows before a painted backdrop of a topiary hedgerow (Figure 15). One girl, standing to the left in the front row, wears a bikini top and shorts with a placard that reads 'Modern Bathing Girl Miss Bikini'. The girl looks to be about six years old. Towards the right of the front row, a smaller, apprehensive-looking girl wears a sign proclaiming her to be 'Too Young at Five'.[67] The girls' outfits, which would probably be deemed inappropriate for prepubescent children to wear today, appear to be making fun of the bikini, which was a new and *risqué* item of clothing in 1953. The reference to 'Miss Bikini' may have been a punning allusion to the fact that bikinis were banned from the 'Miss World'

FIGURE 15 *Photograph of young girls from a Co-operative Society fancy dress event in London, 1953. Courtesy of the Bishopsgate Institute.*

pageant after the contest's first winner, Kiki Hakansson, accepted her prize wearing a bikini, which scandalized the Pope.[68] It is hard to imagine the girls in the photograph understood the meaning of their costumes and placards.

In another photograph from the same event, a pre-teenage boy appears with a body-length sign suspended from his neck (Figure 16). It is decorated with more than 100 matches; many of them used, and bears the text, 'No more strikes'.[69] The reference is to the match girls' strike of July 1888 at the London factory of Bryant and May, Britain's largest match producer. Poorly paid, badly treated and suffering from ill health as a consequence of the use of white phosphorous, female workers led by Annie Besant walked out of Bryant and May's Bow factory and made public their demands for improved pay and conditions. The strike, which lasted almost two weeks, came to be seen as a milestone in the history of the Trade Union movement and organized labour.[70] The subject was appropriate for a costume event organized by the CWS. It also resonated beyond the organization. In the 1930s the strike was deemed to be sufficiently well known to be represented in fancy dress by Weldon's. The firm's catalogue includes an adult woman's 'No more strikes' costume (Figure 8). The outfit consists of a white knee-length dress; a high-collared, waist-length red cape and a hat, shaped and printed in the style of a box of Bryant and May matches. The upper part of the dress bears the demand

FIGURE 16 *Photograph of children from a Co-operative Society fancy dress event in London, 1953. Courtesy of the Bishopsgate Institute.*

'No More Strikes' in red capital letters. The loosely pleated skirt of the dress is decorated with matches, much like the boy's sign. A repeat design of a box of Bryant and May matches runs around the hem.[71] It is conceivable that a woman would purchase the Weldon's costume knowing of its significance forty years after the strikes. It is questionable if the boy understood his sign sixty-five years after the events.

These examples show that fancy dress costume was used to inspire loyalty among CWS members. Competitive encouragement prompted regional societies to organize recurring fancy dress events to demonstrate adherence to key co-operative values. Within these activities, the Society was keen to involve children. Dress-up enabled child participants to become acquainted with the ideals of the Co-operative Society in the frame of an adult world, where marriage and financial management were deemed important. It was hoped this would inculcate loyalty and provide for future co-operatives. However, as much as fancy dress entertainments reveal the importance of children to CWS, it is apparent that they were simultaneously marginalized. Children were frequently not the intended audience for some of the more arresting and time-consuming costumes they wore. Images from CWS events show fancy dress costumes that were probably beyond the social and political register of their pre-pubescent wearers. Moreover, costumes like the 'Miss Bikini' outfits, in which children became spectacles, were very clearly not aligned with the CWS ethos. These sartorial deviations suggest that parents and guardians, who as members were expected to attend the Society's public festivals, conceived of costumes that would provide personal and mutual humour, possibly to make their experience more enjoyable.

Unifying nations - West African fancy dress and masquerade West Africa, *c.*1900 – Present

Masquerade and fancy dress parades have existed within West African culture from at least the end of the nineteenth century. The costumes and the circumstances in which they are worn are 'multisensorial' and the meanings of both are continually evolving.[72] Complex though they are, the performances that occur across West Africa, from Guinea to Cameroon, galvanize people through the physical elucidation of long-standing patterns of belief. Since the twentieth century, it has become possible to separate West African fancy dress performances into two divergent, but interrelated, forms. The first, termed 'masquerade', preserves a spiritual and seriate rite whose origins pre-date European involvement in the continent. The second, termed 'fancy dress', evolved from masquerade and through European cultural exchanges. This form of performance is characterized by a pronounced secularism and a desire to demonstrate social unity through conviviality and competition. The costumes worn at events like Winnneba's Fancy Dress Festival, a civic entertainment that has been held annually since Ghana became independent of British rule in 1957, are visually similar to western fancy dress costume.

In the twenty-first century, masquerade performances in West Africa continue to be organized by societies – sometimes referred to as cults – from across different ethnic groups. There are various types of masquerade across Africa but all involve a series of group dances accompanied by music. The performers are typically men, who wear elaborate masked costumes that invoke spiritual support for a variety of social and political causes, including farming, funerals and warfare. In Nigeria, Gelede masquerades are notable for their use of humour to critique '[a]ctions or attitudes which might endanger traditional life, social cohesion or stability'.[73] The costumes worn by societies are usually visually distinct to those worn at contemporary fancy dress parades (Figure 46). For a western audience, socialized to interpret African art through static displays in museums, the costumes worn by societies are recognizable because of their abstract anthropomorphism, use of natural materials and construction through hand-made techniques. The men – sometimes women – who wear these costumes temporarily lose their human identity and become conduits for specific deities to manifest themselves and influence local events. The spiritual authority accorded to these costumes – particularly the head and face coverings, which become the aesthetic and numinous focus of the garment – prohibits spectators from seeing the wearer dress and undress.[74] Some head and face coverings are deemed sufficiently powerful to warrant separate storage between masking events. Western scholars have long stressed the difficulty of explaining the polyvalent and variant roles of these costumes and the ceremonial occasions at which they are worn.[75] The frenzy unleashed by these costumes is analogous to the *ilinix* and *mimicry* noted by Roger Caillois in his study of play. Where Caillois refers to 'games' in the following passage, I substitute 'performance' that reflects:

[O]n the one hand, the tendencies, tastes, and ways of thought that are prevalent, while, at the same time, in educating and training the [performers[76]] in these very virtues or eccentricities, they subtly confirm them in their habits and preferences. Thus, a [performance] that is esteemed by a people may at the same time be utilized to define the society's moral or intellectual character, provide proof of its precise meaning, and contribute to its popular acceptance by accentuating the relevant qualities.[77]

The second form of costume, fancy dress, is a secular derivation of masquerade and practiced in a limited number of places. Clothes are constructed from a bricolage of African, western- and machine-made materials that do not necessarily carry specific meaning. Many of the objects that decorate these costumes, which include children's toys, product packaging and Christmas decorations, are chosen for their perceived aesthetic value rather than their ability to contribute social commentary. This is also the case for items that would convey specific messages when worn in the west; for example, face masks printed with the visage of political leaders.[78] The costumes are invariably created and worn for group amusement. In a competitive environment, like the Winneba Festival, different groups of people are publicly judged on their dress and dancing.[79]

Despite contrasting appearances, distinctions between the two forms of African costuming should not be rigidly drawn. Western-style masks and decorations can be incorporated into costumes that are ostensibly spiritual and contemporary fancy dress, for all of its apparent frivolity, is influenced by spiritual traditions.[80] West African costume is consequently a complex phenomenon and its inclusion within this study is a deliberate foil to highlight themes that transcend cultures. Three particular caveats should be considered when approaching African costume performances. First, the terms that define African practice are taken from a European vocabulary. Among the languages spoken in Africa, there is also no equivalent, or single, word for 'mask'.[81] Semantic consistency between African, European and American traditions of fancy dress therefore belies divergent practice.[82] Second, although elements of West Africa's performance culture were forged under colonial rule, it is more 'fluidic' than western theatrical traditions where there exists a 'bifurcated understanding of the boundary between theatre and reality'.[83] In an African frame, performance has been defined by Margaret Thomas Drewal as 'the praxis of everyday social life; indeed it is the practical application of embodied skill and knowledge to the task of taking action'.[84] This facilitates a degree of hybridity in public performance that is often absent in western traditions where drama, dance and music tend to be separated.[85] The final consideration, which contrasts with the other examples considered in this chapter, and book, is the spiritual integrity within West African masquerade and fancy dress. Herbert Cole has emphasized that every face mask and head covering 'embodies a spirit', even if this is along a continuum from 'heavy' to 'lighthearted'.[86]

West African masquerade and fancy dress is too large a topic to treat comprehensively here, but there is virtue in considering the similarities that exist between the role and meaning of fancy dress costume in West African, European and American traditions. A further aim is to overcome two specific challenges that hinder researchers. First, the inclination of western scholars to view African culture through a post-colonial prism and attribute contemporary cultural forms almost entirely to European influence. Second, and perhaps opposite to this, the tendency of anthropologists living and working in Africa to focus on specific communities at the expense of making pan-continental – even pan-global – connections. The Winneba Fancy Dress Festival provides the closest parallel to European and American traditions of fancy dress. It was inaugurated by Ghana's first president as a strategy of promoting national unity, along with other initiatives that included 'boat racing, swimming, traditional dancing, cross country'.[87] The Festival is held at the beginning of January. A parade of old costumes is staged in December to raise funds, materials and decorative items for the forthcoming parade and competition. The majority of costumed participants are young men in their teens and early twenties. Group leaders are typically in their thirties and forties.[88] The Festival attracts a large audience, many of whom travel to attend.[89] The number of spectators encourages participants to engage in a 'lively sense of artistic competition'.[90]

The appearance of an anthropomorphized gorilla at the January 2018 Winneba Fancy Dress Festival is typical of the costumes worn (Figure 17). A snarling black gorilla mask covered the face and head of its male wearer. A bright blue sombrero decorated with tinsel was worn on top; silver tinsel was attached to the brim of the hat, gold tinsel was shaped into a point over the crown. The majority of the costume was black and yellow. Green and burgundy provided

FIGURE 17 *Photograph of a gorilla costume at Winneba's Fancy Dress Festival, 2018. © Nii Kotei Nikoi.*

accents. A yellow high-visibility vest, or a garment that approximated one in shape, covered the wearer's torso. Strips of machine-made embroidery, no wider than 15 mm, in black, white and grey, were attached to the hem, cuffs and armholes. Two identically shaped panels of a burgundy fabric were affixed to the front, presumably to represent the gorilla's pectorals. The panels were trimmed with the same embroidery strips used elsewhere on the vest, although with an additional row of red. The pectorals were decorated with several five-pointed gold stars, each with an approximate diameter of 12 mm, and two hanging silver baubles. Two bright yellow tassels were suspended from the top of each panel. Above the pectorals, between the neck and shoulders, more stars, in gold, blue and red, had been added to the vest. Two metallic baubles, in silver and blue, hung on the upper right side. On the opposite side, among the stars, a gold American-style police shield with the number '1038' had been stuck. Unseen from the front, baubles of blue, silver and red lined the back of the vest's collar. More were hung on the back. A black shirt was worn beneath the vest. It had been decorated with three strips of fabric, no more than 15-mm wide, that ran along the outside arm from the shoulder to the cuff. The outer strips were made from an identical and bright yellow material; the middle strip was a paler yellow. This pattern was replicated on the corresponding black trousers that were otherwise plain. A low-slung belt of an indeterminate but flexible material hung around the wearer's thighs. It was predominantly gold but had been decorated with the same embroidery strips as the vest. Two yellow tassels, identical to those on the vest, were attached to each side of the belt. Footwear consisted of a pair of bright yellow high-top trainers with black laces. Latex grey and black gardener's gloves covered the hands.

The sartorial bricolage of this costume reflects a socialized appreciation within Africa of fabric as a 'prestigious commodity' and a fascination for 'lavish display'.[91] The impressive appearance is also influenced by myths that 'equate nakedness with infancy, insanity or the lack of social responsibility'.[92] The appearance and construction of the costume is informed by a specific aesthetic termed 'fancy' and 'fierce' by western scholars that originated in the nineteenth century. Fanciness reflects a temporal desire to create costumes that are joyful. Making use of highly coloured and textured materials, they identify individual, or family, agency and resourcefulness. Fierceness underscores the belief that costumes possess a spiritual authority and should command respect from participants and spectators.[93] The ability of masquerade costumes to invoke spiritual support depends on people adopting an appearance that is at once 'fierce and fancy'.[94] The importance of this aesthetic principle in the more secularized arena of fancy dress competitions is an apt demonstration of the connections between the two forms of African costume performance. Consequently, it would be reductive to look for an overarching message behind the gorilla costume. Nonetheless, it is apparent that the colours and decoration of the outfit derive from the Ghanaian flag, which the wearer held in his right hand as he paraded – three horizontal bands of the Pan-African colours, red, yellow and green, with a black five-pointed star in the middle of the yellow band. The wearer was accompanied by five men, each wearing identical costumes but distinguishable by different head masks, which included a black visor, a wolf and a green zombie.[95]

The costume elucidates Hakeem Adam's belief that Winneba's Festival is 'living museum', a vehicle for 'catalysing conversation on the conditions of the present'.[96] He observes that 'participants do not limit their imagination to the tradition that birthed their beloved festival, but look to themselves and their sociopolitical conditions that permeate society for inspiration for their costumes … the reimagining of predominant images by the masqueraders weaponizes their performance to become a tool for imaginative thinking.'[97] The reference to a museum parallels comments by Colleen McQuillen in her study of nineteenth-century Russian masquerades, where she argues that character costumes are important in 'preserving cultural memory'.[98] Referring to costumed entertainments that draw upon 'cultural patrimony' in which participants dress as historical figures as 'philological masquerades', McQuillen avers that such events have 'a museum-like function of evaluating cultural artifacts through careful curation, like the art museum that perpetuates exclusivity by housing works by and for the elite, [they are] a public exhibition space for erudition and refined taste'.[99] The effect of people dressing as a character is analogous to a museum because their choice of costume parallels the selection of objects and the narration of a particular story for an audience to follow. The experience of West African fancy dress suggests conceptual costumes are no less effective at creating 'museum-like' displays and narratives than character costumes in philological masquerades – if we can extend this category beyond nineteenth-century Europe. Moreover, 'museum-like' displays are not solely focused on the elite. Placed together, the remarks by Adam and McQuillen emphasize how contemporary performance of fancy dress in Ghana achieves social cohesion by harmonizing African and European cultural traditions.

It is generally agreed that African people deepened and developed forms of expression in response to the presence of Europeans. This was particularly the case with fancy dress, which was shaped by western understandings of theatre and costumed entertainments. Twentieth-century English author Maud Diver appeared to empathize, if not altogether sympathize, with the people who confronted European rule. Speaking through her character, Inayat Khan, and remarking upon India rather than Africa, Diver used the advent of fancy dress entertainments to explain the cultural disruption of imperialism:

We Indians who know how little the bulk of India has really changed, could laugh at the tamasha of western fancy-dress, in small matters; but time for laughing has gone by. Time has come for saying firmly – all rights and aspirations will be granted, stopping *short* of actual government – otherwise – ![100]

What Diver wrote of India was true of Africa. If fancy dress entertainments represented European overlordship, western play books, films and fancy dress guides, which included Weldon's catalogue, inspired new forms of drama and costume across the continent.[101] One of the more important changes within West African entertainment traditions that followed in the wake of European involvement was the separation between spectator and performer. Catherine Cole has argued that concert party theatre, a popular African entertainment, did not generally distinguish between actor and audience because it was not habitually performed in a demarcated or raised space. Stages were not used in Africa before European settlement.[102] The adoption of a stage and the delineation of actor and audience were important in the development of African fancy dress because this facilitated an awareness of how existing cultural forms might be used broadly, for the purposes of entertainment and political edification. The impact of Europeans on the genesis of West African fancy dress is perhaps analogous to changes that followed the religious upheavals in sixteenth- and seventeenth-century Europe. Whilst mystery plays in England had been performed in the fourteenth century, Protestant adaptations of carnival, which often created dramatic set pieces, more clearly demarcated participants and spectators.[103]

The European impact on the development of African fancy dress was not benign and events like Winneba's Festival are perhaps best understood as resolutions in a long-running cultural tussle between African and European performance traditions. For example, using Toyne Erekosima and Joanne Eicher's construct of Cultural Authentication, Courtnay Micots has shown how Ghanaian men appeared in nineteenth-century masquerades as the stereotypical plains warrior, or Red Indian, from American culture to challenge European hegemony.[104] The Cultural Authentication Process elucidates how motifs from one culture are borrowed and adapted to occupy new meanings and roles in another culture.[105] In this case, and paralleling equivalent occurrences in Brazil and the Caribbean, the plains warrior, whom Ghanaians became acquainted with through western printed ephemera and Hollywood films, became a symbol of 'heroic courage in the face of insurmountable odds'.[106] Micots quotes one Ghanaian who averred, 'we liked that [the Indians] were fighting white men'.[107] Dressing and performing as 'Indians' amounted to a public show of resistance to European authority. Uniquely, this figure was incorporated into *asafo* performances. *Asafo* ('war people') was a paternally inherited identity among the Akan people 'with paramilitary and community responsibilities'.[108] The adoption of a figure believed to possess positive and courageous associations was presumably conceived to enrich the Ghanaian tradition of masquerading that had existed from at least the seventeenth century. This acculturation shows how experience of European performance traditions facilitated the development of fancy dress costume within Africa through the adaptation of existing forms of entertainment and means of communication.

African fancy dress may have been conceived to challenge European hegemony, but after independence it became a performance in which 'world views and basic human values [were] acted out in striking visual forms at once entertaining, spiritually powerful, and crucial to the continuity and equilibrium of life'.[109] John Nunley has suggested that 'forms of social-political organisation', whilst rooted in performance traditions of liberated slaves, assumed a prominent role in the process of decolonization as they took up 'the slack left by the colonial administration'.[110] In particular, he argues that Ode-lay societies were important in providing a stabilizing focus for younger people after independence, who 'left their rural lifestyles and … entered the national urban mainstream'.[111] Cognizant of the role that masquerade societies had in mediating social tensions, and the ambivalent position of the young after independence, the All People's Congress sponsored costumed performances to broadcast and embed their ideas in Sierra Leone during 1960s and 1970s.[112]

This is not to suggest that the secular and politicized turn within West African costume performance was regarded uncritically. Some commentators were troubled by European intervention and noted the blurring between masquerade, as civic performance, and fancy dress, as social entertainment, with concern. In *The Road* (1965) and *Death and the King's Horseman* (1975), playwright Wole Soyinjka portrays the 'putative immanent power' of *egungun* costume when it is worn by characters who appear to doubt or deride its numinous importance. In *Death and the King's Horseman*, the *egungun* costume is worn to a fancy dress party with negative consequences for its sacrilegious wearer.[113] The impact of European cultural traditions on African performance is still debated but there appears to be a growing consensus that fancy dress, as distinct from masquerade, has become a prominent, and genuinely popular, form of cultural expression. In Ibadan, south west Nigeria, Bolaji Campbell observes that the *egungun* cult 'fosters peaceful coexistence and cooperation in modern Yoruba society'.[114] In Ghana, Micots suggests that fancy dress has grown at the expense of *asafo* performances. She remarks that 'colonial resistance has become entertainment'.[115] The shifting role of Ghanian fancy dress is reflected in the figure of the plains warrior, whose costume was worn during the early years of the Winneba Festival. According to Micots, 'it was needed for unity during political and economic instability. Today, during peaceful and more prosperous times, the Red Indian has faded as a popular character.'[116]

This discussion has sought to clarify how fancy dress entertainments in West Africa are analogous to those in the west, but not identical. Costumes in Africa are more patently polyvalent because of their bricolage construction. Discernible messages of personal and group belonging are nonetheless sufficiently clear to attract the sponsorship of political groups and to foster an instrumental ethnicity in the absence of European rule. Group costumes display individual agency through the selection of personal items to decorate them. Concerns for status definition are also apparent. Post independence, fancy dress competitions appear to have become an important means of channelling the agency of young people – adolescent males in particular – who are the chief competitors, to make them cognizant of their civic role and responsibilities.

Fancy dress - To cohere

The fun of fancy dress is never entirely frivolous, the occasions when it is worn not inherently 'nihilistic' or 'culturally trivial'.[117] The three examples considered in this chapter are celebratory and ludic. They enabled people of different cultures and chronologies to demonstrate and renew shared values. The choice of costumes reflected contemporary preoccupations and tastes. The participants conformed to the social expectations of their respective occasions; bowing to royalty when required, dancing and parading when directed. The attendees at these events may have enjoyed themselves. It is less equivocal that they expressed agency to delineate their place within the interpersonal networks to which they belonged. Four observations can be made by way of summary.

First, participants who wear fancy dress costume when enjoined to do so alongside their peers express support for their community's values. The ludic, perhaps comedic, inversion of order reinforces people's commitment to prevailing structures and mores.

Second, organizers and participants can take advantage of the liminality of costumed entertainments, presented as convivial, politically impartial and symbolically neutral, to engage in acts of individualization to elucidate the importance of themselves and the personal networks to which they belong within their community. The allusion to costumes that perform a 'museum-like' function by facilitating personal expression through the display of shared values is useful in explaining how fancy dress costume can have an edifying and galvanizing function across different cultures and chronologies.

Third, participants assume that conceptual and synecdochic costumes will be understood by legitimate members of their community. An inability to understand a costume demonstrates marginalization, as in the case of spectators at the Devonshire Ball, children at CWS events and western observers in West Africa. People who did not readily understand costumes can become 'unreflective' and 'unanalytical'.[118] The importance of an audience, who can vouchsafe and validate a costume and its wearer, is clarified by the example of West Africa where a westernized form of fancy dress developed after performance traditions defined participants from spectators.

Fourth, children and adolescents can become a symbolic focus within costumed entertainments that are ostensibly organized to promote social cohesion. Juveniles might be oblivious to their social value, but as representatives of their community's future they are often placed in conspicuous and pivotal roles by adults, cognizant that absurdity reinforces order. CWS targeted children in their costumed events. The perceived importance of young women is apparent in Princess Alexandra's Valois court; the primacy of young men is emphasized in West African fancy dress.

2

To Challenge

Costume events that facilitate social and political cohesion may have existed in Ancient Egypt. In 1920, Maximilian Josef Rudwin suggested that European carnival traditions could be traced to the cult of Isis.[1] The history of dressing up to augment interpersonal relationships is certainly long, but these episodes emerge slowly in the written record. Some of the earliest discussions of fancy dress costume are contained within legal documents and concern people who used incongruous and imaginative clothing to assault social and political norms. For as long as people have dressed up, it seems rulers and their governments have been wary of the challenge that masked and costumed individuals could pose to their authority. Accounts of fancy dress in the medieval and early modern periods are typically relayed through the admonishments of officials and moralizers who exercised control over the technology of writing.[2] The apprehension of rulers and their acolytes about costumed insubordination reflect Hannah Arendt's view, summarized by Norma Claire Moruzzi, that 'the public realm and [people's] shared worldliness are the achievements of human artifice'.[3] 'Political practice, especially revolutionary political practice, is inherently theatrical.'[4] The presence of people who are actually masked, anonymized or otherwise incongruently attired therefore threatens the stability of public life.[5] To alter one's public identity is to challenge the 'veneer of consensus' that is foundational to effective human cooperation, as Erving Goffman has shown.[6] During the medieval and early modern periods, the tantalizing and dramatic prospect that costumed revellers could thwart, if not entirely topple, social and political hierarchies was given credence by seasonal ludic rites that inverted authority through fancy dress and raucous behaviour. Whilst these events typically buttressed social structures, the potential for them to disturb was ever-present, and frequently imagined in contemporary culture, as the writings of Shakespeare and Rabelais attest. In Twelfth Night, for example, Sir Andrew declares himself 'a fellow o'th' strangest mind i'th' world' because of his 'delight in masques and revels sometimes altogether'.[7]

Concern about fancy dress and social disorder has died hard. In New Orleans, a city perhaps best known for its annual carnival, head coverings are illegal beyond Mardi Gras.[8] In France, veils and face coverings are prohibited in public. In New York, 'masks, disguises or other "facial alteration"' is forbidden if people are 'congregating in groups or three or more'.[9] Long-standing concerns about masks and masquerades have encouraged scholars to co-opt these terms as analytic concepts to evaluate the duality between character and individual and the tension between self and society.[10]

The episodes of fancy dress costume considered in this chapter – the siege of Kenilworth castle, the assassination of Gustaf III of Sweden and the Reconstruction era Ku-Klux Klan – show how dressing up can challenge ideas, individuals and institutions. Where Chapter 1 reflected on the strategies costumed people adopt to communicate with others, chiefly to delineate their place within a community, the examples here explore how the performance of dressing up to confront and resist a perceived threat can often be of greater consequence to its wearers. If this seems counter-intuitive, especially as some of the people in this chapter were forced, sometimes violently, to engage with the costumes worn, it reveals how wearers' strong emotions can compromise the communicative potential of their outfits. If the previous chapter argued, broadly, that dressing up is an affective form of communicative, this chapter reflects on how it is not always a stable form of communication.

Defying royal authority - The siege of Kenilworth Castle Warwickshire, UK, *c.* 25 June–13 December 1266

The siege of Kenilworth Castle is the longest siege in English history. It lasted for 172 days between June and December 1266.[11] This violent episode occurred during a period of civil strife, ostensibly between King Henry III (r. 1216–72) and his supporters and members of the aristocracy and their supporters. The conflict began in 1264, sparked by criticism of the king's seemingly profligate support of his foreign relatives and penurious scheme to place his second son on the Sicilian throne. The Kenilworth Siege was the third, and final, set piece engagement between the king and his aggrieved subjects. On 14 May 1264, the first major battle of the so-called Barons' War had resulted in Henry's capture and incarceration by his brother-in-law and lead opponent, the Earl of Leicester Simon de Montfort. During the king's captivity, Montfort became the *de facto* governor of England. Henry regained his freedom and throne on 5 August 1265 when Montfort was slain – his neck skewered by a lance – and his forces defeated at the Battle of Evesham. However, the kingdom remained insecure and Henry's authority was not fully restored until the last of the rebels, who had fled to Kenilworth Castle, yielded to him.

Robert of Gloucester's *Metrical Chronicle*, composed contemporaneously in English verse, is one of several accounts of the Kenilworth siege. It is unique, however, for including within its description one of the earliest acts of fancy dress costume to be worn to challenge. A few weeks after the king commenced his siege against the castle, in early July 1266, members of the rebel garrison stood upon the red sandstone ramparts, dressed in makeshift white ecclesiastical vestments, and performed a mock excommunication of Henry and his army. This was an awesome act, for to be excommunicate meant people were forbidden from participation in the seven sacraments. Anyone who died excommunicate would go to Hell. The garrison's defiance of the king, of which the costumed performance was just one, occurred at a liminal moment when political and social roles were in flux. However, instead of pursuing reconciliation, the disruptive actions of the castle's inhabitants indicate they used carnival tropes to create a 'second life outside officialdom' to repudiate royal authority.[12] Simultaneously, there is a sense that they wanted reprieve from their frightening situation, to become in Bakhtin's phrase, 'ambivalent'.[13] At a time of widespread illiteracy, acts of *symbolische kommunikation*, as defined by Gerd Althoff, were prevalent as interpersonal relationships were frequently demonstrated by objects and gestures, particularly between superordinates and subordinates.[14] Within this frame, the use of fancy dress at Kenilworth was one element in an attempt at world making as the trapped garrison relinquished their allegiance to their king and renewed bonds of association among themselves by harnessing the 'second truth' of laughter.[15]

In his account of the siege, Gloucester describes the dramatic moment when local surgeon Philip Porpeis, a member of the garrison who held Kenilworth against Henry III, stood on the fortress's ramparts to excommunicate the royal army. This action meant the king, his soldiers and an attendant papal legate, Ottobuono de Fieschi, were unable to take solace in the sacraments. For the king and the pope's representative, this act more damningly undermined their Christian authority. Porpeis's shocking performance was a comic inversion and rebuttal of an actual sentence of excommunication that had been delivered against the garrison by the papal legate moments before. King Henry had requested Ottobuono's presence and action to intimidate the rebels and induce them to submit. As a surgeon, Porpeis's reciprocal excommunication carried no weight, but it was an important symbolic gesture of the garrison's refusal to yield. The impact of his gesture was enhanced by the costume Porpeis chose to wear. The chief visual difference between the performances of the surgeon and the legate were in the colours of the copes each wore; Porpeis, in imitation, had a makeshift white cope; Ottobuono wore a red cope.

Mid mangenels & ginnes · hor eiþer to oþer caste ·	
Þe legat & þe erchebissop · wiþ hom al so nome ·	
Tueie oþere bissops · & to kennigwurþe come	
To makie acord wiþ þe king · & þe deserites al so ·	
& hom of þe castel · ȝuf it miȝte be ido ·	5
Ac þe deserites nolde noȝt · do al after þe kinge ·	
Ne hii of þe castel naþemo · ne stonde to hor lokinge ·	
Þe legat mid is rede cope · amansede þo ·	
Hom þat in þe castel were · & ȝut þer to wel mo ·	
Alle þat hom holoe · oþer were at hor rede ·	10
Oþer to hom ensentede · in wille oþer in dede ·	
Hii of þe castel tolde · her of gret despit ·	
Cope oþer cloþes · hii lete make of wit ·	
& maister philip porpeis · þat was a quointe man ·	
Clerc and hardi of is dedes · & hor cirurgian ·	15
Hii made a wit legat · in þis cope of wit ·	
Aȝe þe oþer rede · as him in despit ·	
& he stod as a legat · vpe þe castel walle ·	
& amansede king & legat · & hor men alle ·	
Suich game ilaste longe · among hom in such striue ·[16]	20

With mangonels and engines they each other to cast.	
The legate and the archbishop with them also take	
Two other bishops, and to Kenilworth they came.	
To form accord with the king and the disinherited also,	
And with them of the castle, if it might be so.	5
But the disinherited would not do according to the king's will,	
Nor they of the castle either, nor consent to their decision.	
The legate, in his red cope, excommunicated there	

Those who in the castle were, and with them yet many more;
All who abetted him, or were of their counsel,   10
Or consented to them in will or in deed.
They of the castle had of this great indignation;
Copes and clothes, in mockery they bade make,
And master Philip Porpeis, that was a quaint man,
A clerk, and bold of deed, and their surgeon,   15
They make a moral legate, in his white cope,
In opposition to the counsel of the others, and in contempt of them.
And he stood as a legate upon the castle wall,
And cursed king and legate, and their men all.
Such game lasted long among them in such strife,   20
But much good was it not to soul nor to life.[17]

Gloucester suggests that several people assisted Porpeis (lns 10–12) in his defiant and 'bold' act (ln 15). Exactly how they helped is unclear. It is possible those who consented 'in deed' (ln 11) made, or at least found, suitable clothing for him to wear. They may have dressed in mock vestments themselves as Gloucester refers to 'copes and clothes' in the plural (ln 13). Beyond its colour, the costume worn by Porpeis is not described, although if Gloucester reported events faithfully, the implication is that the surgeon deliberately dressed in white to juxtapose the red cope worn by the legate (ln 8). An undyed cloth that appeared white would have been easier to locate than one of a costlier red dye, even allowing for the fact that Kenilworth had been the seat of the king's sister and brother-in-law. However, the account suggests the colour of Porpeis's cope was not happenstance.[18] Gloucester is generally considered to be a reliable commentator and based on our current philological understanding of thirteenth-century English, it is likely that he intended a deliberate pun with his double use of the word 'wit' (ln 16), which could mean both 'white' and 'moral'.[19] Joseph Stevenson translated '*Hii made a wit legat · in þis cope of wit*' as 'They make a mock legate, in his white cope', understanding *wit* in the sense of humour. This reading is plausible, but Porpeis wearing white in contradistinction to the legate's red makes greater sense if this gesture is understood with reference to contemporary colour associations. White was symbolic of purity, innocence, and mourning; allusions that would have had particular significance given Porpeis's predicament.[20] By wearing white, the implication was that Porpeis, and the Kenilworth garrison, possessed a moral authority the legate and king lacked. This point would have been emphasised if he were joined on the castle's ramparts by other people clad in mocking (white) vestments.

Gloucester describes the actions of Porpeis and the Kenilworth garrison as a 'game' (ln 20), but this does not preclude the simultaneous conveyance of a serious message; in fact, it could have made their gesture more effective. Bakhtin and Caillois explain how ludic activities, which follow specific rules and appear to create a distinct timeframe, temporarily remove people from quotidian obligations.[21] Within this ephemeral space, shared values can be critiqued, challenged and confirmed. Paucity of detail means there is a risk of reading too much significance into Porpeis's action. It could be that Gloucester conceived of no *double entendre*; the garment worn by the surgeon was simply a 'mock cope'. However, the communal effort to make costumes during the siege, along with descriptions of the conflict from other chroniclers, provides sufficient evidence to show that the political and psychological strains at this moment in Henry III's reign created an atmosphere that encouraged the use of symbolically charged gestures. To elucidate the motivation and impact of Porpeis's costumed challenge, it is necessary to analyse the circumstances in which it was conceived and executed.

There are three reasons why Kenilworth castle became the focus of Henry III's reign in 1266.[22] First, political. The fortress had been the chief seat of the Earl of Leicester and royal in-law, who had governed England between the battle of Lewes and his death at the Battle of Evesham.[23] During Montfort's governorship of England, the king's brother and his two nephews had been incarcerated in Kenilworth; the king was imprisoned at Woodstock. Second, topographical. According to William Rishanger, a fourteenth-century chronicler of St. Alban's Abbey, Kenilworth was located 'in the middle of the kingdom' and as such, it had to be secure in the king's hands, if peace were 'to smile upon England'.[24] Third, psychological. For the 1,200 men and women who had flocked to Simon de Montfort's banner and been disinherited by the crown after his death, the castle was a safe haven.[25] Located in a region known for its support of Montfort, it was also a beacon of resistance.[26] For as long as Kenilworth held out, Henry III's position was insecure.

To achieve the quick victory that he needed, and perhaps to demonstrate that his authority had not been irrevocably weakened by his captivity, Henry III pursued several strategies to impress and intimidate the garrison upon his arrival at Kenilworth in June.[27] Nine siege engines were erected around the castle and hurled stone missiles day and night.[28] Siege towers were also constructed. These movable wooden structures, as high as the castle's walls, gave the soldiers protected within greater scope for attack. One of the towers, 'of remarkable height and width', contained 200 crossbowmen.[29] In an act that may assume greater significance given the garrison's use of clothing to challenge royal authority, accounts of the royal wardrobe indicate that Henry was provided with a new military tunic during the siege. A description of the gambeson, which was made of quilted fabric, states that it was decorated with gold embroidery and dags, pointed pieces of fabric attached to the hem or shoulders of a garment typically in a contrasting colour.[30] The description of the garment, which was geared to hand combat rather than siege warfare, suggests it resembled a surviving jupon of the Black Prince (1330–76). Consequently, it seems to have been worn chiefly for its visual impact, to demonstrate Henry's commitment to the siege. The king had, after all, made a conscious, possibly public, decision to remain at Kenilworth until the siege was over.[31]

Alongside these acts of bellicosity, King Henry initiated gestures of benevolence. Royal accounts reveal that he distributed larger quantities of plate and jewellery as gifts and oblations during the period of the Kenilworth siege than ever previously.[32] One hundred paupers were fed daily, which maintained the king's customary level of almsgiving.[33] On 15 August, the Assumption of the Virgin Mary was celebrated with a sumptuous feast that cost £50 7s. 5d.[34] This large sum was roughly equivalent to the annual income of a knight. There was probably an element of psychological warfare here, as the king tormented the starving and besieged garrison with the sight and smell of eating and drinking. In July, the rebel garrison had witnessed an equally impressive sight, when a dead whale was brought to Kenilworth.[35] The carcass would have provided cheap and plentiful food for the royal army, and much-needed oil for light and lubrication. It is also possible the king intended to make a more symbolic point. By having the whale brought to Kenilworth, he may have been trying to demonstrate his singular prerogative, because he had the right to claim such beasts when they washed ashore. If the siege sought to demonstrate Henry's power over men, it could be that the dead whale demonstrated his mastery over animals. As Paul Edward Dutton notes of the role and meaning of animals under the Carolingians, '[i]n a hierarchical world of competing forces it was necessary for kings to demonstrate their superior control of animals'.[36] Henry appears to have understood the awesome impression that exotic creatures could create in the minds of his subjects. He kept a menagerie at the entrance to the Tower of London, which included, briefly, a polar bear and elephant.[37]

Prosaically, dead marine mammals were unlikely to induce the Kenilworth garrison to surrender. The decision that Legate Ottobuono should travel to the castle in the same month, whereupon he excommunicated the garrison, was acknowledgement that Henry's various strategies were not working. In fact, Ottobuono had already expressed concern about the king's paradoxical actions, observing 'after strong faith nothing shines greater in a prince than, in justice, to serve clemency'.[38] The advice, which advocated benevolence over bellicosity, was accurate because the use of intimidating gestures against the garrison encouraged reciprocal behaviour. Throughout the siege, the gates of Kenilworth remained open, possibly to taunt the royalists who struggled to gain access.[39] Members of the garrison had also severed the hand of a royal messenger sent to talk with them.[40] These gestures were made in the face of illness, hunger and increasing division among the garrison. Gloucester indicates that some of the castle's defenders had refused to participate in Philip Porpeis's mock excommunication (lns 10–11). According to another account of the siege, a renegade group hoisted the royal standard from the ramparts. These quislings were besieged, subjected to some form of trial, before being pulled by horses and hanged. The events were visible to the royal army, presumably because of the castle's open gates.[41]

It is difficult to reconcile the actions of the garrison, which were simultaneously confident and confused, with Claire Valente's model of political resistance in medieval England. Valente suggests that acts of rebellion, whether passive or physical, were usually calculated to broker a settlement; the repudiation of royal authority was a means to an end, rarely an end in itself. In this period of Henry's reign, she argues that raids by the 'disinherited' contributed to a political hegemony over the kingdom and thus perpetuated something akin to a 'holy war'.[42] This claim is hard to substantiate considering the garrisons' refusal to negotiate. Their prolonged challenge suggests they did not expect to be pardoned. Some may have remembered the siege of Bedford castle of 1224, when Henry had over eighty of the garrison hanged.[43] The evidence suggests the men and women within Kenilworth interpreted the siege as a last stand.

Consequently, the garrison's challenging actions were probably conceived to give themselves a sense of mastery over their fate. Assembling Porpeis's costume, as much as convening a mock trial, enabled the garrison to control a moment within an episode over which they were otherwise powerless. According to anthropologist David Kertzer, the appeal of ritual actions that do not appreciably benefit the people performing them is 'psychological; they reduce people's anxiety level and give them the healthier impression that they do have some control over their lives'.[44] The actions of the garrison were not wholly intangible, for they not only criticized existing political structures, but seemed to offer alternatives to them. Porpeis's performance through fancy dress discredited the authority of the king and the legate and implied that someone else could assume the mantle of church leader. Gloucester emphasizes Porpeis's learning and standing as a surgeon in his verse (lns 14–15) and, if my translation is accepted, he implied the surgeon had a moral authority the legate lacked (ln 16). In a similar way, the mock trial and punishment of dissidents within the garrison rejected and replaced the role of the king as font of justice. The actions of the garrison amounted to a repudiation and reconstitution of royal and ecclesiastical authority. It is unlikely the garrison conceived of fundamental political reform. Their dauntless challenges, which most stridently expressed through Porpeis's excommunication of Henry III through fancy dress, aimed at world making to give them a psychological control over their fate.

King killers - The Assassination of Gustaf III of Sweden
Stockholm, Sweden, 16 March 1792

On the evening of 16 March 1792, Gustaf III of Sweden was shot and stabbed in the lower left of his back during a masquerade ball at Stockholm's Royal Opera House. He had been wearing a fancy dress costume, but one that did not conceal his regal identity. The shooter, ironically a former captain of the king's lifeguard, Jakob John Anckarström, was dressed as a black domino, as were his aristocratic accomplices. Shortly after the king had arrived at the Opera House, an anonymous hand-delivered letter warned of an imminent attempt on his life. These threats were not uncommon and the danger was downplayed. Even after the attack, the king retained his composure. He did not complain of excessive pain and was able to walk. Noise and crowding meant that many revellers were initially oblivious to the attempted regicide. Panic only set in when shouts of 'Fire!', a ruse to create pandemonium and allow the attackers to flee, sparked a rush for the Opera House's exits. The king's injury was serious. The shot, which had contained two lead balls, rusted tacks and scraps of lead and iron, was not easily extracted and the wound turned septic. Thirteen days later, on 29 March, Gustaf died. Throughout the medieval and early modern periods rulers had feared the unrest that masks were thought to facilitate, but Gustaf III's death is the first known case of regicide through fancy dress costume.

The garments worn by Gustaf and Anckarström were kept as evidence for the murder investigation and survive in the collection of Stockholm's *Livrustkammeran*. Both are interesting for what they suggest about their wearer's attitude to the challenge that was made against royal authority. Engaging with a growing body of scholarship, chiefly by literary scholars, which considers the dynamic relationship between theatre and political discourse during the early modern period, I want to suggest that fancy dress costume had a deliberate and central role in framing how the assailants, their victim, and subsequently the public, made sense of this awesome event and understood their roles within it.[45] If Anckarström conceived of his costume to comprehend the personal implications of his challenge to royal authority, and to bolster his resolve, Gustaf III used his dress and a series of atypical public gestures to mount a counter challenge and to refute the attack.

After Gustaf's death, his masquerade clothing was placed in a wooden chest lined with blue silk that had originally been made for the 'death clothes' of his predecessor, Gustaf II Adolf.[46] The grey silk suit and contrasting blue and gold striped stockings that Gustaf wore on the evening of the attack are not fancy dress costume (Figure 18).[47] The king had worn these clothes to a performance of *Les Foiles Amoureuses* at the Bollhus Theatre earlier that evening. On arrival at the Opera House, he adorned the suit with costume accessories. A large selection of fancy dress clothing was kept in the royal apartments at Stockholm's Opera House, expressly for the king's use. A contemporary inventory recorded twenty-six masks and domino coats of white, black, brown, grey and green (*celadonfärgad*) taffeta.[48] On the evening of the assault, royal footman Elfström claimed the king was unable to find anything suitable to wear. He eventually chose a black cloak, described as 'Venetian', to drape over his suit.[49] French historian Artaud de Montor, who published an eyewitness account of the regicide in 1797 suggested the king's 'manteau l'essemblait parfaitement à celui des abbés de France'.[50] This sartorial connection may have been easier to establish after the king's death; throughout his account Montor refers to 'l'unfortune monarque', which implies his analysis is not wholly dispassionate.[51] A triangular black hat of beaver fur with white plumes and a white mask of oiled cloth covered much of the king's face and completed his improvised costume.[52] Captain Gustaf Löwenheim expressed surprise at the

FIGURE 18 *Photograph of Gustaf III of Sweden's masquerade costume, March 1792. Courtesy of Livrustkammeran, Stockholm.*

king's choice of dress. The star of the Order of the Seraphim, a chivalric order whose members included Swedish royals and foreign heads of state alone, was embroidered on the right breast of Gustaf's suit and remained visible beneath his costume, prompting Löwenheim to remark[53]:

Han var så igenkännlig, som om han varit omaskerad.
He was so recognizable, as if he were unmasked.[54]

Like Montor's history, Löwenheim's observation was made after the attack and needs to be treated cautiously. Nevertheless, the king's sartorial ambivalence is curious considering his fondness for the masquerade and theatre. During his reign, Gustaf had attended court events in theatrical costume following rehearsals with his actors. According to courtier and royal emissary Hans Axel von Fersten, the king made 'a jester of himself'.[55] Peter Cassirer argues that the king's interest in French and Italianate modes of performance made him a 'stranger' among his court.[56] In view of this criticism, it is conceivable that on the evening of 16 March Gustaf wanted to retain his regal identity, and the authority this conferred upon him, in response to the assassination threat. One account of the assault states the cautionary letter arrived whilst the king was being dressed, which may explain his quandary over what to wear.[57] Whilst Gustaf determined to attend the ball, the warning did alter his behaviour. It is reported that before entering the ball room, he stood in the royal box accompanied by his equerry Hans Henrik von Essen. After surveying the masked revellers, he is said to have remarked, 'Well, now they've had their chance to shoot. Come, let's go down'.[58] This version of events is relayed in various contemporary and near contemporary accounts and is likely accurate.[59] The king's action hints at bravado and seems to have been an attempt to challenge his would-be assailants.

Anckarström's costume was a domino. The surviving white face mask is of a waxed linen that has been folded to form a pronounced nose. The mask, which terminates in a point over the mouth, covered his eyes, and two oval holes 40-mm wide are cut into the cloth. A rectangle of black cloth is affixed to the bottom of the mask to conceal Anckarström's mouth.[60] The sixteen men who accompanied him, ostensibly to ensure the deed was successful, were dressed identically; several had hired their costumes from Stockholm hatmaker Hartins for thirty-two shillings.[61] The two guns, their grisly shot, and three knives that Anckarström carried with him, also formed part of the material evidence collected by police and now form part of the *Livrustkammeran* collection.[62]

The conspirators' choice of costume is interesting. Terry Castle describes the domino suit, characterized by its cloak, tricorn hat and full or partial face mask, all typically in black, as 'a kind of Ur-costume' on account of its monotone and ill-defined silhouette, 'from which any sartorial fancy might be formed'.[63] The ability to inscribe meaning onto the domino costume made it a symbolically compelling choice for political revolutionaries. In her study of literary depictions of fancy dress in nineteenth- and twentieth-century Russia, Colleen McQuillen explains how author Boris Savinov conceived of a political activist's fractured identity with reference to the domino's half mask, which corresponds to an 'existential loss of self'.[64] Focused on the revolutionary act, the terrorist renunciates personal relationships and property and becomes an 'invisible man'.[65] This psychological state is manifest in the domino costume. McQuillen asserts that it 'efface[s] identity' without providing a substitute. 'The absence of a decipherable identity is the most epistemologically unsettling kind of mask: it is simultaneously a blank page on which anything can be written and a vacuum into which everything collapses.'[66] The implication of this for Anckarström and his conspirators is that the domino was selected at least in part because it helped them to stabilize the vortex of emotions their planned action unleashed. This was costume as psychological salve. Moreover, by dressing alike, as though in uniform, the men gave tangible expression to the bonds that existed between them and galvanized their resolve.

An approach to dress that prioritized psychological wants is suggested by at least two practical missteps. First, dressing alike facilitated the men's identification and capture. Witness reports taken after the attack suggest the premature arrival at the Opera House of numerous dominoes, and their subsequent surrounding of the king before he was shot and stabbed, had been noted with suspicion.[67] Naturally, such observations were easier to make with the benefit of hindsight. Second, the decision to wear the same style of costume created the problem of distinguishing one another during the ball. The group relied on distinctive squared-toed boots to identify one another within the Opera House.[68]

The conspiracy against Gustaf III developed over a three-month period although concerns about the king's autocratic methods and his ambitious foreign policy were long-standing. Between 1788 and 1790, he had led Sweden into to an expensive and near-disastrous confrontation with Russia. In 1790, his emissary Hans Axel von Fersen had been instrumental in arranging Louis XVI's and Marie Antoinette's ill-fated flight to Varennes.[69] In 1792, he seemed poised to commit Swedish troops to the reinstatement of the French king, which the country could ill afford, politically or financially. Removal of Gustaf seemed urgent. From the outset, Anckarström had seemed intent on exploiting the opportunities for regicide that a masked ball created.[70] Crowds of people confined within a relatively small space, rendered anonymous by their incongruous clothing, facilitated a surprise attack and swift escape. Moreover, before Lent the king's penchant for fancy dress entertainments provided a frequent schedule of events at which the assassin could plan his strike. Masked balls were announced in advance in Stockholm's newspaper *Dagligt Allehanda* and Gustaf's attendance, whilst not guaranteed, was likely.[71] Prior to the 16 March, Anckarström had made several attempts on the king's life. Four of these occasions – 19 January, 21 February, 2 March and 9 March – had been at masked balls.[72] The circumstances were not always propitious. On 2 March, he aborted his plan because too few people had attended the ball, which was unusual for being held during Lent, and he risked exposure.[73] If fancy dress costume facilitated regicide by concealing the identity of Anckarström, it is possible the masked ball was identified as a suitable venue for the king's murder for another reason. To attack the king whilst he was engaged in an activity that appeared to epitomize his capricious exercise of authority was to make a legitimate challenge to his rule.[74] After their arrest, the conspirators maintained they were acting in the interests of the nation. They had needed to convince the people of Stockholm, and Sweden, of the rightness of their action and choosing to strike at a costumed entertainment may have strengthened their argument.

Denunciating rulers and regimes by focusing on their extravagant private pursuits was, and remains, a tactic commonly adopted by critics. For example, in 1906, Russian satirical magazine *Leshii* published a cartoon that criticized the outlook of the country's elite by remarking on their attendance at fancy dress balls (Figure 19).[75] The image depicts two men who are making hanging garlands from human skulls. One man, seated on a bench in the middle of the scene, appears to be a military officer judging by his uniform. Over the top of this he wears an apron. The man is using a hand-operated bradawl to bore holes into the sides of skulls so they can be threaded with string and hung. A second man, observing this work, stands to the left. He wears a civil uniform decorated with gold braid. Both men wear face masks of an equivalent shape to that worn by Anckarström in 1792. A caption explains that they are decorating the Tauride Palace in St Petersburg, which was the seat of the Tsar's parliament. The message of the cartoon is that Russia's callous aristocrats were enjoying themselves at the expense of the Russian people. For the privileged few, the Palace was not a place for discussing political reform, but merriment. Their indifference was perpetuating Russia's suffering, as represented by the hollowed hanging skulls.

FIGURE 19 *'The Decoration of the Tauride Palace', N. Brute,* Leshii, *4, 1906.*

In Sweden, Gustaf III's patronage of the dramatic arts was well known and, analogous to the *Leshii* cartoon, had come to symbolize the ills of his reign; chiefly, his perceived predilection for personal fulfilment at the expense of his nation's needs. The king's enjoyment of dramatic performance was not atypical. Various Scandinavian monarchs patronized the theatre and paid for the enlargement or construction of new performance spaces during the seventeenth and eighteenth centuries.[76] However, the influence of the theatre on the appearance and practice of Gustaf's kingship was distinctive. Stig Fogelmarck suggests 'drama, both on stage and in politics, was Gustaf's natural mode of self expression'.[77] The king wrote librettos, which he pressed into propaganda, and his script of *Siri Brahe* was translated widely after his death.[78] He acted the title role in several court performances, including the seventeenth-century French play *Cinna*. This was particularly prophetic because Cinna connives to kill the Emperor Augustus. In spite of his stooped and unprepossessing physique, Gustaf was also said to charm and persuade audiences with his oratorical skill.[79] The king's clothing may also have been inspired by the theatre. Gustaf's characteristic knitted silk stockings were similar to those worn by hussars, whose costume was popular throughout the early eighteenth century as fashion and fancy dress costume. Lena Rangström suggests the king's adoption of these garments was influenced by a specific visit he made to Italy between 1783 and 1784. On stage, Gustaf would have seen Italian actors wearing skin-coloured stockings in an allusion to ancient nakedness.[80] Patterned and coloured variations of the silk stockings were also worn by the *Commedia dell' arte* character Pantalone.[81] Royal accounts show that Gustaf personally paid for the costumes of actors within the Swedish Royal Theatre and silk stockings, in various colours, are itemized. It is possible that some of the stockings purchased by the king were intended for his daily attire and personal fancy dress costumes. According to Rangström, a payment was made to Mazar of Stockholm on 19 March 1792 for eighteen pairs of stockings. The order included a pair described as 'raye' (striped), which could have been those that Gustaf wore on the evening he was attacked.[82]

The theatrical mode of Gustaf's kingship appears to have become more pronounced in the circumstances of Anckarström's attack. The shooting and stabbing was a moment of acute personal and political crisis but their occurrence at a masked ball may have heighted the king's awareness of the symbolic potential of violence against him. Prior to the attack, Ronald Gerste avers that Gustaf had become fearful of the 'dark prophecy' (*dunklen Prophezeiung*) of Julius Caesar's murder following his reform of the Swedish constitution at the commencement of his reign.[83] Contemporaries were quick to connect the date of Anckarström's attack, which followed the Ides of March, with Caesar's fate.[84] Rangström identifies another figure whom Gustaf may have recalled; Henri III of France, who was assassinated by Jacques Clément, disguised as a priest.[85] The king's familiarity with *Cinna* certainly meant he was alive to the idea and implications of regicide.

Placing the king's actions in a theatrical frame can help to explain his apparently lacklustre costume. It can also clarify the king's dramatically inspired actions after the attack. The implication is that Gustaf anticipated death and sought to direct his exit from the world. Rangström argues that Gustaf's decision to be placed in the state bedchamber after his removal from the Opera House was governed by the 'impression of maintaining order', because it was from here that he had traditionally performed his *levée* and held audiences.[86] There is clearly an element of informed speculation about some of these suggestions but contemporaries did remark on the king's unusually calm demeanour during his final days and his attempt to stage manage events within the royal court. John Brown's nineteenth-century description of Gustaf's return to the palace is worth quoting in full because it shows how spectators were inclined to interpret the shooting and its aftermath as a theatrical set piece:

This great diversity of splendid costume; the melancholy state of the king, stretched on the bier, lying on his side, his pale face resting on his right hand, his features expressive of pain subdued by fortitude; the varied countenances of the surrounding throng, wherein grief, consternation, and dismay were forcibly depicted; the blaze of numerous torches and flambeaux borne aloft by the military; the glitter and burnished helmets, embroidered and spangled robes, mixed with the flashes of drawn sabres and fixed bayonets; the strong and condensed light thrown on the king's figure, countenance, litter and surrounding group; the deep, dark masses of shade that seemed to flitter high above and far below the principal group, and the occasional illumination of the vast and magnificent outline of the structure, – formed, on the whole, a spectacle more grand, impressive, and picturesque than any state or theatrical procession on the arrangement of which the tasteful Gustavus had ever been engaged.[87]

Gustaf's intentions are unknowable, but it is interesting to observe parallels between his actions and those of England's Charles I, who was executed on 30 January 1649 after being found guilty of treason by his subjects. Charles was noted for his aestheticism of politics and participation in masked performances. In a study of reactions to the king's execution, Nancy Klein Maguire argues that Charles closely controlled his public appearances during his trial and prior to its sentence being carried out. She suggests the king may have thought that, 'much as he dispelled the antimasques [whilst in costume at] Whitehall, he could dispel the "antimasque" of the civil wars by his death; his statement on the scaffold, "I am the Martyr of the People", suggests such a notion.'[88] Charles's words express a similar sentiment to those of Gustaf, who apparently remarked, 'I can almost rejoice at the wound that has stretched me here, and think it smart overpaid, since it has reconciled me to my friends'.[89]

In the Swedish and English examples, the theatrical analogies of kings making defiant last stands appear to have helped Gustaf and Charles to comprehend an attack upon their God-ordained status and imminent death. It enabled royal supporters to come to terms with their immediate grief and the longer-term decline in their political and social fortunes. Dramatic framing also aided the regicides. In the case of Charles I, Maguire suggests the king's theatrical execution and trial, where the lord president of the High Court of Justice was sat upon a chair of cushioned crimson velvet and the jurors on cloth of scarlet, helped to 'legitimize the new regime and abolish the mystique of kingship'.[90] This elaborate panoply may have also worked to provide psychological comfort and ballast to the people who were tasked with challenging the monarch and, more awesomely, the fundamental nature of the institution of monarchy. In the case of Sweden, the quantity of weapons that Anckarström carried with him, the brutality of his attack, and the premature arrival of sixteen identically clad dominoes in the auditorium of the Opera House, seems comically exaggerated. In view of the fact that these men were poised to kill a king, their risible behaviour is probably best understood as a coping strategy that anesthetized them to the import of their purpose.

In the early modern period, the boundary between politics and theatre was porous. Maguire asserts, with reference to England, that '[t]heater and politics were so closely meshed by 1649 that they became nearly indistinguishable, metaphorically contaminating each other in many ways. Politicians, playwrights, and audiences experienced considerable ambivalence about the two forms.'[91] This was less apparent after the seventeenth century, but it clearly influenced the political discourse of Gustaf's reign. The dramatic framing of his murder also continued after his death. Subsequent generations interpreted the king's death in theatrical terms, and by using fancy dress costume, perhaps to eschew its horror as much to clarify a point that may have been intended by the conspirators about the capricious nature of absolutism. French authors were particularly interested in the circumstances of Gustaf's death after the Revolution that toppled Louis XVI. In the nineteenth century, interpretations of Gustaf's murder reached a global audience. From 1840, Samuel Kinser notes that participants in New Orleans's carnival parade went to the Orleans Theater to join actors on stage in the final scene of Daniel Auber's opera, *Gustave*, which features a gallopade.[92] The practice apparently mirrored a Parisian tradition.[93] Guiseppe Verdi's opera *Un Ballo in Maschera* of 1859 was based on the narrative of Gustaf's assassination, although specific reference to the king had to be removed by anxious censors.[94] In 1897, American singer Frances Ronalds attended the Devonshire House Ball as Euterpe, the spirit of music. Her yellow satin dress was decorated with bars from Verdi's opera.[95] August Strindberg's six-hour historical play *Gustav III* of 1902 was adapted for Swedish television in 1972. In the immediate circumstances of the attack upon Gustaf, fancy dress enabled people to define their roles in a chaotic situation. Subsequently, the popularity of this sartorial form helped people to understand the tumultuous event and make its implications relevant to their circumstances.

Resisting change - The Reconstruction Era Ku-Klux Klan Southern American States, 1866–71

Between mid-1866 and early 1871, the Ku-Klux Klan existed as an inchoate group within the southern American states. This was the region that had seceded from the Union prior to the Civil War of 1861–65. To challenge the perceived hegemony and deleterious effects of black culture in the period of Reconstruction, klansmen drew upon a number of performance traditions to create and wear purposefully frightening forms of fancy dress costume. Influences included the *charivari* and carnival, which incorporated elements of African performance brought to America through the slave trade, and contemporary entertainments like Mardi Gras, minstrelsy and the burlesque.[96] To explain how the klansmen challenged social and political norms within the American south, and the position of black people specifically, Elaine Frantz Parsons uses Victor Turner's concept of social drama. She suggests the klan occupied a liminal position; geographically – because its ideas and actions were shaped by a north–south discourse on American unity after the War – chronologically – because it harnessed traditional and contemporary elements within popular culture to manifest its concerns – psychologically – because klansmen perceived themselves to be at the periphery of their communities and wanted to recover, or to claim, positions of respect – and culturally – because its violent actions, invariably perpetrated at night, led many people, particularly in the north, to question the veracity of its existence.[97] Situating the klan at the margins of nineteenth-century American life, Parsons argues that it was 'epiphenomenal'.[98] The hatred and violence used by klansmen was conceived, however fitfully, to contribute to formal and informal dialogues about America's future. This section is informed by Parsons's thesis, but modifies her contention that 'costuming carried with it a modern, urban feel'.[99] Interpreting the intentions of the Ku-Klux Klan through its dress and behaviour suggests their chief concern was to resist changes to political and social hierarchies.[100]

Klansmen typically attacked black households at night, travelling in groups of between five and ten men.[101] Sometimes there were as many as twenty to thirty.[102] They were almost invariably dressed in costume, which extended to their horses.[103] The klansmen entered homes whilst the occupants slept and forcibly removed male residents.[104] Outside, victims were verbally assaulted and threatened. Some klansmen carried guns to convey the seriousness of their intent.[105] Victims were whipped.[106] Others had their possessions stolen.[107] Stories circulated of klansmen raping black women, although these were often difficult to verify.[108] The assailants often made music, performed dance or imitated animal noises to disorientate their targets.[109]

The form of klan attacks is well-established, but the interpretation of evidence, particularly concerning the role and meaning of their attire, is not straightforward. The controversial nature of klan apparel continues to make its study and display problematic in the twenty-first century.[110] Few klan costumes survive. In part, this is because klansmen were expected to keep their dress hidden and to discard evidence after capture.[111] Contemporaries charged with investigating the klan after the Civil War did attempt to collect items of dress.[112] In one example, a circuit court trial in the state of North Carolina, defendant T.J. Downey was asked to wear his confiscated costume.[113] If government officials sought klan costumes primarily as evidence, it seems they were equally keen to take possession of them to dispel lingering notions that they harboured spectral powers. Augustus Wright, a former judge and congressman, expressed his sympathy 'with the negro; he is ignorant, to some extent confiding, superstitious, and easily made to believe anything in the world, especially by white men, and more especially by those white men who profess to be his friends'.[114] Black people harassed by the klan also preserved masks and caps that were dropped during attacks.[115] Some did think the klansmen were invulnerable and likened them to devilish avatars, but many quite literally saw through their costumes and identified the people beneath the makeshift coverings, who could be neighbours.[116] In the case of witness Alfred Robinson, who had a collection of at least seven klan caps and a horn, which 'they blow when they are gathering', there seems to have been a genuine fascination with imaginative and gruesome garments that had taken time to produce (Figure 20).[117]

Another historiographical consideration relates to the written testimonies of klan members and victims collected after the War by a Joint Select Committee of Congress. Published in thirteen volumes, the interviews elucidate klan motivations and operations. They also contain the fullest descriptions of klan costumes. However, despite their apparent pellucidity they are a product of contemporary prejudice and political machination.[118] As Parsons notes, Committee interviews were overly reliant on the testimony of white people; black witnesses were frequently deferential, if not defensive, and northern interviewers, possibly bored with the task assigned to them, were too inclined to accept stories of klan competence.[119] On the one hand, the notion that white people were ordered and black people were disordered sustained a socialized narrative about race relationships within America.[120] Whilst the nineteenth-century klan only existed in America's southern states, Parsons argues that people in the north inadvertently sanctioned its outlook and activities through the social and political frame in which they discussed it.[121] On the other hand, perceiving the klan to be coordinated and labelling the South violent conveniently explained the slow pace of Reconstruction.[122]

Descriptions and survivals reveal costumes worn by the klan were not of a standard design. Some klansmen participated in attacks without altering their appearance. Virtually all testimonies that mention klan costume describe face coverings, sometimes decorated with beards, and hats that were typically pointed, occasionally adorned with horns (Figures 21 and 22).[123] Garments that covered the body, which were worn over conventional clothing, are generally described in lesser detail, presumably because their appearance was less striking, and thus less memorable. Similar costumes for horses are also described:

MISSISSIPPI KU-KLUX IN THE DISGUISES IN WHICH THEY WERE CAPTURED.
[FROM A PHOTOGRAPH.]

FIGURE 20 'Mississippi Ku-Klux Klan in the disguises in which they were captured', engraving. No date. © Getty Images.

This chief was dressed in a white pair of pants. With a red shirt on with two crosses before and one behind, and he had a white cloth over his face, bound around the eyes with red, and he had on his head a big horn, about three feet high; it nearly touched the top of the loft. But I tell it was the scariest sight, though he didn't look as scary as them that had four horns.[124]

Question: Barton Biggerstaff?
Answer: He was in the house disguised only with a necklace and cravat.
Q: What was it made of?
A: Made with wool with horns.
Q: Where was that tied?
A: Just around the back part of his head.
Q: How wide?
A: It was wide enough to come down to his throat. They called them a cravat.
Q: He had a cravat tied around his face and the back of his head?
A: Yes, sir. That came off. The Early Boys tied nothing over their face. Their coats were only turned wrong side outward. If they had anything tied over their faces I didn't see it at all.[125]

North Carolina: testimony of Mary Anne Norvill

There was also found a piece of white osnaburg [a coarse fabric], which had covered a horse down to the knees. These things were found where the firing took place. After a while we went on around, and I suppose some two or three hours after the firing it was announced that there was a man found near the corner where they had turned … There was a man lying on his back, with dark clothing; he had on a kind of dark sack, which they said afterward was black calico; I did not examine very carefully the texture of the cloth. It was a loose sack, reaching down to about the hips; his pants had a broad stripe, about an inch wide, reaching all the way from the hips down. He also wore a mask which reached to the bosom. It had holes cut out for eyes, but none for the mouth, because it hung loose, and there was no difficulty in breathing … The hat that was worn on that occasion was a white-looking hat that stood up high. I suppose those saddle-bags were for the purpose of putting disguises in, because the hats in the saddle-bags were citizens' hats – common hats. When the disguise was removed it was found that the man had on his full suit of common clothes under the disguise.[126]

Mississippi: testimony of Richard W. Flournoy

Despite variations in dress, witness testimony that refers to 'regular disguise' indicates there were similarities between klan groups.[127] Evidence shows that some klan leaders deliberately gave their followers a coherent appearance. Outwardly, this may have made the men appear more intimidating; inwardly, an instrumental group identity may have given them confidence. In one example, James M. Justice tells how Turner 'brought the cloth to make the disguises, and the bolt made five disguises, and … Decatur bought a redder kind of goods to make his disguise … There were seven at Birge's, six of whom were disguised, and one not in disguise.'[128] In other cases, klansmen were told what to wear, but had to provision cloth themselves. Klan member James Grant explained that all men in his group had to have 'disguises', 'that is, to have their head and horns; and then they were to have a gown made to wear', but 'each member was to get one himself'.[129] The onus on individuals to dress themselves, combined no doubt with the experience of participating in raids, encouraged sartorial experimentation. In the following exchange, the apparent frustration of a cross-examiner for the defence, who had difficulty visualizing what was being described to him, and the short, often monosyllabic responses from interviewee Aaron Biggerstaff, support the idea that klan victims came to expect sartorial cunning. The transcript also hints at the Committee's lack of empathy:

Question: Were they disguised?
Answer: One of them were.
Q: Well, Hunt didn't have on anything?
A: His hat lining was over his forehead.
Q: Was it put there to disguise himself?
A: It was.
Q: Just the lining pulled over his head?
A: Yes sir.
Q: Pulled from the inside of his hat?
A: Yes, sir.
Q: How low did it come?
A: Close to his eyes....

Q: What color hat was this; what was the color of the lining?
A: Well, you know, hats is generally lined with a dark color.
Q: You cannot tell the color of the hat?
A: It was a black hat.
Q: With a dark lining?
A: Yes, sir.[130]

The ability of some victims to recall exact details and to recognize similarities between the dress of klan groups indicates that those targeted were adept at understanding how clothes were made and how they communicated intent. This was almost certainly what the klan intended. In the nineteenth century, a majority of people made their own clothes and possessed knowledge of different fabrics, which are frequently speculated upon in klan reports. The costumes worn by the klan were also encountered in popular forms of entertainment, including carnival, minstrelsy and burlesque performances. Parsons has drawn attention to the klan's Pulaski founders, who had participated in staged fancy dress musical performances to raise funds for Confederate amputees and to convey political messages about a resurgent South.[131] For her, 'the klan was conceived in a *tableau vivant*, nurtured by minstrels and serenaders, housed by circuses and masquerades, and given an afterlife in Mardi Gras processions'.[132]

Black people's comprehension of klan costume was not entirely borne of spectatorship. In some cases, the grotesque masks worn by klansmen appear to have been based on black costumes of parody and protest. Samuel Kinser discusses troupes of black 'John Canoe' entertainers who performed along the North Carolinian coast before the klan emerged.[133] Contemporary descriptions refer to 'kuner faces ... painted upon something like bukram [that] presented features most remarkably distorted, enormous noses, widely grinning mouths, horns, and beards, fierce and terrifying to behold'.[134] The head coverings described here anticipate those worn by the state's klansmen, below:

The greatest number had nothing to disguise them except over their heads and faces a mask, as far as I could understand it, with a large-crown piece, and with a very large face. The places where the eye-holes and the mouth were cut was bound around with some reddish stuff; and something painted, for a nose. Some had very long beards; one that I have examined since, that I saw at Raleigh, was made of the tail of a cow. I did not know what it was, but some of them had white beards. Some had horns which were erect; others had horns which lopped over like a mule's ears, and their caps ran up to a point with tassels.[135]

The depiction of this head covering is similar to one that survives from the klan in The North Carolina Museum of History, which is adorned with three horns (Figure 21). Two horns, which are noticeably curved and approximately 410 mm long, project horizontally from each side of the mask. The third horn, approximately 460 mm long, is straighter and projects vertically from the crown. The horns are stuffed to retain their shape and red and black ribbon is wrapped around each. A beard and sideburns have been fashioned from brown rabbit fur and three vampyric-looking teeth, each approximately 60 mm long, protrude from the mouth.[136] Two differently sized eyeholes (right: approximately 40 mm; left approximately 65 mm) have

FIGURE 21 *A head covering associated with John Campbell, jr, Roxoboro, North Carolina. H.1996.102.1. Courtesy of The North Carolina Museum of History, Raleigh.*

been cut for the wearer to see. The holes are ringed with red paint. Directly above, two black eyebrows have been affixed at acute angles of approximately 35° (left) and 45° (right) to create an aggressive appearance.

Descriptions of many klan costumes reveal the prevalence of black, red and white, the potential significance of which has never been considered. The three colours had specific meaning in the west. Since the Middle Ages, black, red and white had symbolized virtues and vices – black: humility, sorrow, death; red: charity, faith, pride; white: innocence, death.[137] The colours appeared together in popular culture. For example, and although later, Edvard Munch used a scheme of black, red and white in the 'Frieze of Life' project he began in the 1890s. For the klan, it is possible the colours referred to West African masquerade traditions, where they were invested with particular importance.[138] It is unlikely that klansmen viewed African masks directly. These were not widely displayed until the twentieth century. Instead, elements of African performance traditions were incorporated into American carnival traditions by slaves, as the description above reveals.[139] Red and white are common colours in *Egungun* costumes where they represent Shango, a former king of Oyo.[140] Red can also refer to the Mother of *Egungun*, who is said to give birth 'not to black children but red ones'.[141] In another myth, black, red and white are linked to *Ijmere*, the Patas monkey, whom the *Egbado* Yoruba suggest was the first masquerader. According to Margaret Thomas Drewal and Henry John Drewal, the fur of the Patas monkey

> May be a "bright brick-red," and adults have a distinctive, dark reddish-brown mantle of fur around the neck and shoulders and a "top-knot" on the crown of the head … The face of the Patas monkey is light to dark grey with a black eyebrow ridge that contrasts with the white skin of the upper and lower eyelids and the white moustache.[142]

It is possible that nineteenth-century klan members appropriated images and artefacts from African traditions of masquerade in their aim to challenge and dominate black people in America's southern states.

If, as Eric Lott suggests in his study of blackface minstrelsy, black performers had used parodying entertainments 'to indulge their felt sense of difference', the klan's usurpation of these tropes had, on one level, the effect of negating them.[143] The extent to which victims of klan violence were forced into the passive position of spectator, as Parsons suggests, is, however, questionable.[144] The forces at work were likely more complex than this binary interpretation allows. As Lott observes, referring to the minstrel show and drawing on the work of Clifford Geertz, whilst nineteenth-century entertainments maligned black society and sought to '[defend] white America against it', the adaptation of black cultural forms simultaneously demonstrated their absorption into American life. In a similar way, whilst klansmen deliberately used elements of popular black performance to challenge and forestall blacks' increasing social mobility, their action indicated an awareness that they were unable to halt this progress. After the Civil War, in which black men had fought, and the emancipation of slaves, which led to many freed people becoming landowners, the klan was never likely to realize what many people perceived to be its aim of 'keep[ing] the colored people down to keep them in subordination'.[145]

In seeking to challenge the ascendancy of black people and their culture, there is a sense that klan members were involved in world making to preserve their hegemony. In contrast to Parsons, I would suggest the klan's behaviour is analogous to what sociologist Norbert Elias terms a 'drag effect', whereby people remain wedded to ideas and traditions of their existing association in the face of social change.[146] Parsons argues that the klan were 'distinctly modern' and '*au courant*', but the clever adoption and manipulation of contemporary popular culture did not necessarily make klansmen less 'idiosyncratic and desperate', as she claims.[147] Fancy dress was used by the klan less because it made them seem 'modern' but because it was efficacious in helping them to defend and demonstrate what it perceived to be traditional and immutable (Southern) American values. To reconfigure Marshall McLuhan's memorable phrase, here the message was not entirely synonymous with the message. New technologies and commercial innovation facilitated the popularity and spread of fancy dress within nineteenth-century America, but these developments were rarely important in their own right. Cameras, catalogues, carnivalesque entertainments and new types of cloth were important collectively because they enabled costumed revellers to experience the compelling sensation of teetering on the cusp between 'the now' and 'the neverland'. New technologies provided fancy dress entertainments with sufficient credibility and escapism to make them compelling. Whilst people were in the transitory state that costume facilitated, thoughts and feelings dimly perceived and felt were often crystallized.[148] The liminality of fancy dress was its attraction to the klan who could use this popular recreation to communicate with diverse groups of people.

The liminality of klan activities is expressed most clearly in Select Committee interviews that describe klansmen wearing women's clothing:

Some of them had on some women's clothes. It looked like a sort of paper or sheep-skin; it was a sort of black thing; some had one thing and some another; it was not all of one part.[149] He had his wife's old dress on; a dress I have seen many a time.[150]

North Carolina: testimony of Mary Anne Norvill

Broadly, klansmen's decision to wear women's costume was probably a subconscious response to the contemporary recognition that male and female bodies were anatomically different. An insistence on 'biological divergence' had crystallized during the late-eighteenth century. This meant that sex replaced gender as a 'primary foundational category'.[151] It apparently followed that the roles and appearance of men and women should be more clearly delineated, even though censures for cross dressing are recorded in Deuteronomy, which forbids men and women dressing in the clothes of the other sex.[152]

To conceal one's sexual identity though dress, and to commit the 'crime of falsity', created a stigma around cross-dressing that was to endure for at least the next century.[153] The specific intentions of klansmen who dressed as women are harder to define. This is especially the case when articles of women's clothing were worn over their conventional clothing, meaning they were clothed as both sexes simultaneously. The genderless costumes described above could also be worn over conventional dress, as (Figure 22) shows. In these circumstances, Alison Bancroft's observation is apposite:

The body is inevitably deceptive, to ourselves and to others, and shows that notions of gender are often in conflict with the lived experience of sexed subjectivity. The question of meaning attached to one's status as a man or a woman is unanswerable. Corporeal integrity is shown to be a myth.[154]

By wearing female clothing, it has been suggested that klansmen were seeking to assert their 'white manhood' and to 'ward off castration anxiety'.[155] The act of symbolic inversion ostensibly demonstrated that men were secure in their gendered roles. Of course, the need to

FIGURE 22 *'Klu Klux Klan Murder of John Campbell', engraving, 1891. © Getty Images.*

prove this suggests otherwise. Some men probably did experience feelings of emasculation after the Civil War. The point should not be overstated, but the conflict did have an emancipatory effect for American women. Whilst many women resumed their former lives after 1865, the conflict exposed gendered roles for the social constructs they were. Approximately 250 women, black and white, are known to have fought in the armies of the north and south between 1861 and 1865 disguised as men.[156] Women's reasons for fighting were rarely different to those of the opposite sex, but some specifically cited the unwillingness of males to enlist as their motivation.[157] Still others wanted to leave lives restricted by patriarchal obeisance.[158] Contemporary fiction conceived of daring and headstrong women, whom the press sought to locate in reality during the war, such that some female soldiers became 'media darlings'.[159] The challenge women's actions could pose to men is documented during the War. In one case, Confederate Mary Ann Clark was captured by Unionist soldiers. Before her release, she was forced into 'female apparel'.[160] By dressing as women after the War, it could be that klansmen were also attempting to assert their authority over women by demonstrating possession and control over their clothing.

Alternative readings of why klansmen dressed as women are possible. It could be that they wanted to represent the plight of both genders in the face of a common threat that black people were thought to pose. Here, parallels can be drawn between the klan and the English Luddites. The Luddites were followers of a fictitious Ned Ludd. In groups, costumed men attacked newly installed machines in factories and mills across the north of England between 1811 and 1816. These machines precipitated unemployment and constituted a threat to established social hierarchies.[161] In their attacks, the Luddites often dressed as women. Contemporary descriptions of the men's costumes are similar to those of the klan.

> Late of a Saturday night a number of men with faces blacked and their dress disguised, some wearing women's gowns and others a strange headgear, broke into the dressing shop of Mr Joseph Hirst.
>   Some were dressed in smocks, and all had their faces part concealed, either by a mask or by a 'kerchief drawn across the lower face. One gaunt being strode on before us dressed up in women's skirts; but a pair of men's trousers, that showed at every step, and a manly stride were all in ill-keeping with the skirt.[162]

According to Norman Simms, Luddites who dressed as women were demonstrating that their 'masculine identity' had been undermined by the newly installed machines, which effectively made women of them (Figure 23). Simultaneously, the men identified 'with the women most affected by the breakdown of the village economy'.[163] By representing the concerns of both sexes through their costumes, the men asserted their role as the 'virile force of the community's power'.[164] It is possible klansmen who dressed as women intended a similar statement. That the klansmen did think their actions protected wider social interests is evidenced by testimony given to the post-War Select Committee. Some interviewees expressed a belief that the klan existed to prevent black men from voting and marrying white women.[165] Respondents also stated that klansmen performed their violence because the federal government was doing too little to maintain order. Men of the south were therefore performing a duty beholden of their gendered role to uphold traditional values.[166] In essence, they were performing a nineteenth-century *charivari* to maintain norms of belief and behaviour.

If the actions and apparel of the klan were conceived to convey the group's purposes, the adoption of women's dress emphasizes how their use of fancy dress costume was double-edged. Historians are generally persuaded that the klan drew strength from its similitude to traditional and popular entertainments. To an extent this is true, but in the longer term this relationship seems to have had the effect of diluting the klan's message. The problem of adopting a popular form of entertainment to pursue a serious political and social challenge was that contemporaries, both victims and observers, sometimes did not recognize the implications of the klan's activities. This is apparent when black people had to be guided through klansmen's costumes and told that they represented Confederate ghosts or moonmen.[167] Ambiguity is equally apparent when costumed entertainments parodied the klan by dressing like them.[168] To some degree, confusion about the klan's nature stoked fears, but it strongly implies the costumes were worn chiefly to galvanize their wearers. These were men who felt a sense of dislocation from contemporary American society and wanted to be part of something larger than themselves. There was perhaps also a need to sustain morale and a sense of control when they conducted their attacks, much like Gustaf III's regicides.

The instability of fancy dress as a communicator probably explains why uniforms were introduced when the klan re-emerged in the twentieth century. As Robert Ross observes, uniforms are unambiguous in their depiction and promotion of rank.[169] The anonymizing white

FIGURE 23 *'The Leader of the Luddites', anonymous coloured engraving, 1812. © Heritage Image Partnership Limited/Alamy Stock Photo.*

dress, face covering and conical hat that is conventionally associated with the Ku-Klux Klan was likely inspired by the film *Birth of a Nation* (1915). The film's final scene shows a band of klansmen on horseback dressed entirely in white muslin. Various klan costumes appear in the film, but Alison Kinney suggests this new design, conceived in part by director D.W. Griffith, whose mother had made klan costumes during the Reconstruction era, may have inspired the future uniform.[170] A decade after the film's release, the klan published a catalogue of its banners and uniforms, which bear a strong resemblance to the film's costumes.[171] The silhouette of the klan's dress has become indelibly pressed into people's consciousness, although in the twentieth century its incongruity still made it a subject of parody in fancy dress. In the 1930s, the outfit features in a catalogue published by fancy dress supplier Weldon's (Figure 9).[172] Nonetheless, homogeneity of dress reflected a communal will and consolidated power that did much to show how the reformed Ku-Klux Klan of 1915 was a more effective and challenging political force than its Reconstruction-era precursor.[173]

Fancy dress - To challenge

Ostensibly, the wearing of fancy dress to challenge a political and social consensus is a clamorous act. Within each of the episodes considered in this chapter, costume is a conspicuous element that shaped the perceptions and behaviours of participants and spectators. However, the different circumstances in which this sartorial form was conceived and worn complicates conventional and binary discussions about the extent to which fancy dress is affective. The evidence suggests that a fancy dress costume could influence its wearer's behaviour and simultaneously become a less effective communicator due to their troubled psychological state. Four observations can be made. First, the examples considered – a thirteenth-century siege, an eighteenth-century regicide, a nineteenth-century terrorist group – emphasize the liminal circumstances in which fancy dress costume is worn and, correlatively, the rarity of surviving examples. This is undoubtedly frustrating, although the extent to which it constitutes an investigative limitation is arguably down to the resourcefulness of individual researchers. The examples in this chapter make it apparent that the frame in which fancy dress costume is conceived and worn needs to be understood if the performance of this sartorial form is to become clearer. In each episode the decision to wear fancy dress was informed by its perceived ability to symbolize, for the wearers if not always for its spectators, quotidian and more lofty concerns. This requires scholars to be attendant to issues beyond materiality and to consider, as Rachel Hann, Hajo Adam and Adam Galinsky urge, the reciprocal relationship that exists between the action, body and material affectiveness of costume; what Hann specifically identifies as the 'hug of costuming'.[174]

Second, fancy dress costume that is worn to challenge normative ideas and behaviours can appear aggressive to those confronted by it, a primary purpose it serves is to bolster the psychological resolve of its wearer as a form or world making. Fancy dress sustains its wearer in their struggle against an individual or group that is perceived to pose a threat. This observation chimes with empirical research that suggests the wearing of costume leads to deinviduation.[175] Deinviduation occurs when a person's self-awareness and social identity is reduced. Experiments have shown that fancy dress costume can alter its wearer's behaviour by distancing them from their immediate social roles and obligations. This is most apparent when people dress as a popular figure with well-known characteristics. For example, a study by Rachel White has shown that children costumed as Batman had an increased concentration span, possibly because their clothing enabled them to channel the character's known fortitude.[176] Similar experiments suggest costume role playing increases a wearer's propensity for risk taking.[177] The three examples considered in this chapter suggest that deinviduation occurred as a consequence of wearing fancy dress and, furthermore, that this temporary suspension of self was necessary for the wearers to undertake the actions they did when in costume: the repudiation of royal authority, regicide, and the perpetration of acts of terror.

Third, costume becomes imbued with its wearer's emotional turmoil. This can make fancy dress costume an unstable and unclear communicator to individuals and groups who do not immediately empathize with the wearer's concerns. The psychological volatility evinced by costume is more likely to render it polyvalent and, simultaneously, to create to a sense of farce or menace through misperception.

Fourth, the three episodes emphasize the dynamic and complex relationship between costumed and normative behaviour. Helpful in understanding this connection is Colleen McQuillen's adaptation of Yuri Lotman's 'translator code'.[178] Lotman has argued that theatre is adept at representing life and conveying important semiotic messages because the flow of a performance mirrors the course of people's lives. Moreover, a performance has the ability to 'isolate' 'integral, discrete units' that contain meaningful messages for their creators and audiences.[179] The dynamic relationship between representation and reality also facilitates the contra-tendency for life to imitate theatre.[180] McQuillen suggests that eighteenth-century western masquerade – I would assert, fancy dress costume broadly – occupies a similar 'interstitial place' because it 'assimilates the flow and punctuation of time'.[181] In this way, a theatrical performance facilitates analysis of human ideas and behaviour. She asserts that the freedom and unpredictability of costumed entertainments 'align them more closely with life' than theatrical performances.[182] The episodes in this chapter, which to varying degrees involve contemporaries drawing on their experiences of live performance, would support this assessment. The creativity evinced through the combination of artistic modes eventuates a 'productive metaphor for memory and a tool for inscribing historical experience into personal biography, or writing oneself into cultural tradition'.[183] In their various ways, and with different motivations, the people considered in this chapter, who sought to challenge and face down a physical or psychological threat, could all be said to have been seeking this.

3

To Clarify

An enduring delight and dilemma of fancy dress costume is its at least dual ability to conceal and clarify aspects of its wearer's character. The recognition that masked and costumed entertainments could create a liminal space in which reality and romance, fact and fiction, became malleable made them widely popular across Europe and the United States of America from the eighteenth and nineteenth centuries. For the same reasons, moralists inveighed against these festivities, believing them to encourage socially harmful behaviour. The controversy of fancy dress costume heightened its appeal and the theme of dressing up was widely depicted in literature, painting and the decorative arts. In some of the more unusual examples, diamond-studded finger rings featured masked cameos (Figures 24 and 25), taffeta hand fans depicted scenes from imagined *bals costumés* and, in Sweden, Baron Bengt Rosenhane commissioned portraits of his friends in fancy dress to line the walls of a small cabinet in Tista Manor, which he built between 1766 and 1771.[1]

These artworks are attempts to prolong the exhilaration experienced when wearing fancy dress costume. They show how the physical and psychological space that dressing up established fascinated people with the prospect of exploring their own identity and that of others. Satires against fancy dress frequently ridiculed this solipsistic pursuit for revelation. Celia Marshik's study of British fancy dress costume during the early twentieth century elides with excoriating commentaries that suggest the transnaturing ability of dress up was largely imaginary.[2] Her evidence indicates that fancy dress could even be menacing and alter people in ways they did not anticipate.[3] The complex relationship between a wearer and their costumed wardrobe, which became apparent in the previous chapter, where both can be seen to influence a fancy dress performance, suggest Marshik's explanations are not wholly sufficient. Whilst her evidence explains some attitudes towards aristocratic and plebeian dressing up in twentieth-century metropolitan Britain – specifically London – the synchronic snapshot she provides, largely pieced together from the views of critical social observers, does not convey the diverse experiences that people were having simultaneously in other parts of the world. A more nuanced view, albeit one that still emphasizes the malevolence of dressing up, is offered by Colleen McQuillen, who links costume concerns to contemporary musings about individual identity. Focusing on nineteenth- and twentieth-century Russian literature, she opines:

Writers used the costume party scene as a social satire to unmask their respective eras' social ills. In correlating appearance and essence, aesthetics and ethics, they perpetuated certain

FIGURE 24 *Photograph of a masquerade locket ring with flower shoulder details (shut)*, c. 1750. © *Fauna Jewelry*.

FIGURE 25 *Photograph of a masquerade locket ring with flower shoulder details (open)*, c. 1750. © *Fauna Jewelry*.

cultural beliefs that had influenced early nineteenth-century society-tale representations of the demonic masquerade. The implicit link between mask and menace, disguise and demonism, provides a counterpoint to the emergent understanding of identity as a temporary social construct.[4]

Academic debates aside, the simple, seductive and unsubstantiated view that costume is revelatory and diagnostic of a person's true self has continued to compel. It is frequently repeated in media commentary when public figures wear questionable fancy dress. For example, in 2005, Britain's Prince Harry dressed in a makeshift Afrika Korps suit with a red swastika armband. His choice was globally condemned. Some critics argued the outfit demonstrated the prince's unsuitability for the Royal Military Academy at Sandhurst and suggested he be removed.[5]

The apparent need to explain the connection between impersonation and identity has been most evident in cases of cross-dressing. Examples of gender inversion are long-standing and reliably documented from at least the medieval period.[6] Attitudes became notably intolerant from the eighteenth century because of a scientific belief that men and women were biologically diverse. This problematized the issue of people wearing clothing of the now opposed sex and a stigma was created around cross-dressing which constituted a counter narrative to the dominance of heteronormativity.[7] For the people who committed the supposed crime of falsity, however, the intention was probably less to challenge than to clarify their place in society. This is particularly apparent within America's ballroom scene, which is documented in Jennie Livingston's film documentary *Paris Is Burning*.[8] Lucas Hilderbrand explains that the film 'appeared [in 1991] just as the very category of "identity" was beginning to be interrogated (particularly gender identity), and the intersections of race, gender, and sexuality were being recognised'.[9] The film and the lives it documents was consequently a powerful demonstration of 'the possibility of queer world-making'.[10] The balls, which involve homosexual men parading in specific costume categories from 'Butch Queen' and 'Schoolboy/Schoolgirl' to 'Military', parody conventional gender distinctions in a safe and liminal space with surrogate families or 'houses'.[11] The ballroom scene helps (young) men, who are often without the support of their biological family and kin, without regular work and food, to mediate the reality of their situation with their aspirations. One anonymous interviewee in the film avers of the ballroom scene, 'It's like crossing into the looking glass, in Wonderland. You go in there and you feel; you feel 100 per cent right being gay ... it's not what it's like in the world'.[12]

Where chapters one and two ostensibly explore what might be termed the binary role of fancy dress costume, its ability to unite and to separate people, the episodes in this chapter – European depictions of harlequin and pierrot between the eighteenth and twentieth centuries, homosexual balls in Wilhelmine and Weimar Germany and fancy dress within Britain's Royal Navy during the First and Second World Wars – confront more directly the ambiguities of this sartorial form and consider a possible middle ground. They investigate how people seek elucidation of, and escape from, stifling or frightening political and social situations through dressing up.

Artistic avatars - Harlequin and pierrot Continental Europe, *c*.1700–1945

The potential for fancy dress costume to clarify personal roles and interpersonal relationships when it ostensibly confounded them through incongruent clothing is most clearly expressed through the characters of harlequin and pierrot. During the early eighteenth century, Peter Stallybrass and Allon White have argued that there was 'veritable explosion of artistic *representations*' of these figures, along with other carnivalesque characters.[13] Interest in the harlequin and pierrot, which continued into the first half of the twentieth century, was not solely, or even chiefly, aesthetic or dramatic.[14] In painting, poetry and music, to a lesser extent literature, these characters became avatars. Through their associated traits and duelling partnership, which was widely understood across Europe, harlequin and pierrot enabled artist and audience to convey deeply felt personal views and feelings that would have otherwise been difficult to express because of censorious social mores. Assuming the 'explosion' of interest in the harlequin and pierrot were responses to a common stimulus, I argue that the prevalence of these characters within fancy dress events is an example, at once more widespread and nebulous than others considered so far, of people, mindful of restrictive social attitudes, seeking a means to assert themselves. Furthermore, the use of fancy dress costume in this way demonstrates how the sartorial phenomenon facilitated new modes of expression and became something of a cultural conduit as its popularity grew.

The harlequin and pierrot were among the most popular characters of the *Comédie-Française*, the French derivation of Italy's *Commedia dell' Arte*. Harlequin, in his earliest incarnation, wore a costume covered with multicoloured patches. Later, this became a suit of regular, interlocking triangles.[15] A mask with a hooked nose covered his eyes and a bicorn hat was positioned horizontally across his head. He carried a baton, or wand, that transformed whatever it touched. Harlequin's character, a quick-witted and fast-paced trickster, was defined in the sixteenth century by actor Tristano Martinelli.[16] The origins of harlequin's malevolence were medieval and most likely derived from devilish creatures in plays and *charivari*.[17] By the fourteenth century it was understood that harlequin had a satanic progeny, and in Cantos XXI and XXII of *The Divine Comedy* a shape-shifting devil, Alichino, makes an appearance.[18] The devilish aspect of harlequin's character made him a *mixta persona*; he acted within this world and yet remained apart from it. Yve-Alain Bois has called him a 'hybrid', 'diversity personified', who belonged to 'two mutually exclusive worlds and [was] thus capable of making them communicate'.[19]

Harlequin was traditionally paired with pierrot, his rival in love for female character Columbine (Figure 26). The defining traits of pierrot were opposite to those of harlequin. He was physically cumbersome, naïve and unfortunate. Helen Borowitz has questioned whether early eighteenth-century depictions of pierrot were conceived to be sad, but whatever Antoine Watteau had intended in his paintings, this idea became prevalent.[20] Pierrot's rotund appearance was emphasized by a voluminous white costume that was conventionally decorated with a ruff and frilled cuffs. His face was unmasked but painted white, occasionally with rouged cheeks, and framed with a wide-brimmed, often conical, hat.[21] He carried a cithara. Jean Starobinski has emphasized the difference between the devilish harlequin and innocent pierrot by suggesting that the suffering of this tragic clown was analogous to the Passion of Christ.[22]

The paradoxical coupling of harlequin and pierrot meant that they continued to be compelling and popular characters long after the *Comédie-Française* had been banned in 1697. In fact, by freeing them from physical constraints, the pair developed a wider signification as their meaning was explored and augmented by successive writers, painters, musicians, and revellers in fancy dress. Starobinski concludes:

Mais ces significations ne sont-elles pas contradictoires? Ne s'excluent-elles pas l'une l'autre? Certes. Le clown balourd ne ressemble en rien au pitre agile. L'Auguste n'est pas Arlequin.

FIGURE 26 *'All for Columbine'*, M. Vollon Fils, *supplement to* Le Petit Journal, *1 August 1891.* © *Art Media/Print Collector/Getty Images.*

Le clowne-victime (simulacre du Christ) ne paraît rien avoir en commun avec l'Arlequin transgressor (succédané du diable). Mais, en s'idenifiant tantôt avec l'un, tantôt avec l'autre, l'artiste nous indique une resemblance possible, dans la mesure même où angélisme et satanisme et ressemblent. Ce sont les directions inverses et complémentaires que prend le désir de dépasser le monde, ou plus exactement d'introduire dans le monde le témoignage d'une passion *venue d'ailleurs* ou *visant un ailleurs*.[23]

The appeal of harlequin (in particular) stemmed from the character's *mixta persona* that enabled him simultaneously to conceal and convey messages about the zeitgeist and contemporary mores. Wolfgang Zucker, pre-empting Starobinski, suggested harlequin was a 'counter image of the sublime'.[24] By inverting, or appearing to oppose, conventional public beliefs and behaviour, harlequin's mischievous deeds served to reaffirm them. Moreover, and crucial for the character's relevance, if harlequin or clown – the two figures were frequently conflated[25] – were akin to the devil, Zucker reasoned that 'he must always change his face as the sacred order undergoes changes'.[26]

The development of the harlequin clown from the eighteenth century, as described by Zucker, helps to explain how harlequin's character maintained its relevance and appeal after the decline of the *Comédie-Française*.[27] It can be briefly summarized. As 'the deistic god [was] relegated into a dangerless remoteness', the devil lost his 'personal directness and deft monstrosity' and the harlequin became harmless and melancholic.[28] After the French Revolution, and drawing on Enlightenment ideals of openness and transparency, a belief that role-playing was 'dishonest' further weakened the appeal of the trickster character. The clowning figure was considered more favourably in the nineteenth century, but as a 'picturesque archaism', a 'nostalgic remembrance'.[29] Unable or more likely unwilling to trick, the harlequin clown became a tragic, displaced and bewildered figure.[30] Zucker suggests he wore 'the face of Camus' *Stranger*, the image of marginality'.[31] In the twentieth century, the figure of the harlequin clown was revived, once again as a 'mirror' to public sentiment.[32] In this incarnation, Zucker suggests the harlequin clown's estrangement in place and time provided something of a psychological salve for audiences who, in a position of 'bewildered helplessness', sensed the possibility of hope:

> In a world which tends toward an absolute functionalization of the human, where man, faced with the myth of an unchangeable mechanism, drops into stupor, while he is manipulated and directed by powers out of his reach and his understanding – in such a world the clown becomes necessary again, as the one who affirms by denying.[33]

In this dystopic formulation, and by insisting that 'the ridiculous presupposes the sublime, and the sublime in princely graciousness permits the presence of the ridiculous', Zucker suggests the harlequin clown offered the possibility of hope by being the abnegation of it, in much the same way that he had indicted the presence of god by aping the devil.[34] The audience were not alone in identifying with the tragic figure of harlequin. In a study of the work of Russian poet Elena Guro, Milicia Banjanan argues that 'through the buffoon, *saltimbanque*, and the clown the artists and poets were able to present their own condition as well as that of art. By the end of the nineteenth century, both harlequin and pierrot became associated with the condition of the poet and poetry, as, in some cases tragic alter egos of the poet'.[35]

The perception that the harlequin clown could reflect the zeitgeist was broadly appealing in the eighteenth and nineteenth centuries, as were the carnivalesque settings where he could be seen, notably the circus or *fête foraine*. As Jean Starobinski asserts:

> Le monde du cirque et de la fête foraine rèprésentant dans l'atmosphère charbonneuse d'un societé en voie d'industrialisation, un îlot chatoyant de merveilleux, un morceaux demeuré intact du pays d'enfancé, un domaine où la spontaneité vitale, l'illusion, les prodiges simples

de l'adresse ou de la maladresse mêlaient leurs seduction pour le spectateur lassé de la monotonie des taches de la vie serieuse.[36]

Richard Thomson makes a similar point in the context of his examination of Georges Seurat's painting *Parade de cirque* (Circus Sideshow) (Figure 27): 'In a decade [1890s] that saw the rise of socialism in France and growing tensions between the capital and labor, artists of leftist sympathies were drawn to the imagery of the *fête foraine*, not least because *saltimbanques* immediately conjured up associations of marginality and alienation.'[37] In a society that was becoming increasingly complex and where the consequences of modernization were creating innovative problems of identity, as Richard Sennett has brilliantly shown, the *mixta persona* of the harlequin-clown enabled artists to express deeply held feelings of anxiety in a publicly acceptable form, more especially when his antics were juxtaposed against those of pierrot. And what artists expressed, I would suggest, many contemporaries felt.[38]

Stallybrass and White argue that adoption of harlequin and pierrot amounted to a 'refined mimicry' that was conditioned by disapproving attitudes towards the body. They suggest the 'the imagery, masks and costumes of the popular carnival [were] being (literally) put on by the aristocracy and the bourgeoisie in order to simultaneously express and conceal their sexual desire and the pleasures of the body'.[39] There is some truth in this point.[40] The masquerade was certainly associated with amorous and erotic encounters in eighteenth- and nineteenth-century literature, as Terry Castle and Colleen McQuillen have shown.[41] Harlequin and pierrot rarely

FIGURE 27 *'Parade de Cirque', Georges Seurat, 1887–81, 61.101.17. Courtesy of Metropolitan Museum of Art, New York.*

featured in fiction, however, presumably because their firmly established and widely understood traits inhibited authorial creativity. The pair's symbolism was better suited to visual depictions, where viewers could use their understanding of the characters to readily comprehend an artist's meaning. Frequently, harlequin and pierrot were associated with the illicit liaisons that were linked, enthusiastically and excoriatingly, to fancy dress events.

Amorous encounters and 'sexual desire' are more patently the theme of Konstantin Somov's paintings, which tend to focus on harlequin. *Lady and Harlequin* (1912) depicts a masked soirée in the grounds of a wooded estate or pleasure garden (Figure 28).[42] In the foreground, a man dressed as harlequin and a woman dressed in a faux-historic fancy dress costume inspired by eighteenth-century vogues, have removed themselves from the main party, which can be glimpsed through the trees behind them. They have retreated to a secluded part of the garden behind an ornamental hedge. Two costumed men evidently had a similar idea. This couple huddle between a row of trees just beyond the man and woman. One of the men wears a vertically striped two-piece suit, a ruff and bicorn hat, mixing elements of pierrot and harlequin's dress. The other man wears another faux-historic costume that is partially covered by a tree and an ankle-length black cape. The vertically striped lining of his dress corresponds to his partner's suit. The implication is that the men are a homosexual couple. The man in the striped suit has his left hand placed around the other's waist, who raises his hands to the man's ruff in response. The men's eyes are covered by black masks, but they smile knowingly because their assignation has been unexpectedly interrupted by the viewer, whom they look towards. The desire for greater secrecy is apparently shared by the heterosexual couple in the foreground. The woman leans against the man who, true to harlequin's character, is portrayed as dominant: the woman's left hand is raised across the man's chest, her right hand reaches back to connect with his left hand, as he extends his arm around her. The woman's blue scarf hangs, forgotten, over her hooped skirt and trails behind. Her black eye mask has been removed. With his left hand, the man harlequin gestures to another part of the garden, beyond the confines of the canvas, to the viewer's right. He seems eager to continue their amorous liaison in greater seclusion. The painting is almost a direct inversion of Somov's *Pierrot and a Lady* (1910).[43] In a nearly identical setting, Somov depicts a man and woman on a secluded stone bench. The masked woman, in faux historic costume, embraces a man, dressed as pierrot. According to the traits of this character, the man is portrayed passively; his head and right arm recline and his body appears to wilt in the embrace of the dominant woman, who leans in to kiss him.

The quest for love or sexual satisfaction at masked balls was a recurring theme in the lithographs of Paul Gavarni. Focusing on the naivety of pierrot, who became something of a stock character that Gavarni depicted many times in his work, men are typically depicted as incompetent seducers of women, who almost always have the upper hand.[44] The theme is evident from a lithograph of 1851 that features a tired-looking man dressed as pierrot. He stands with his back to a wall in a small private room. His mask is in the process of being removed by an inquisitive woman dressed entirely in black.[45] In a scene that anticipates Somov's *Pierrot and a Lady*, the woman, whose face remains masked, appears younger than the man. She is certainly more assertive and leans in to examine his face, which is vacant. The weakness of the man and the assertiveness of the woman scrutinizing him is summarized by the title, '*Le masque tombe, l'homme reste, et le pierrot s'evanouit*' (The mask falls, the man remains and the pierrot vanishes) (Figure 29).

The physical longing and sexual freedom evident in the images of Somov and Gavarni bear out Stallybrass and White's point that harlequin and pierrot, and the carnivalesque setting more

FIGURE 28 *'Harlequin and Lady', Konstantin Somov, 1912, State Tretyakov Gallery, Moscow.* © *Getty Images.*

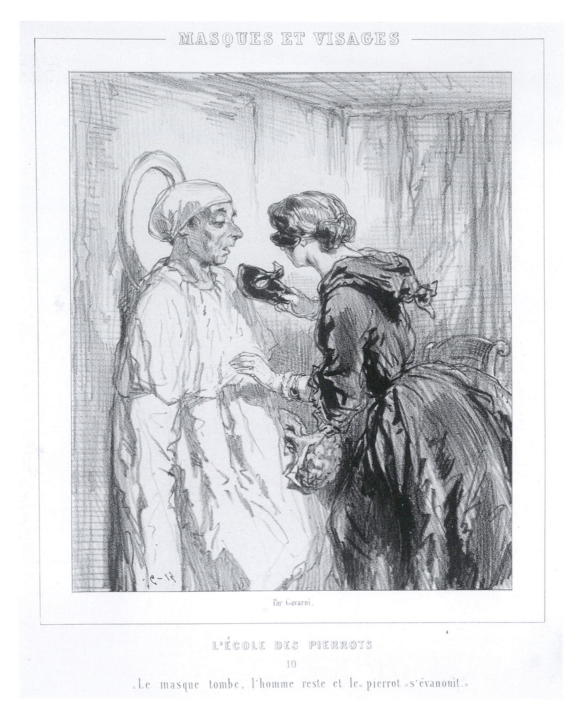

FIGURE 29 *'Le masque tombe, l'homme reste, et "le pierrot" s'evanouit.' Paul Gavarni, lithograph, 1851. Courtesy of Yale University Art Gallery.*

generally, enabled people to flout contemporary moralizing about the sensuality of the body and to enjoy physical love. If this were the most overt message from these works, it is not the only one, or, perhaps, the most important. Somov and Gavarni, in particular, show how the inhibitions of people wearing the costumes of harlequin and pierrot were lessened. By concealing their conventional identity and adopting the clothing of these characters, fancy dress participants experienced a greater emotional and intellectual clarity. However, the ability to transcend social criticism and restraints was temporary and never entire; in portraying the euphoria of the two male lovers, Somov, who was homosexual himself, emphasized the difficulties he faced because of laws and taboos against same-sex partnerships.[46] Gavarni's lithographs seem to go further than this and suggest the act of concealment clarified social realities.

Gavarni produced over 150 prints relating to the carnival. Nancy Olson suggests this body of work amounts to a 'pictorial record of human behaviour [that] anticipates the findings of modern sociology'.[47] Many of Gavarni's carnival lithographs explore how an environment in which everything was either concealed or false heightened people's natures and their response to contemporary ideas and events. For example, in *D'Apres Nature*, a lithograph of 1858, two identically dressed pierrots walk along a corridor of closed doors, presumably heading out to a costume ball (Figure 30).[48] On the left, the bearded man focuses on pulling on his gloves. His companion, on the right, looks ahead. In his left hand, he holds a thin rod. The man enquires, jokingly, of his bearded friend, '*Y es-tu? L'Esculape*'. After a pause, his companion responds, '*Attends! Demosthenes*'. By rejecting the characterization of Asclepios, Greek god of healing, in favour of the orator Demosthenes, the bearded man denies the insinuation that he intends to rely on his considerate nature this evening. Instead, like Demosthenes, he will use his ability to persuade. The implication is that the men are referring to their intention of finding sexual partners during the masquerade.[49] In view of the fact that the bearded man is first associated with a god of healing, and is pulling on gloves akin to a doctor – in French, *Esculape* can refer to a skilful doctor and Asclepios – his self-assessment, in which he likens himself to a fiery rhetorician, seems misplaced. Gavarni seems to suggest the man, in misjudging his nature and overestimating his abilities, will not fair well during the forthcoming evening. The rod carried by the man on the right may reinforce this point. A rod was conventionally associated with harlequin, and was similar to the *caduceus* carried by the trickster god, Hermes. The fact that this object is carried by the companion, rather than the man claiming to act contrary to his nature, may serve to emphasize how futile his efforts to overcome himself will prove.[50] In sum, Gavarni is using the characteristics of pierrot – naïve and unfortunate – to suggest that whilst his costume emboldens its wearer, it does not, to borrow a term of Ann Rosalind Jones and Peter Stallybrass, possess a '"transnaturing" power' and fundamentally change his character.[51] Instead, the concealment clarifies his nature.

If this psychoanalytical interpretation seems overwrought, it should be remembered that many contemporaries appreciated how the figures of harlequin and pierrot could be simultaneously escapist and explanatory. Several artists and poets, not least Pablo Piccasso, Abraham Mintchine and Elena Guro depicted themselves as harlequin in self-portraits.[52] Russian artists Vasily Shukhaev and Alexandre Jacovleff painted a joint self-portrait of harlequin (Jacovleff) and pierrot (Shukhaev).[53] Cézanne painted his son, William, as harlequin; Picasso painted his son, Paul, as harlequin and pierrot in separate portraits.[54] In eighteenth-century Britain, the traits of harlequin were so widely understood that a newspaper claimed the country was 'no better than a "nation of harlequins"'.[55] It was this broad understanding of what harlequin and pierrot represented, as individual characters and as a pair, that made them compelling, and popular, choices for fancy dress costume.

FIGURE 30 *'Y es-tu? L'Esculape. – Attends! Demosthenes!'. Paul Gavarni, lithograph, 1858. Courtesy of Yale University Art Gallery.*

Photographs of adults and children dressed as harlequins, pierrots and pierrettes frequently appeared in the pages of *Vogue* between the nineteenth and twentieth centuries.[56] If the variety of designs available from costume suppliers accurately reflected demand, in London, harlequin and pierrot were the most popular fancy dress subjects during the first half of the twentieth century. Theatrical costumier and wigmaker Chas H. Fox provided five costume variations for harlequin and seventeen for pierrot and his female variant, peirrette.[57] Weldon's offered a similar number; five for harlequin and fifteen for pierrot and peirette.[58] No other character had as many different costume options (Figures 7, 9, 10). The greater number of outfits for pierrot was likely prosaic and reflected the fact that the costume was less prescriptive than that of the harlequin, who seems to have been the more widely depicted of the two in contemporary culture. Choices of pierrot costume ranged from the piratic 'Pierrotic' – an orange pyjama-style suit with white gauntlet gloves and collar trimmed with black, worn with an oversized black belt around the waist and a black bandana hat – to the 'Black and White Pierrette' – a low-cut, single-button black jacket worn over a vertically striped black and white knee-length skirt. The ensemble included a stylized ruff and a simple black tricorn hat decorated with three white pom-poms.[59] In many cases, the popularity of the harlequin and pierrot costumes was likely a reflection of their simplicity to make and wear. In both cases, the outfits were more creative than the anonymizing and potentially menacing domino, and they were usually cheaper.[60] The most expensive pierrot costume sold by Chas H. Fox was the 'Purple Pierrot' that cost £2 10s. 6d. The majority of their pierrot costumes were £1 7s. 6d. By contrast, the firm's 'Domino Masque' cost £2 7s. 6d.[61]

Prosaic reasons must go some way to explain the ubiquity of the harlequin and pierrot in fancy dress entertainments between the eighteenth and twentieth centuries, but the prevalence of these characters in contemporary culture suggests they had a deeper resonance for many costumed revellers. Like many authors and artists they identified with these maligned characters. I want to consider this point with reference to one further painting, *March of the Clowns* (1941), by American-domiciled German Jewish émigré Albert Bloch (Figure 31).[62]

A line of at least fifty marching clowns, dressed in multicoloured suits that appear to be more elaborate versions of those associated with pierrot, are walking the perimeter of a performance arena. The clowns are masked or have brightly painted faces. Most wear conical hats. Near to the front of the line, two clowns play musical instruments. In front of them, the leading clown is dressed in a scarlet military-style tunic. In his hands, he clutches a tall pole to which pieces of string, or streamers, are attached. A swastika is fixed to the top of the pole. From this, hanging on a short length of string, is a small effigy of Adolf Hitler. The troupe of clowns is led by a tall, black man, dressed as a soldier. Instead of camouflaged fatigues, his tunic and trousers are covered in a multicoloured grid that resembles the clothing of harlequin. The solider appears to puff on a cigarette as he simultaneously plays the bassoon, which resembles a gun from the manner in which it is held. An audience is stood around the perimeter of the performance arena. The boundary between performers and spectators is far from distinct. For example, in the foreground to the right, a bearded man wears a jacket made of the same harlequinesque material worn by the solider. On the left, audience members include characters from American cartoons of the 1920s and 1930s; Popeye, Olive Oyl, Ignatz Mouse and Krazy Kat. To gain entrance to the arena, the clowns have marched under a tall arch atop of which is a crucifix, a symbol of Christianity. To the left, a crescent moon and star, symbolic of Islam, appears to float above a section of the audience; to the right, a star of David, a symbol of Judaism, floats above the swastika.

FIGURE 31 *'March of the Clowns', Albert Bloch, 1941, 2001–42. © The Jewish Museum, New York.*

The meaning of the painting is enigmatic. The focus on jubilant clowns and crowds may relate to the Jewish festival of Purim, which celebrates the saving of the Jews from Haman, as told in the Old Testament Book of Esther.[63] During a day of carnivalesque revelry, masks and disguises are worn publicly, as they are in Bloch's painting, in part to symbolize how God guided the Jews' salvation but remained unseen.[64] Haman was hanged for his attempted genocide, which may explain Bloch's depiction of Hitler, who had banned celebration of Purim in Germany in 1938. The significance of a festival in which Jews celebrated the overthrow of their enemies was not lost on Hitler. In a speech of 1944, he acknowledged that German defeat in the Second World War would become a second Purim for Jewish people.[65] If Purim guided the composition of Bloch's painting, it was not his only reference. Bloch was influenced by Wassily Kandinsky, who bemoaned people's obsession with materialism, and this may account for the cartoon figures.[66] Richard Green observes that '[t]here are no flags, no soldiers or politicians, no heroes. The religious symbols suggest the triumph of Christianity and Judaism, but that may also be misleading, and the viewer is left to supply his own score.'[67] Whatever its precise meaning, the painting shows how the liminality of carnival and fancy dress facilitates the exploration and expression of deeper, rawer emotions. In particular, it suggests the traits associated with harlequin and pierrot had become socialized, such that they could become a conduit for people to express their views about the perceived wrongs in society, and the Second World War in particular. The act of concealing their conventional identity and donning the costume of harlequin and pierrot enabled people to enter a liminal space and to articulate their views with greater confidence, if not precision.

Escapism under scrutiny - Homosexual balls during the Wilhelmine and Weimar era Berlin, Germany, 1918–33

The atmosphere in Germany after the First World War was akin to a world turned upside down. The country's military defeat was the cause of confusion and anger; the Treaty of Versailles, which blamed Germany for starting the War, a source of long-standing and widespread shame. The abdication of Kaiser Wilhelm II and the establishment of a republic in place of a hereditary monarchy were no less bewildering. For nationalists, conservatives, and more radical elements of the right wing, whose views had generally been ascendant under the autocracy, the Weimar Republic, headed by Social Democrat ministers, who had accepted the terms of the Versailles settlement, was a particular humiliation. According to Eric Weitz, 'the result was lack of consensus and constant debate. The most basic matters of how Germans would live together and with their neighbors were subject to unending strife.'[68] In this political and social limbo, where many Germans were cognizant of being betwixt and between different stages in their young country's development, the arts – understood in the broadest of senses – provided an immediate, flexible and compelling conduit for people to comprehend, and seek to clarify, their sense of place, figuratively and literally. Fancy dress costume, which features in contemporary entertainments, paintings, films, social commentary and diaries, was adept at conveying the zeitgeist and enabling people to pursue alternative identities, however temporarily. To repurpose a contemporary observation by author Alfred Döblin, the liminality of fancy dress was enticing to people 'who filled out a human skin … [and] happen[ed] to want more from life than a piece of bread'.[69] This was especially the case for homosexuals in Germany because social stigmas and legislation (against male–male sex relationships) prompted people to conceal their sexual identities in public.

The paintings of George Grosz and Otto Dix, two of the more well-known contemporary artists working in Weimar Germany, suggest the clothes Germans wore became acute signifiers of status and allegiance after the War, as social and political hierarchies, and the socialized assumptions that underpinned them, tottered. Grosz's *Grey Day* of 1921, now in Berlin's Nationalgalerie, with its depiction of four men in a nondescript city, all walking on different levels and in different directions, their eyes closed, downcast or crossed, provides an immediate insight into the divisions that clothing proclaimed so clearly: two bespectacled men wear black suits and carry leather cases, one has a black-white-red lapel pin – the colours of Germany's imperial flag – to show his lingering support for the monarchy; a wounded veteran wears a uniform denuded of its military insignia; the fourth man, in drab and rudimentary clothing, is the most indistinct. The shovel he carries identifies him as a labourer. Grosz's purpose may have been to heighten social and political contrasts, but across Germany the divisions he suggests would have been clear to see. They would have become clearer in the 1930s, as the Depression washed away people's newly gained wealth and prosperity. The composition of Grosz's painting, in which buildings look like stage scenery and the four men carry props and themselves as though taking cues from a director, seems to reflect the many performances of reality that people played or observed across Weimar Germany. Drawing from contemporary accounts, historians allude to the blurring of the public and private, the factual and the fictional, in people's lives. Wounded veterans wore masks to conceal facial injuries.[70] In towns and cities, political parties organized parades and street-side skits.[71] The grotesque, as discussed by Mikhail Bakhtin, seemed ever present and it appears that Germans used laughter, black as their comedy often was, as an anaesthetic to explore the new social and political possibilities, and to heal. It is understandable why the *Münchener Neusten Nachrichten* reported that there was a 'carnival atmosphere' in southern Germany in November 1918, the month World War One ended.[72]

Themes of the carnivalesque and grotesque converge in Otto Dix's *The Seven Deadly Sins* of 1933, now in the Kunsthalle Karlsruhe. Seven people, potentially adolescents judging from their physical size, are dressed in costumes and masks that depict one of the deadly sins. The symbolically charged painting has been the subject of much discussion, not least because Dix added a Hitler-style moustache to the mask of the person representing envy in 1945.[73] This addition has persuaded many scholars that the painting is a critique of National Socialism. James van Dyke follows Birgit Schwarz and offers a nuanced view, in which personal and pan-national ideas coexist.[74] If some of the sins represent people associated with the Dresden art scene, and reflect Dix's feelings about his enforced resignation from the city's Academy of Arts, it is apparent that the painting's 'fantastic masked procession' – a phrase used by Dix to describe his work – which is disorderly, rather than regimented, and enacted by ghouls rather than able-bodied people, mocks the street parades and theatre that were organized by the National Socialists and other political groups. Van Dyke suggests the painting 'affirmed a vulgar, obscene, intoxicated, cruel – Dionysian, in a word – folk culture that threw the racial ideology of National Socialism into question.'[75] The painting emphasizes how fancy dress costume could convey complex and widely felt feelings because it was a peripheral art from and not beholden to convention. Consequently, Dix's work implies that fancy dress was regarded with caution and suspicion in early twentieth-century Germany.

Costumed entertainments in Weimar Germany were typically associated with homosexuality, transvestism and immorality.[76] In a telling insight of how fancy dress events and homosexuality had become conflated in the minds of contemporaries, Richard Oswald's *Anders als die Andern* (Different from the Others) features a costume ball in one of its central scenes. Premiered in 1919 and regarded as one of the first homosexual-themed movies, *Anders als die Andern* is as much documentary as it is drama.[77] Championing the repeal of Paragraph 175 from Germany's penal code, which made it illegal for men to engage in mutual sexual acts, or acts that simulated them, the film sought to debunk demonizing myths about male and female homosexuality.[78] To highlight the shortcomings of Paragraph 175, and perhaps to guide discussion about its repeal by speaking to people's common humanity, the film shows how Germany's legal situation encouraged the morally unscrupulous to blackmail people they suspected of homosexuality to prevent their exposure to the authorities. The film's lead character, violinist Paul Körner, first meets his tormenter and blackmailer, Franz Bollek, at a fancy dress ball. As the two men converse, a circle of men and women dressed variously as pierrots, jockeys, cowboys, eighteenth-century courtiers and Arabian characters dance obliviously behind them.[79] Towards the end of the film, a lecture by leading contemporary sexologist Dr Magnus Hirschfeld and head of the *Institut für Sexualwissenschaft*, who plays himself, includes a series of photographs of transvestites and homosexuals. In one of the images, labelled 'Homosexual couple', two women appear to be preparing for a costume ball; one of the women wears a black evening gown and matching eye mask.⁸⁰ In another image, labelled 'Female Narcissist', a middle-aged man wearing an evening gown sits in front of a mirror applying make-up, presumably to attend a costume party.⁸¹

In *Homosexualität des Mannes und des Weibes*, published before the War, Hirschfeld describes the organization and form of Germany's homosexual costumed balls. Between October and Easter, several balls were held each night in major cities. Before the republic, censorship laws meant there was no overt advertising, chiefly because there were no homosexual newspapers, so details spread by word of mouth.⁸² Venues would open around ten in the evening, although most attendees arrived from eleven; peak entry was between midnight and one o'clock.⁸³ At two o'clock there was a break for coffee, which is when the building's owners made most of their money.⁸⁴ Entry fees were relatively steep at one mark and fifty *pfennigs*, but this was most likely a measure to deter people intent on causing trouble. Guests were certainly subject to some form of vetting before they entered the ball because police informed organizers only to admit people whom they knew to be homosexual.⁸⁵ Throughout the Wilhelmine and Weimar periods, homosexual balls were attended by police, who had a special department to monitor these events.⁸⁶ Organizers generally appear to have informed police of an upcoming ball to ensure cooperation.⁸⁷

In sanctioning balls, the police were pragmatic rather than an altruistic. Journalist Paul Lindenberg, who published *Polizei und Verbrechertum* in 1892, averred that balls were tolerated so that police officials were 'better able to monitor the unclean elements (*die unsauberen Elemente*) in society, most of whom had already been punished, and united in a certain gang of the criminal album, for which reason even the so-called "criminal cellars" (*Verbrecherkeller*) are tolerated.'⁸⁸ Balls were also attended by journalists, writers and physicians. The Swedish author August Strindberg attended a ball with police and sat along one side of the hall, 'where all the couples had to pass'. 'The most interesting' (*die interessantesten*) people were called over to the table by a police officer, apparently to afford Strindberg a closer look.⁸⁹ It was noted that 'some come with grim, unconscious, sad and evasive answers; others shy, with childlike gestures, as if they were playing'.⁹⁰

Hirschfeld found the costumes particularly interesting and described their appearance at length. Discussing a New Year Homosexual Men and Women's Ball (*homosexuellen Männerund Frauenballes*) in Berlin's dock lands that he had attended with colleagues, he records costumes worn by the 800 revellers.⁹¹ Some people were 'heavily masked in impenetrable dominoes, they come and go without anyone suspecting who they are'.⁹² Others wore phantasy costumes (*in Phantasiegewämndern*), simple clothing (*in einfachen Toiletten*) or more costly garments (*in sehr kostbaren*).⁹³ Hirschfeld recalls the account of an 'old homosexual count (*Grafen*)', who had a 'wonderful' new dress made by a Parisian couturier during the winter months, so it could be ready for the new season's entertainments.⁹⁴ At the New Year ball he spotted a South American man wearing a Parisian robe that he believed had cost more than 2,000 francs.⁹⁵ Hirschfeld implies that most men at the ball dressed as women (*in Damenkliedern*).⁹⁶ The opposite was apparently true at balls organized specifically for homosexual women, where Hirschfeld noted that most dressed as men. Describing another ball, he lists the presence of 'a fat capuchin, in front of whom are awe-inspiring gypsies, pierrots, sailors, clowns, bakers, mercenaries, handsome officers, gentlemen and ladies in riding gear, Boers, Japanese, and petite geishas' (Figure 32).⁹⁷ As a homosexual, Hirschfeld was doubtless never a wholly dispassionate observer. Some of his comments indicate that he developed an attachment and empathy, if not complete sympathy, for the people he studied. He describes a 'glowing-eyed Carmen' who 'ignited' a jockey and a 'fiery Italian' who sealed his heartfelt friendship with a snowman.⁹⁸ Hirschfeld's affection towards the people he documented is also evidenced in his concluding remarks:

FIGURE 32 *Photograph of objects and people dressed in costume for 'Masks Exhibition', Berlin, published in* Berliner Morgenpost, *16 June 1929. © Ullstein Bild/Getty Images.*

The cheerful crowd, shimmering in the most colourful colours, offers a highly peculiar, attractive image … No misunderstanding clouds people's enjoyment, until the last attendees, in the dim gloom of the February morning, leave the place where they were allowed to dream for a few hours among sympathisers, what they inwardly are.[99]

Whilst Hirschfeld was attempting to record the activities of homosexual men and women dispassionately, in seeking to encourage a reappraisal of homosexuality within Germany he stops short of reflecting on the implications of what he observed; namely, why so many people attended balls that were not inexpensive or publicly advertised, and why people were prepared to spend large sums of money and time preparing costumes to wear (Figure 32).

One possible reason for Hirschfeld's cursory enquiry is that he enjoyed similar entertainments to those he recorded. An undated photograph shows him sitting in costume among fourteen others, also in costume. The men and women may have been colleagues from his Institute. Rainer Herrn suggests their costumes may have been worn to a ball or for 'public purposes'.[100] The relationship between the group members, conveyed by their physical gestures, makes the first suggestion more convincing. Hirschfeld's left hand is placed tenderly on the shoulder of a masked woman, who sits immediately in front of him. His right hand is clasped by Karl Giese, his colleague and homosexual partner. In the centre of the image, two men lean into each other; one places his left arm across the other's lap and his eyes are closed, as though rapt in a moment of emotional intensity. These 'intimate gestures' were permissible within the Institute, but problematic beyond it, where they would have been 'judged harshly'.[101] For Herrn, the photograph reveals how 'privacy requires shields from public judgement, yet private selves also need to be publicly revealed'.[102] Cognizant that he needed to monitor, and to conceal, aspects of his character in public, Hirschfeld would have been acutely aware of similar restraints on the people he observed for his research.

If Hirschfeld were wary of asserting conclusions that were too intrusive and disruptive about his subjects' lives, his writing still provides insights into the public revelation – the clarification – that fellow homosexuals seemed to yearn for. This desire is most apparent from the care and effort people invested in the fancy dress costumes they wore at balls. Hirschfeld notes the costly attire of a count and South American man. Whilst no fancy dress costumes from Wilhelmine or Weimar balls are known to survive, a woman's costume dating from the first half of the twentieth century, which was bought for the Chelsea Arts Club archive, provides an idea of how they would have looked and how long they would have taken to create.[103]

The Arts Club costume is said to depict a bull, although this is questionable.[104] The outfit is hand-made and consists of an unlined dress of black silk, and an elaborate mask that would have entirely covered the wearer's head and much of their face. The dress has a round neckline and is approximately 1422 mm long; dried mud on the hem suggests it dragged along the ground. Three-quarter-length bell-shaped sleeves – measuring 686 mm on the outer arm and 533 mm on the inner arm – add to the dress' voluminous appearance. The inside of the sleeves, which where potentially visible when the gown was worn, are lined with orange silk. A vertical band of black silk runs down the front of the dress, from the neck to the hem, and conceals ten hook and eye clasps. The dress and sleeves are decorated with bands of black sequins (diameters varying from 7 mm to 9 mm) of different lengths. Identical sequins are used to decorate the striking head mask, which in outline shape resembles the *kabuto*, a Samurai helmet. The mask, made in the same black silk of the dress, is approximately 304 mm high. The two pieces of cloth that form the mask have been cut so that a point, or 'tail', of approximately 1232 mm long hangs down the wearer's back. The 'tail' is decorated with bands of sequins to match the dress and sleeves. Two triangular pieces of fabric, similar to the *fukigaeshi* of a *kabuto*, are attached to the sides of the mask. The fronts of these panels are covered entirely with sequins. The panels are faced in black silk and backed with hessian to retain their shape. Hessian has also been stitched behind a 470 mm × 63 mm band of black silk that runs along the opening of the mask, across the forehead. This presumably supports two horns that protrude from either side of the mask. The horns, 216 mm in length, are spongy and covered entirely with the black sequins. A veil of ruched black lace, measuring 127 mm × 279 mm, hangs from the front of the mask. The mask appears to have been conceived to sit low on the wearer's head, so the veil, which is not easy to move aside, would have curtailed visibility. A chin strap with a hook and eye fastening helps to ensure the mask remains in place. Attached to the rear and bottom of the mask, a 139-mm band of silk, akin to a small shawl, has been added to cover the neck. The band is decorated with a uniform grid pattern of 3-mm sequins. On top of this, larger sequins of 7 mm to 9 mm have been affixed in the shape of four-pointed stars, or flowers, and swirls. The band is trimmed with ruched black lace. Three hook and eyes positioned at the front of the band help further to secure the unwieldy mask on the wearer's head. The costume would have taken many hours to model and to decorate. There are indications that it was worn multiple times and that it was maintained. On the upper right side of the dress the edges of a small hole, similar to a cigarette burn with a diameter of approximately 10 mm, have been hand-stitched with black cotton thread to prevent the silk from fraying. The damage was unlikely to have been noticed when the dress was worn; that it was repaired is consequently suggestive of how an owner felt towards the costume.

The views of English homosexuals, who visited Germany during the interwar period and described the nightlife of its cities, generally more dispassionately than Hirschfeld because of their non-domiciled status, help to clarify why people spent time and effort constructing costumes. They suggest costume facilitated world making and provided wearers with a sense of public clarity and control that was otherwise absent from their lives. Author Christopher Isherwood lived in Berlin between 1929 and 1933. As a young man questioning his sexuality, he felt stifled by the legal restrictions and social conservatism that existed in England and enjoyed the greater (sexual) freedom that Germany offered, Berlin particularly. He writes, 'To Christopher, Berlin meant boys.'[105] He describes 'screaming boys in drag and monocle, Eton-cropped girls in dinner jackets [who] play-acted the high jinks of Sodom and Gomorrah'.[106] Similar scenes are described by Isherwood's friend and fellow author Stephen Spender, who visited Germany in 1929 and stayed in Hamburg in 1930. He describes a photograph of 'self-consciously factitious [young] people in fancy dress, making faces or gesturing at the camera'.[107] He recalls his friend 'Heinrich', who 'kept his lederhosen for fancy dress parties', which 'were very popular'.[108]

Brief though they are, these vignettes emphasize the ostentatious and performative behaviour of people in costume. The accounts convey what Hirschfeld never seems to have been able to do in his writing, but presumably felt, as evidenced by the photograph of him mentioned above. Writing after the events documented and beyond Germany, Isherwood and Spender may have been emboldened to write freely, if still somewhat abstractly because of the illegality of homosexuality. True as this was, this is unlikely to have been the most important reason for the differing accounts of homosexual life in early twentieth-century Germany left us by the authors and academic. Isherwood met Hirschfeld and toured his Institute. Afterwards, he described the academic's public restraint as a 'visible guarantee of his scientific respectability'.[109] Whether he fully grasped it at the time, Isherwood's description of Hirschfeld as a 'silly solemn old professor' explained the duality of his existence.[110] A façade that 'reassured the timid and the conservative' was prerequisite if he were to lead a public life as a Jewish homosexual and further the cause of homosexuality through his Institute.[111]

The façade Hirschfeld constructed was similar to that which homosexuals across Germany wore. It was arguably also similar to the façades that everyone in Germany wore after the War, if the emphasis on clothing in the paintings of Grosz and Dix is an accurate reflection of contemporary realities. Costume is a form of concealment because it effaces elements of its wearer's conventional identity. Equally, it is revealing. When worn by homosexual people and giving physical expression to the censorship that was imposed on their daily lives in Wilhelmine and Weimar Germany, it became a form of clarification. It enabled men and women to transcend and block out criticism and judgement of their lives, if temporarily. People could experience the public revelation that Rainer Herrn refers to, the fact that private selves need public acknowledgement. Understood in this frame, the making and wearing of costume in nineteenth and early twentieth-century Germany afforded its wearer a greater sense of self-awareness, public security and control.

Galvanizing distractions - The Royal Navy at sea, 1914–45

Fancy dress costume and conflict might seem diametrically opposed, but periods of warfare constitute a liminal time that encourages non-normative behaviours characteristic of this sartorial form. Military conflicts disrupt people's lives and the values that substantiate them because of the imposition of a fighting front, which dominates a community's economic, political and social priorities, and a subordinate home front, in which the scope of people's lives is either partially suspended, through fear and regulation, or enlarged, through the unique demands that fighting generates. On the home front, the sense of bewilderment, of existing betwixt and between normal states of being, is exacerbated by the knowledge that warfare is usually impermanent but continues without a fixed end. Historically, gender roles undergo marked change in wartime as women assume positions vacated by fighting men. Women also adopt male identities to fight.[112] Shifts in the responsibilities undertaken by women and men expose gendered roles as social constructs and facilitate new forms of expression and action as normative modes of behaviour, and the ideas that reinforce them, are questioned. As people search to uphold or to undermine conventional gendered roles during periods of military conflict, dress tends to assume a more prominent role because of its singular and immediate ability to clarify its wearer's attitudes to sex and status.

Scholars have long recognized how the wardrobes of the home front are changed by warfare, but they have only recently started to consider how the garb of a society's guardians is affected by their resolution to fight.[113] Germane to the topic of fancy dress are the studies of David Boxwell and Alon Rachamimov, which consider ludic performances, featuring costume and cross-dressing, that were staged by soldiers of the First World War, by the British serving on the Western Front and by Austrians in captivity on the Eastern Front.[114] Boxwell and Rachamimov use Turner's concept of social drama to show how costume, as a form of world making, enabled these men to comprehend, and to cope, with the physical and psychological strains that war placed upon them. This section contributes to Boxwell and Rachamimov's research by looking at fancy dress costume within the British Royal Navy during the First and Second World Wars.

The feeling of displacement, of existing in a liminal place and time, is particularly great for sailors serving at sea and during periods of conflict. Fancy dress and dramatic performance have therefore long had an important role within the navies of many countries, including the United States of America, Britain, Denmark, France and Germany. They comfort sailors far from home and enforce acceptable naval attitudes and behaviours, specifically with regards to hierarchy, gender and sexual conduct. A tradition in many navies is the 'Crossing the Line' ceremony. First recorded by French sailors in the sixteenth century, it provided an opportunity to '[instill] as no classroom session could, values essential to the navy'.[115] The ceremony was staged to initiate naval recruits at their first crossing of the equator. As the lines of latitude and longitude converged at zero, sailors entered a time and place that 'literally inverted their world'.[116] Older crewmen ('shellbacks') lead newer recruits ('pollywogs') through a series of choreographed performances in which they could be shaved, stripped, imprisoned and plunged into water, before being judged a loyal subject by Neptune, God of the Seas.[117] The identity of pollywogs, who occupied a liminal position as they were betwixt and between roles, was deliberately effaced and they wore clothing associated with women and animals to 'represent an ambiguous, undifferentiated state in which [they] possess[ed] no status, property, or insignia'. Their clothing also 'distinguish[ed] the neophyte from his initiators and the dominant structure aboard ship'.[118] Naval uniforms were ostensibly earned after the sailor had completed the ceremony (Figure 33). Similar ludic performances were staged during the First and Second World Wars. Testimonies gathered by the Imperial War Museum, London, from retired sailors show how the effacement of conventional identities through fancy dress costume enabled men to clarify their place as individuals and as fighters in environments that were pressured, confused and frightening.

H. M. S. Southampton. Having this day visited our Royal Domain, the undermentioned person has received our ancient requisite initiation and certificate to become one of our loyal subjects.

We do signify to all whom it may concern that it is our Royal will and pleasure to confer upon him the freedom of the Seas and to exempt him from further homage, and should he fall overboard, all Sharks, Dolphins, Whales, Crabs and other dwellers of the deep are to abstain from maltreating his person.

Given at our Court on the Equator Long.........................

this .... day of .... 1922.

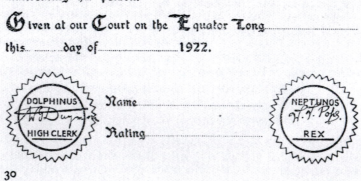

30

FIGURE 33 *Part of an address given to sailors after the Crossing the Line ceremony.* 'Bunx', Crossing the Line in H.M.S. 'Southampton' (A Naval Episode). *London: Arden Press, no date), 31.*

The memoirs of naval rating turned sailor Joseph Murray include an account of a fancy dress competition that was held prior to the ill-fated Gallipoli campaign. In early 1915, Australia, Britain and New Zealand determined to open a second front against Turkey to pressure Germany into diverting soldiers from France and to gain access to Russian resources by opening trade routes to the Black Sea. On 15 April 1915, Murray recalls how the Hood Battalion of the 63rd Royal Naval Division, sailing aboard the transport ship *Grantully Castle*, was informed of its involvement in the Gallipoli campaign during the judging of a fancy dress ball. The news was announced by the Battalion's commander, Lieutenant-Colonel John Quilter and recorded by Murray as follows:

> Anyhow, he come along and said, "Well, now we'll give the prizes [for the fancy dress costumes] and by tomorrow we're going to give the Turks hell. By tomorrow, I mean, that we're going to land on the Gallipoli peninsula at the toe [ie. Cape Helles], failing that, we're going to Bulair Lines and failing that, we're going to land at Enos, that's on the [unclear]. He says, "and the eyes of the world will be on you and the whole course of the war will be altered. We must take Constantinople from the Turks, and the eyes of the world will be on you." That's the first official recognition we've had that we were really going anywhere.[119]

Prior to this announcement, Murray joked that it felt as if he had been on a 'Cook's tour', a reference to the British tour operator, Thomas Cook. Murray's written account indicates the men aboard the *Grantully Castle* knew they had been heading to the Dardanelles from at least January 1915, but were unaware of the scale of the upcoming operation and their exact role within it.[120] If the sailors had been largely ignorant of their purpose, the fancy dress ball in which they participated had been planned because the costumes Murray describes took time to create:

> … and one fella, he made himself a suit of armour out of Huntley and Palmers biscuit tins, funny [?you know]. Another one was dressed as a zulu with a grass skirt [laughs], you know, and a bloody big axe [laughs] made out of a biscuit tin, and there was another young fella, oh dear me, dressed in a beautiful silk; very seductive.[121]

Assuming Murray's recollection is correct and the announcement of the Gallipoli campaign was incorporated into the judging of the fancy dress costumes, it is possible the event and statement were planned to coincide. Fancy dress events aboard naval ships were not uncommon, but Murray's reaction to the costumes implies they had not been worn previously. Furthermore, it would have been necessary to ensure all personnel were told at the same time about the ship's destination, to avoid confusion. It does not appear that the Navy's objective was relayed simultaneously between its ships. For example, the account of Norman Woodcock, who served aboard *HMS Euryalus*, implies the crew had been informed that Gallipoli was their destination when they were at Chaty-les-Bains, a neighbourhood within Alexandria, Egypt, several weeks earlier.[122]

The longevity of the Crossing the Line ceremony helps to explain why such weighty news was conveyed to the crew of *Grantully Castle* during a fancy dress entertainment. In his study of the tradition, Simon Bronner suggests the narrative structure of the drama facilitated a 'withdrawal from reality … [by] leaving behind the familiar realm of home to create a reversed divided world'.[123] In the new environment that was created through the ceremony, Bronner argues 'There is a sense in which the bonded, isolated ship becomes a small island culture' (Figure 33).[124] In a similar way, the jovial, incongruous costumes worn during the fancy dress competition aboard the *Grantully Castle* temporarily effaced the traditional hierarchy and established equality between the crew. The absurdity of the event in this military frame – a ship sailing closer to the enemy during a global conflict – may have provided a momentary release from the strains of conflict, especially if the sailors were unsure of their destination. Simultaneously, the wearing of fancy dress placed the relationships between sailors into sharper relief. The sense of togetherness in this fantasy emphasized the need for cooperation in reality.

Communal tasks that reminded a ship's crew of their shared values and objectives were important when their 'withdrawal from reality' became more apparent during festive periods. A written account by signalman G.F. Wilson of Christmas Day spent aboard *HMS Valiant* in 1916 describes the efforts of sailors and officers to maintain their 'island culture'. In the case of *Valiant*, this may have been more pressing in 1916. Serving with Britain's Grand Fleet, the ship had participated in the largest naval battle of the First World War between Britain and Germany, the Battle of Jutland, in June. The ship and its crew were unharmed, but the loss of fourteen ships and 6,784 lives from the Grand Fleet had been a bruising first encounter between the British and German navies, and they were not to know it was to be their last.[125] Between 24 August and 18 September, *Valiant* had also been under repairs following a night-time collision with *HMS Warspite*, which meant a long period of enforced inaction. The feelings of loneliness and isolation that Christmas could engender may have surfaced with greater intensity during wartime, but the nature of naval service could make any sailor susceptible at this time of the year. In interviews with serving American sailors during the 1990s, Steven Zeeland interviewed 'Lieutenant Tim', who claimed that Christmas depressed him:

> Rather than degrade myself by participating in some ritual display of forced, artificial cheer I prefer to spend the day wallowing in sadness and honest resignation – listening to depressing music or watching movies about the Holocaust. It is my way of purging a year's accumulation of disappointment and despair in safe advance of January 1 – the day statistics show Americans most favor for suicide.[126]

The 'ritual display of forced, artificial cheer' would probably be Tim's response to the festivities described by Signalman Wilson. The account he has written is ostensibly a factual narrative of events aboard *Valiant* from the evening of 24 December to midnight on 25 December.[127] Wilson makes it clear that this episode was a tradition and he expected it to be occurring simultaneously on other Royal Navy ships. The account is written in the first-person plural. This form of address is suggestive of how pervasive the festive atmosphere abroad *Valiant* was. Wilson frames his response as though his readers – presumably family members – were alongside him. The account emphasizes the liminality of this episode, which enabled him to connect the festive world of his ship with the festive atmosphere he assumed existed at home. In the process, Wilson affirmed relationships with crew and estranged family that he clearly held dear.

To establish a festive environment, decorations – Chinese lanterns, flags and 'fancy paper' cut into shapes – were hung up around the ship. Tables in the canteen were 'tastefully laid out as if for a bazaar' and covered with fruit, vegetables ('some with grotesque faces carved out'), cards and photographs. After a service led by the padre and captain ('which remind us of the spiritual import of the day, and of Christmas mornings spent in happier and more peaceful surroundings'), the men exchanged their uniforms for costumes. To some extent, the costumes worn were determined by age. In an act of symbolic inversion, which recalls the medieval Feast of

Fools by emphasizing the place of adolescents in the community, Wilson notes that the youngest of the crew appeared as officers. By contrast, older seamen appear to have dressed as they pleased:

> On returning to the mess deck, not only do we find the decorations complete, but wondrous changes wrought in the appearance of the men themselves. Mere boys are wearing the badges of petty officers; two youths are walking the bridge, with telescope under arm, in suits of the Chief Yeoman and signals; and many other ratings are garbed in the cast-off uniforms of Officers. Some of the men are dressed and bewigged as girls, some as clowns, and others in ever more fantastic disguise. One company of stokers attracted great attention by impersonating a band of Maoris. They were naked except for rabbit-skin loin cloths and feather head-dresses, with their skins blackened, and strange figures and designs patterned thereon in red lead.

As with the fancy dress ball held aboard *Grantully Castle*, some of the costumes described in this account took time to create. Coordination is also implied by the company of stokers, who decided to dress as a group. Planning would have been required to secure their rabbit skins and headdresses, even if substituted materials had been used in place of fur and feathers. The reaction of Wilson suggests he had not seen the costumes on display before, although later in the account he suggests that garments were re-worn. During the evening of 25 December, whilst 'some messes had their own private parties', others formed together to provide a concert programme. As part of this, Wilson notes that several officers were 'arrayed in the fancy dresses worn at the concert the previous week'.

Conspicuous within the accounts of Wilson and Murray is the presence of sailors who dressed as tribal warriors and women. These characters appear diametrically opposed but they demonstrate how fancy dress costume enabled sailors to rationalize their situation, which deprived them of personal and psychological comforts whilst simultaneously demanding greater mental attentiveness and physical discipline. Expressed prosaically, these men were required to exercise a mastery over their conventional gendered traits whilst being unable to engage in the defining heteronormative act of sexual intercourse. In their studies of cross-dressing among First World War soldiers and prisoners of war, Boxwell and Rachamimov suggest men's adoption of female attire enabled them to assert their masculine identities by abnegating them. War risked the 'potential unmanning of the male body'.[128] By dressing as women or hyper-masculine near-naked tribal warriors, men could make light of the phallus, and even joke at losing it, to emphasize they had it.[129] Costume that appeared to flout naval conventions was therefore important in galvanizing the men. Boxwell uses Turner's concept of social drama to explain how a social breach – here, in 'male homosociality' caused by the war – was remedied through the performative genre of cross-dressing.[130] This explains why such acts were tolerated, even encouraged, by officers.[131]

Aboard *HMS Valiant* Wilson describes how the transformed environment simultaneously flouted and fostered naval hierarchies. The captain toured the crew's rooms, 'complimenting the men on their decorations and displaying great interest in their masquerades'. No sooner had he performed his rounds and returned to the quarter deck, however, 'he was placed upon a chair and carried shoulder high to the hatchway above his cabin'. 'Remonstrating in vain', he was called upon to make a speech:

> Evidently embarrassed, he responded, remarking that from the moment when he commenced his round, surprise after surprise had been sprung upon him, and the heartiness of the

welcome he received, and the extent and excellence of the decorations and masquerades, far surpassed anything he had witnessed in any other ship.[132]

The extent to which the captain feigned his embarrassment is uncertain, but his service aboard other Royal Navy ships suggests he anticipated the 'surprises'. His reaction and comments were important less for their accuracy than for their acknowledgement that all men on board *Valiant* served together. This sentiment was conveyed in a slightly different manner after dinner, when officers visited the messes of their units. Some of the officers were requested to make speeches and were carried in chairs by their subordinates. In the case of the Engineer Commander, who found himself being paraded in a chair, there may have been a case of symbolic punishment, for he was treated with less obvious respect than the captain:

The Engineer Commander … much to our amusement, did not altogether appreciate the honour. The angle at which he was being carried, the proximity of his head to the beams, as he was being pushed along the mess deck, evidently caused him a good deal of anxiety and discomfort, and he would quickly have alighted from his chair had this been possible.[133]

The enchantment of the day ended as swiftly as it began, at midnight. In a histrionic conclusion to his account, which emphasizes the transition from recreation to reality, Wilson remarks:

"Eight bells" again peals out in the midnight air. The dancing and the music cease! For a second a magic stillness reigns. But this is quickly broken, as the band strikes up crew and officers and men, in the words of "Auld Lang Syne", herald together the dawn of another day.[134]

During the Second World War, the importance of world making is apparent from the oral testimony of Charles Gordon Stringer. Recalling a journey from Liverpool to Mombasa, Stringer describes the nightly tension caused by the threat of a German U-boat pack, which he called 'an absolute brute'. On the first night of their journey, 17 December 1942, nine ships in his convoy had been sunk. By the third night, Stringer estimated that over half of the convoy had been destroyed.[135] 'The feeling amongst us all was one of inevitable doom because when you're threatened, you're not frightened, you just accept it; you don't think about [if] you're going to go up in the sea because you know you are, so you just accept it.'[136] He attributed the death of his ship's captain to a stroke brought on by the 'shock of being in the bridge night and day'.[137]

Sailing from Montevideo on the last stretch of his journey, Stringer describes a fancy dress ball in which people dressed as leading Nazi officials:

On the way, in Mid-Atlantic, we had a fancy dress ball. And we had Hitler, Göring, Göbbels and sundry other eminent people. And while we were having dinner, the captain dropped his spoon into his soup … ran up onto the bridge and he knew, by a certain vibration that he felt, that a torpedo had been fired at us in Mid-Atlantic, all by ourselves. And it had been fired too close and it had just gone under the ship. But it's quite boggling to imagine what would've happened if he'd hit us because the German U-boat would have been faced with all these people in fancy dress, and he'd wonder what on earth was going on.[138]

The absurdity of this gathering emphasizes how fancy dress provided a physical and psychological space that enabled sailors to cope with fears. The alleviating effect that costume provided was such that recalling the incident fifty years later, Stringer speaks with humour rather than horror.

Just as soldiers of the First World War used fancy dress costume to facilitate world making to bolster their resolve and to rationalize the physical and psychological transformations that military conflict engendered, sailors of the First and Second World Wars harnessed traditions of dressing up and did likewise to clarify their place within their community and to face down the more frightening aspects of their service.

Fancy dress - To clarify

Fancy dress costume wholly or partially conceals its wearer's identity, sex and status. The temporary effacement of self, the eschewing of normative roles and attendant expectations of behaviour, disrupts the place of the individual within their community and facilitates the exploration of an individual's public and private situation. Concealment through costume can therefore lead to a greater sense of self-awareness and clarity. Contrary to view that emerges through Marshik's study, where fancy dress tends to reveal its wearer's (negative) characteristics, the evidence in this chapter develops observations made in Chapter 2 and suggests a more complex, symbiotic, relationship between an individual's intent and their chosen costume, where each shape the performance and affectiveness of fancy dress. Three themes emerge from the foregoing discussion.

First, however public the performative act of fancy dress, its meaning is often greater to its wearer than their community and immediate audience. This observation may appear counter-intuitive but the examples considered suggest the conception, creation and performance of fancy dress is often undertaken, however consciously, to facilitate world making. This enables people to reflect critically upon the meaning of their identity and place within their community. The psychological comfort provided by dressing up is acute when personal roles and physical safety are threatened. A threat could be a tangible and specific (i.e. the likelihood of injury or death from an enemy power) or intangible and imprecise (i.e. the intimidation caused by social taboos). The expression of personal feelings through an imaginative and incongruous sartorial form that often relies on humour and parody assists people in probing and rationalizing worrying topics. In this way, fancy dress is akin to the performative genres that emerge through Turner's social drama and which enable social rifts to be clarified and calmed.

Second, the liminal nature of fancy dress costume emboldens people, enabling them to express aspects of their characters, and to articulate ideas about themselves, that would be otherwise difficult whilst maintaining their conventional identity and social positions.

Third, fancy dress costume has an ambivalent relationship with the human body. Reflecting on evidence considered here and in the previous chapter, it is apparent that fancy dress can conceal its wearer's sex and status and clarify them. Consequently, it can be used to critique and to enforce normative ideas about gendered roles. This means that dressing up can be a flexible, but potentially confusing communicator and underscores the deeply personal nature of this sartorial form in which wearer and wardrobe conjointly influence a fancy dress performance.

4

To Champion

Previous chapters have considered how fancy dress costume can affirm interpersonal relationships and tear them asunder. It can support individuals who query their self-perception and social identity. For all of these reasons, fancy dress has long been worn to effect change by people championing social and political causes. Much of this activity has occurred within urban environments, centres of economic, political and social authority, where people seeking to initiate reform are likely to have most impact. The transformation of urban spaces during the eighteenth and nineteenth centuries was important for creating an environment that facilitated the formation of social movements, which often used fancy dress to further their cause. Two seemingly opposed developments were paramount. First, urbanization formalized human interactions as large numbers of strangers from different social tiers cohabited in a relatively small space.[1] Second, networks of streets seamlessly connected diverse neighbourhoods and cultures.[2] The sensation of feeling isolated and in want of belonging within a populous and culturally dynamic environment that assisted socialization created an arena in which social movements could emerge.

An early and quixotic street demonstration that involved fancy dress costume occurred in London on 12 January 1821. Eight knights in shining armour, accompanied by squires, trumpeters and approximately 1,800 people filed along the Strand to protest George IV's treatment of his estranged wife Queen Caroline. The marchers wanted to persuade the monarch to behave in a more chivalric, certainly gentlemanly, manner towards his consort. The event's aristocratic backers also sought to remind the king of their potential political authority.[3] Nearly 200 years later, on 5 July 2017, 1000GESTALTEN staged a similarly dramatic costumed demonstration on the streets of Hamburg. Hundreds of people in clay-soaked suits marched to express 'their criticism o[f] the G20-summit in a two hour choreography'. The 'crusted shapes' of the costumes represented 'a society that ha[d] lost [its] belie[f] in solidarity and in which everyone fights for their own progress only. During the course of the performance [the marchers] dropped off their grey costumes where underneath their colorful T-Shirts appeared. In this way they symbolically freed themselves from their petrified structures' and 'called up on more humanity and self-responsibility'.[4]

In the twenty-first century, the staging of costumed marches appears to be increasing as reports on people's disillusionment with the political process multiply. In October 2017, Catalans who sought independence from the Spanish government wrapped themselves in the red and yellow striped flag of their community and wore decorated white face masks. The silhouette of a dove was outlined in blue across their foreheads and alternating streams of yellow and red paint were added below the eye holes to resemble tears.[5] In May 2018, white clowns marched in Acapulco, Mexico, to urge their government to intervene and stop rising crime rates.[6]

The three episodes considered in this final chapter – the Sherborne pageant of 1905, Sydney's Mardi Gras and the global women's march of 2017 – brings the study of fancy dress costume firmly into the twenty-first century. In so doing, it pursues arguments made in previous chapters to consider the potential and problems of using fancy dress costume to gain recognition and support for causes that seek to alleviate the suffering of local and international communities. The examples also question what fancy dress has come to mean in modern and contemporary times and how it is used alongside other forms of human performance.

Civic pride - The Sherborne pageant, Dorset, UK, 12–14 June 1905

In 1905, the 1200th anniversary of the foundation of the Dorset town of Sherborne by St Aldhelm in 705 provided an opportunity to champion domestic industries and patriotism within the frame of a local commemoration. Staging an elaborate entertainment within the ruins of the town's twelfth-century castle and using a unique scheme of coloured costumes to provide narrative and dramatic cohesion Louis Napoleon Parker, a former Sherborne resident and master of music at Sherborne School, wanted to recreate a form of dramatic performance and story telling that had fallen into abeyance. He attributed the decline to the fact that people had 'very little leisure or inclination to read anything' and were 'almost oblivious of the past'.[7] Ambitious for what could be achieved, Parker wanted all townspeople to be involved. In outline, eleven musically accompanied dramatic performances, or episodes, conveyed Sherborne's defining historical moments from its foundation in 705 to the arrival of Sir Walter Raleigh in 1592. The idea of a pseudo-historical entertainment that combined commerce and civic pride was timely as the affects of industrialization became ever more apparent and engendered a persistent, if nebulous, sense of unease. As organizers employed the latest technology and arranged for 'special fast trains' to bring Londoners to Dorset, the play's narrative appeared to advocate a return to more community-centred modes of living.[8] The novelty of the entertainment proved popular and sparked 'pageantitis', as similar events were organized across England during the first half of the twentieth century.[9]

From its inception, Sherborne's creation story drama was referred to as a 'pageant', but this edifying entertainment was innovative and defied classification, which is why I think it can be included in a study of fancy dress costume (Figure 34).[10] Contemporaries linked the anniversary festivities to miracle plays, which continued to be held in the north of England,[11] folk plays,[12] morality plays, masques,[13] *tableaux vivants*[14] and 'the great continental outdoor fêtes',[15] most notably the once-a-decade Passion Play that had been performed in the Bavarian town of Oberammergau since 1634.[16] If people recognized that Parker was drawing on a European theatrical tradition, they nevertheless perceived that his ambition was to reinterpret rather than merely revive. Two weeks before the pageant opened, on 7 June 1905, an article in *Today* suggested that success in Sherborne would 'mark an important step towards the conversion of our country into the "Merry England" of ancient fame'.[17]

A patriotic sentiment that challenged the absolutization of everything, to paraphrase Bakhtin, was at the core of Parker's project.[18] When the plan was presented to the people of Sherborne

FIGURE 34 *The Final Tableaux of the Sherborne Pageant, 1905. Courtesy of Sherborne School.*

in 1904, he exhorted townspeople to recognize the opportunity 'of making a stir in England'.[19] He suggested neighbouring towns that were preparing to honour the life of St Aldhelm were usurping their prerogative. He roused his audience to take action:

> Thus, while you yourselves shew [*sic*] you are not forgetful of your own privileges as citizens of no mean city, you will be teaching your children the truer and higher patriotism. For the love [of] country is founded on the love of home, and that deepens and deepens and broadens the better the home is known, and the more we are taught of its twelve hundred years of unbroken stately history.[20]

To persuade his listeners, Parker compared Sherborne to Bruges and Venice and drew attention to the historic costumed entertainments staged annually within each city. If spectators of these festivities had an 'ache at their hearts' because they acknowledged their communities were 'dead and their sons degenerate', Sherborne 'is alive; she is prospering; her people are as sturdy as they were twelve hundred years ago, by means of the youth and energy she sends out from her great school, her influence is felt wherever the banner of England flouts the wind.'[21]

Prosaically, but no less importantly for the townspeople, the pageant provided an opportunity to showcase the skill of Sherborne's domestic industries; chiefly its manufacture of leather and silk.[22] On 24 April 1905, just over a month before the pageant opened, the *Standard* reported that Parker's drama had 'already done much good locally' because it focused attention on the silk industry, which was 'hundreds of years old [and] one of two or three remaining in all England.'[23] The article appears to criticize the practise by which silk was made in England and sent to France where it 'comes back to us as Lyons silk'.[24] A belief that fancy dress entertainments benefited domestic textile industries was long-standing. In 1837, a costume ball was said to have reinvigorated the silk trade of London's Spitalfields.[25] In 1897, to assuage criticism of a costumed ball that may have cost as much as £4million in twenty-first-century sums, the Bradley-Martins of New York insisted they sent invitations late to ensure guests patronized American costumiers and native industries, rather than Worth in Paris.[26]

If Sherborne's pageant costumes provided economic sustenance in the longer term, in the shorter term they were important in realizing Parker's dramatic plans. To provide coherence to the pageant's narrative, and to create a visual crescendo, a new colour was added to participants' clothing and dress accessories in each of the eleven episodes. In a concluding set piece, actors and costumes came together in a final tableau (Figure 34). The use of colour in each episode is not clearly described in contemporary accounts, but it can be roughly reconstructed (see Table 1).

Table 1 Attempted reconstruction of the colour scheme employed in the Sherborne Pageant, 1905

Pageant episode	Historical year	Colour of costumes
1. The coming of Aldhelm	705	?White
2. The defeat of the Danes	845	Orange
3. Death of Aethelbald and the coming of Alfred	860	Mauve, purple and white[a]
4. Benedictine rule introduced	998	Black[b]
5. William the Conqueror removes the bishopric of Sherborne to Sarum (Salisbury)	1015	Armour[c]
6. Roger of Caen lays the foundation stone of the castle	1107	Girls wore white with silver, gold, blue and pink[d]
7. Quarrel between the town and monastery	1437	Brown and green[e]
8. Foundation of the Almshouse	1437	Red
9. Expulsion of the monks	1539	Black, brown, grey
10. School receives royal charter	1550	'subdued colours'[f]
11. Sir Walter Raleigh comes to Sherborne	1592	Dark green[g]
Final Tableau	1905	All colours

a Cecil P. Godden, *The Story of the Sherborne Pageant* (Sherborne: F. Bennett, 1905), 20.
b Ibid., 21.
c Ibid., 21.
d Ibid., 22.
e Ibid., 23.
f Ibid., 25.
g Ibid., 25.

The unique colour scheme was important in generating advance publicity for the event, which was doubtless intentional. The Pageant's Honorary Committee were adept at distributing copy for the national and international press to use in their reports. On several occasions verbatim accounts of the town's preparations appeared in publications across England and the Atlantic.[27] On 8 April 1905, *The Irish Times* described the colour scheme in similar terms to those that appear in a draft leaflet[28]:

> Each episode will be distinguished by a special colour scheme, and as each turn is produced the body of the performers in the arena will increase until all is blended in a gorgeous whole in the final tableau.[29]

As this appetizing preview indicates, colour helped to create a clear and dramatic narrative that would, in the final tableau, demonstrate the accomplishments of the town through the past and present. An awareness that the colour scheme carried this deeper significance is apparent from contemporary newspaper accounts and the private diaries of people who saw the pageant. Teenager Jane Mary Deane recorded her impressions in a private diary. Her rhapsodic description indicates the experience was akin to a *gesamtkunstwerk* where scenery, staging, acting and music created an immersive environment:

> The favourite feature, or that which struck me most, was the gorgeous mass of colour. Besides the principal figures in each scene there is in all except episode eleven, which represents Sir Walter and Lady Raleigh in their castle home, a large crowd in various dresses at the back, young girls in white dresses with mauve capes and white flowers in their hair, (mourners for King Ethelbald) girls in loose blue or drab coloured dresses, with their long hair confined within a circlet of gold (apparent) or some other metal, monks in reddish brown, greys or black gowns with ropes girdles [*sic.*] round the waist, Tall girls with their long hair floating over their shoulders, soft loose dresses of various delicate colours with garlands of flowers, little children in white on pale blue, Robin Hood's men, in their red capes and green suits and Maid Marian's attendants with their red capes, green dresses with red showing below and garlands of green, red and white flowers, all these and many more were there, their many coloured dresses making a beautiful contrast to the bright green of the grass on which they stood and the gray old ruins with their festoons of dark green ivy behind them. The whole thing – the brilliant colouring, the sunlight glitterings on the armour of the warriors, the natural movements … and the music – was like a glorious, ever changing dream.[30]

Deane's account suggests that Parker's ambition to demonstrate Sherborne's historical and contemporary importance was effective. It might be said, too affective, for the dramatic entertainment appears to have distracted Deane from the pageant's Sherborne-focused narrative, which here seems incidental. The account is interesting because of how Deane appears to construe what she saw in a highly personal manner. It is possible to interpret the diary entry as an example of a 'saturated experience', as described by Beverly Gordon.[31] Whilst Deane did not make any of the costumes, her detailed account that considers their colour, feel and affect, suggests she empathized with the women's work, possibly through the recollection of similar experiences from her life. Whilst this point cannot be substantiated it is noteworthy, if anecdotal, that contemporary publications which discussed the pageant and aimed at a female readership devoted more space to descriptions of costumes and scenery than publications whose readers also included men.[32] Accounts of the pageant in female-focused publications also emphasized how the exertions of Sherborne's women reflected skills that all of their sex possessed. *The Ladies' Field* asserted that the 'skilful fingers' of Sherborne women provided 'proof that English housewives have not yet lost their cunning in needle-work'.[33]

The women of Sherborne certainly had a major role in making the pageant's costumes. The heavy labour and cost that was required to produce clothes and dress accessories had been noted by Parker when he presented his anniversary scheme. He estimated that costumes would be needed for 'three-hundred men and women figuring at the same time, and many of them will require two dresses'.[34] By the day of performance, there were 'no fewer than 700 old English costumes'.[35] A register of participants compiled after the event suggests 944 people had been involved, although not all of these would have required unique outfits.[36]

The responsibility for making the pageant's costumes was devolved to committees, chiefly consisting of women from the town, who worked under the supervision of Frances Macadam (Figure 35).[37] *The Manchester Courier* estimated that 'nearly two hundred ladies of the neighbourhood' cooperated with the town's tailors and dressmakers.[38] Assuming the pageant's surviving costumes, now in Sherborne Museum, are representative, they involved multiple and complex patterns, made use of durable cloth and fabric and would have been time consuming to assemble. These were precisely the circumstances Gordon suggests nineteenth-century women sought because of the practical enjoyment and opportunities for socializing they provided.[39] A staged photograph shows a working party of fourteen women working outside and around a table, upon which three hand-operated sewing machines have been positioned. The impression

A WORKING PARTY OF SHERBORNE LADIES MAKING COSTUMES FOR THE PAGEANT

FIGURE 35 *'A working party of Sherborne ladies making costumes for the pageant'*, Ladies' Field, *24 June 1905. Courtesy of Sherborne School.*

this photograph creates of independent female agency is misleading. If participants in nineteenth-century fancy dress entertainments simultaneously demonstrated the power and powerlessness of women, this was no less true of the preparations required to stage them.[40] A number of studies have shown how women were crucial in the construction of fancy dress garments, but it was typically men who designed them.[41] This was the case in Sherborne.

The majority of pageant costumes were designed by Sherborne School's art master Henry Hudson and Florence Drewe. Parker also had input, presumably to oversee his plans for the synchronizing colour scheme. On 21 December 1904, the headmaster of Sherborne School borrowed a book from the school's library on Parker's behalf, Joseph Strutt's two-volume survey *A Complete View of the Dress & Habits of the People of England*. The book includes 144 hand-coloured engraved plates of historic costume.[42] Strutt asserted that his illustrations were authentic replications from medieval and early modern art, 'without an additional fold being made to the draperies, or the least deviation from the form of the garments'.[43] In reality a degree of creative licence was employed because all of the images are anachronistically coloured. In one scene, 'Hunting habits of the 13 Century', a bullseye target foregrounds three young male archers (Figure 36). The scene is rendered in complementary shades of red and pink.[44] In another scene, 'Ladies of Rank of the 15th & 16th Centuries and their head dresses satirized', five women, each wearing a tall headdress appear deep in conversation (Figure 37). Their gowns are painted subtle tones of purple, maroon and blue.[45] None of the plates can be linked directly to surviving pageant costumes, although it is clear why the books appealed to Parker, who kept them for just over six weeks. Volumes like this were widely consulted for fancy dress costume during the nineteenth and early twentieth centuries. The colours used for the plate depicting 'Ladies of rank' recalls those worn by Princess Alexandra and her daughters at the Devonshire Ball, although there is no explicit evidence that this source provided inspiration.[46]

Women's creative autonomy may have been circumscribed, but their 'skilful fingers' are evident when surviving pageant costumes are examined. A morris dancer's outfit, which appeared in episode seven consists of six items, all of which were hand-made: waistcoat, shirt, breeches, hose, hat and pointed red leather shoes (see Figure 38).[47] The waistcoat and breeches are made of brown serge lined with light orange silk. Many of the items that make up this outfit are machine-stitched, but intricate work was completed by hand. For example, internal patch pockets of red cotton were attached by hand. Fourteen small bells that decorate the edges of the waistcoat's dags, along with a larger bell sewn onto the dag's point, were also attached by hand. On the whole, the stitching is neat, but in places the fabric appears to have been roughly cut and it has now frayed. A red silk dress embroidered with a repeat floriate pattern in gold that was worn in episode eight by Mary Field, mother of Sherborne's vicar, shows signs of hasty construction. The stitches that attach the pale red silk lining are long and irregular.[48] These minor imperfections are on the inside of the garment and would not have been seen by the audience, but they emphasize the enormity of the task that the women working under Frances Macadam had and the limited time to complete it. The importance of the costume makers' role is emphasized in the pageant's financial account, which reveals the cost of costumes (£209 2s. 1d.), props (£151 2s. 10d.), 'wigs and sundries' (£105 17s. 6d.) was £465 2s. 5d., or £36,500 in twenty-first century sums, 16 per cent of total expenditure for the event. These were second only to the costs of constructing the grandstand (£587 8s. 10d.).[49]

The cost of individual costumes is unknown except for those worn by the pupils of Sherborne School. In a letter to parents, headmaster Canon Westmacott explained that 'a sketch of the required costume has already been made, and it is estimated that the cost for each boy will

FIGURE 36 *Plate LIII, 'Hunting Habits of the 13 century', from Joseph Strutt,* A Complete View of the Dress and Habits of the People of England, From the Establishment of the Saxons in Britain to the Present Time, *2 vols. London: J. Nichols, 1796. Courtesy of Sherborne School.*

FIGURE 37 *Plate CXXVII, 'Ladies of rank of the 15th and 16th centuries and their head dresses satirised', from Joseph Strutt,* A Complete View of the Dress and Habits of the People of England, From the Establishment of the Saxons in Britain to the Present Time, *2 vols. London: J. Nichols, 1796. Courtesy of Sherborne School.*

FIGURE 38 *Morris Dancers in Episode Nine of the Sherborne Pageant, 1905. Courtesy of Sherborne School.*

be about ten shillings (Figure 39). This it is hoped Parents and Friends will be ready to pay; for the dress will be an interesting souvenir of a truly historic occasion'.[50] It says much about Sherborne's hopes for the pageant that Westmacott assumed all parents would contribute the equivalent of approximately £40 in twenty-first-century sums to support their son's mandatory involvement. His letter also indicates that people were thinking of mementoes, no doubt to keep alive their association with an event many hoped would transform the town's fortunes. The sense of self regard engendered by Parker's event, and the desire to champion Sherborne before the widest possible audience, also explains why a copy of the pageant script, 'bound in Morocco leather', but presumably prepared in Sherborne, was sent to Edward VII along with an invitation to attend the event.[51] The royal response is not recorded, but the king did not come.

For a significant minority of people posterity was perhaps less important than personal pride. On 12 June, the *Manchester Guardian* ran a story that explained how the number of performers, the materials and cost of the costumes had increased due to competition between Sherborne's residents:

Its ideas ran in cloth in serge, with a few hired properties and not more than about a hundred performers. But local rivalries made sport of the idea. From the beginning there was no question of clique, but there was such a large field to draw from – twelve centuries to cover,

FIGURE 39 *Sherborne School's boys in costume for the Sherborne Pageant, 1905. Courtesy of Sherborne School.*

the history of a town, an abbey, a school, and a castle to epitomize – that the modest scheme extended itself unbidden. It was not to cost more money, so all the performers were called upon to make their own clothes. Thereupon the performers began vying with one another for splendour of attire. They set the silk mills of Sherborne to weave them wonderful stuffs, and while keeping to a set design, let their imaginations play for once in colour schemes and draperies. All the while there was room for the costumes of the simplest, and as the idea grew, more of the townsfolk and countryside joined in, till at least there were eight hundred performers.[52]

Negative or dismissive accounts of Sherborne's pageant from newspapers in regions that routinely staged traditional folk plays should be treated cautiously. Some accounts imply that Sherborne's venture was considered competition. Consequently, they describe lapses in historical accuracy and the existence of long-standing community plays to question the legitimacy and value of the town's efforts.[53] The comments of the *Manchester Guardian*, published on the opening day of the pageant, could reflect envy more than certainty. Nonetheless, the pageant's financial accounts, along with the surviving garments, indicate the total cost of the costumes was high. An anguished letter from Parker in which he admonishes the townspeople for not working sufficiently hard or in unison is unusual for being signed off with his title, which was underlined: 'Louis N. Parker. Master of the Pageant'. This apparently angry gesture gives credence to the idea of personal rivalry and contrary objectives.[54]

Contemporary responses from those who saw the pageant or considered it competition suggest Parker's novel and edifying entertainment did achieve some success at championing

Sherborne to audiences local and further afield. As Paul Readman has argued, interest in the past during the nineteenth century was genuine and 'active'.[55] However, the existence of interpersonal rivalries, which led to escalating costs, indicates that Parker's script and historical accuracy were not the sole determinants of what people wore. In addition to fulfilling their scripted roles, the people of Sherborne used costumes to convey specific information about their position and status within their community to champion themselves as much as their town. Another narrative is discernible in the commentary on Sherborne's women, whose work making costumes was used to advocate the skill of English women. In conceiving of a novel entertainment to promote Sherborne to a national, even international, audience, Parker inadvertently, perhaps ruefully, created an opportunity for participants and spectators to communicate concerns of their own.

Finding a voice - Sydney Mardi Gras Australia, 1978–*c.*1990

Sydney has hosted an annual Mardi Gras for forty consecutive years since 24 June 1978. The date of the first event, which involved approximately 1,500 participants, was chosen to coincide with the ninth anniversary of New York's Stonewall riots.[56] The spur for Sydney's Mardi Gras was not merely commemorative, a means of showing support for the social and legal position of homosexuals in another part of the world. The decision to organize an event that focused on homosexual lives and rights was more directly a response to political and cultural attitudes within Australia that continued to deem same-sex relationships illegal.[57] The role of the United States of America as activist lodestar was nevertheless important because Australia's history of social movements and protest remained incipient during the 1970s, even after demonstrations against the Vietnam War in the previous decade.[58] The furtherance of homosexual rights in America, which included a more diverse and public gay subculture than that in Australia, provided strategies the residents of Sydney could harness.[59] The combination of limited activist experience, the illegality of homosexuality, and the ignorance and suspicion surrounding same-sex relationships in Australia meant there could be no verbatim exchange and organizers and participants debated whether their event was, at its core, a protest – which sought to improve the lives of homosexual people by drawing attention to their current difficulties – or a celebration – which demonstrated the diversity and cohesion of Australia's homosexual community. These two visions were not mutually exclusive, but they engendered a long-running, at times acrimonious, debate about the purpose of Sydney's Mardi Gras during its early years. Within these discussions, which were largely resolved by the mid-1980s, when the argument in favour of celebration became dominant, the usage and meaning of fancy dress costume was reviewed. The formative years of the parade, when the purpose of the event was much debated, are consequently useful for exploring the challenges of harnessing fancy dress as a form of civic protest from the perspective of participants and spectators.

The earliest costume from Sydney's Mardi Gras to survive in a public dress collection dates from the twelfth annual parade of 1990 (Figure 40).[60] Photographic and film evidence provide the best opportunity to examine costumes prior to this, although images are frequently blurred and it is often impossible to determine the materials and techniques of construction. A documentary about the sixth Mardi Gras in 1984, 'We'll Dance If We Want To', which aired on Australian channel *SBS* in the same year, includes a six-minute clip of various costumed participants.[61] In this, one woman wears a sleeveless denim jacket embellished with metallic decoration, black gloves and an imitation chastity belt over a pair of light-coloured trousers.[62]

FIGURE 40 *A Mardi Gras costume designed by Peter Tully, 1990. © Marlene Gibson. Collection: Museum of Applied Arts and Sciences. Purchased 1995. Photo: Sue Stafford*

Five people, their sex disguised by their costumes, wear white shirts and baggy trousers with a red belt tied at the waist.[63] Floor-length white capes attached at the wearers' shoulders are decorated around the hem with red musical notes. The group members are only distinguishable by their white headdresses, which are uniquely decorated; one includes five red and white striped rods, approximately 500 mm long, that project vertically from a gold scaffold in the shape of a five-pointed star attached to the back of the wearer's head and neck. A large white eighth note is also affixed to the gold structure. One man wears full evening dress.[64] Two men wear black leotards, or singlets, with low-cut v-neck fronts and suspenders. Across their faces they wear oversized pink-rimmed sunglasses and false pointed noses. Curled shoulder-length wigs – one red, one black – and matching pairs of fluffy white bunny ears cover their heads.[65] Photographs by William Yang, who documented the early years of Sydney's Mardi Gras, show similar outfits, including groups of men in army uniform and mock construction gear.[66] Some costumes were overtly political. In one image by Yang from the 1983 parade, a bearded man wears a white spotted wedding dress, costume tiara and cuffed fingerless lace gloves. In his right hand he holds a placard, decorated with what appears to be silver tinsel, that proclaims in capitals, 'IT TAKES BALLS TO BE A FAIRY'. In another photograph, from the 1984 parade, a group of four men stand in a row facing the viewer, their arms linked behind their backs. They wear identical oversized sunglasses, similarly styled denim jeans and matching white crew-neck T-shirts, which are differentiated by a single letter printed on the chest of each to spell 'P.O.O.F'.

The challenge of purposefully incorporating fancy dress costumes that were variously idiosyncratic, personal and political into Sydney's Mardi Gras was practical, ideological and long-standing. Practical, because prior to 1981 Mardi Gras had been held during the winter, which made warm clothing more appealing than costume; ideological and long-standing because dressing up had formed a minor part in Australia's limited history of public campaigning. The decision to move Mardi Gras to the summer in 1981 exacerbated these tensions. By severing the link to Stonewall, the nature of Sydney's event appeared to become immediately less political and more celebratory. This was a point of contention for activists who initiated further discussions about the overarching purpose of Mardi Gras. In 1980, the Mardi Gras Task Group asked baldly, 'What is the goal of Mardi Gras? Is it a political demonstration to defend gay rights, or is it a celebration of coming out, with its only political goals being to demonstrate the size and variety of the gay community and to establish its right to be?'[67] Within the debates that followed, the efficacy of using fancy dress costume was cogitated.

In the early 1980s, the number of participants dressing up remained small, but the visual potency of fancy dress costume made it an important issue. A report compiled by the Task Group on the parade of 1980 revealed that 'probably only 25 percent of the crowd were in costume [c. 750 people[68]], partly – no doubt – due to the cold, but clearly Sydney's gays are not yet accustomed to costume parades'.[69] The report notes that some costumes 'really did catch the spirit of celebration and a number of groups and mini-acts performed pieces of street theatre'.[70] The remark implies that the parade's organizing committee considered Mardi Gras to be essentially unpolitical and deemed fancy dress costume to be inherently benign, lacking coercive force or communicating potential. Campaigners who wanted the event to champion homosexual rights thought differently. They challenged the incorporation of fancy dress in the parade for being, at best, trivial and, at worst, a potentially offensive distraction. In an article of December 1980 that appeared in *Klick*, a newspaper for the homosexual community, Terry Goulden articulated concerns about the event's direction and averred that 'frivolity was only ideologically sound when it had a decent purpose'.[71] Interestingly, the only recorded disturbance during the 1980 parade was sparked by a costume, when a woman attempted to climb onto a float to challenge what she perceived to be the racist use of blackface.[72]

Disapproval of fancy dress costume in Mardi Gras stemmed from its perceived instability as a medium of communication. Three concerns stood out. First, the performative display of sexuality reinforced negative assumptions about homosexuality. An anonymous interviewee in the documentary *Feed Them to the Cannibals*, which first aired on *ABC* in 1993, suggested that 'society allowed us to have drag because they didn't see it as challenging. In a way it reinforced their view of us as being women anyway; that we weren't really men.'[73] Throughout the 1960s and 1970s, defamatory pamphlets depicted homosexual men as self-consciously performative – wearing particular clothes, effecting particular gestures and speaking in a particular manner – and it could easily be assumed that the wearing of costume perpetuated this spiteful fallacy.[74] Some homosexuals confronted critics directly by engaging in radical drag or genderfuck – bearded men wore dresses and cosmetics; women cut their hair short and kept their body hair – but this tactic worried participants and committee members who thought the parade was already too political.[75] Second, the provocative gathering of a large number of homosexuals could divide the community, particularly between men and women, and alienate heterosexual support. In the initial years of Mardi Gras, female homosexuals spoke of their marginalization, which they felt dressing up exacerbated. In 1996, participant Kate Rowe recalled how she had been 'uncomfortable around men in drag and there was a lot of misogyny.'[76] By contrast, participant Kimberly O'Sullivan considered her involvement in the Mardi Gras parade to be liberating. However, her comments highlight the fragile basis on which the event – commandeering public space and organized by people whose sexuality made them criminals – took place. She suggested the event,

> almost, like, turns the normal dynamic of society on its head, where the heterosexuals are behind the barricades, held back, coming out to watch us as we take over the streets, because that is truly one night when you can have hundreds and thousands of people coming to see you being completely outrageous and over the top, and having those streets to yourself is incredibly empowering.[77]

Third, the serious intent of the public demonstration was trivialized and undermined by costumed participants. Barry Cecchini, who ran Sydney's Beresford Hotel, a popular homosexual venue, was critical of street demonstrations and marches. In a letter of March 1981, published in Sydney newspaper *The Star*, he explained that they did 'not constitute a prudent move'. He thought they were more likely to 'threaten' people, or at least make 'the average Australian … feel more protective towards his children'. Looking to the United States of America, he argued, 'we can dance or march ourselves through a dozen pair of sneakers and still not win'. Perhaps reflective of his occupation, Cecchini advocated the use of money to effect 'influential persuasion'.[78]

There were no straightforward solutions to these interrelated concerns but Cecchini's thoughts became mainstream as event organizers determined to champion the political rights of homosexuals by asserting their moral rights. This would be achieved by increasing the number of people who participated in Mardi Gras. Crucial to this change in outlook were two decisions. First, the creation of an elected organizing committee and, second, the involvement of non-activist groups.[79] Ironically for Cecchini, these organizational changes, along with the resolution to raise more money and levy more marchers, facilitated the wearing of fancy dress costume. If Mardi Gras was increasingly conceived as an inclusive event for homosexual men, women and heterosexuals, the polyvalence of dressing up would become less of an issue. In fact, it could become an advantage if the anonymity of dressing up flattened social and political hierarchies and lessened their correlative tensions. In 1982, the first costumed after show party, the Sleaze Ball, was organized to raise funds for the following year's parade. Ticket sales for the Ball increased yearly through to 1994.[80] In 1983, artist Peter Tully was appointed to run the newly created Mardi Gras Workshop, which was responsible for the creation and construction of parade costumes and floats.[81] The extent to which this development facilitated aesthetic cohesion across the parade is unclear because costuming groups still exercised autonomy over their costumes and floats.[82] Nevertheless, this innovation indicated a more favourable attitude towards fancy dress costume.

Concerns about the role and meaning of dress up were not wholly resolved. Prior to 1980, discussions about fancy dress had tended to focus on the meaning of costume within Mardi Gras, as it was understood by homosexual participants. The broadening of the event after 1980 established a greater need to clarify what homosexuals in dress-up meant to a heterosexual audience, even if contemporary surveys implied a more sympathetic public attitude towards the legalization of same-sex relationships.[83] The question was prompted by increasing national and global interest in Sydney's Mardi Gras and the problematic nature of its reporting. It is evident that newspapers and documentaries, which were predominantly written and edited by heterosexuals, highlighted aspects of the event they presumed would pique the curiosity of their audiences, who were also predominantly heterosexual. Consequently, contemporary discussions of Mardi Gras frequently involved extensive consideration of costumes that were deemed unusual and risqué. This means that much of the commentary on the first decades of Sydney's Mardi Gras is problematic as a historical source. For example, the parade footage in *We'll Dance If We Want To* appears to have been edited to juxtapose striking costumes and performances. In a similar way, some journalists evidently thought that Mardi Gras provided an opportunity to write with atypical humour and hyperbole. An article of 2 September 1987 from *Sydney's Star Observer* appeared under the heading, 'Pre-Sleaze with ease', and opens with the line, 'A ridiculous title to match a ridiculous concept for a column'. After a tongue-in-check explanation of the column's genesis, Gareth Paull outlines 'suggestions for a Pre-Sleaze Ball party' with a discussion of 'The cossie'. He suggests, 'Simply think of something outrageous. That's all. "Caution to the winds" is the motto. Wasn't *that* easy! Ditto for makeup, which can be the best substitute for costume. You still need to wear *some* clothes (I think) but fun stage paint can be real Sleaze!'.[84] In circumstances where fancy dress costume could be considered an asset to Mardi Gras, it continued to raise questions about what participants wanted, and more fundamentally, who they were.

A complete costume from the twelfth Mardi Gras in 1990, now in the collection of Sydney's Museum of Applied Arts and Sciences, can clarify this point (Figure 40).[85] The costume was created by Peter Tully, artistic director of Mardi Gras, between 1983 and 1986.[86] The ambiguous garment is approximately 3302 mm tall and 2489 mm wide. It consists of three main parts – a purple V-neck T-shirt, black and white trousers and multicoloured headdress – that are overlaid with numerous and brightly coloured recycled objects, or 'reverse garbage'. Much of the T-shirt is covered by a circular breastplate trimmed with lime green fur and decorated with vertical bands of blended yellow, red and blue that radiate from a central metal boss like a sun burst. The arms of the T-shirt, which are visible when the costume is worn, have been cut with vertical incisions to create rectangular tassels. The black cotton trousers are decorated with a bricolage of white patterns and objects. Prints of a mock keyboard are pinned on the outside of both legs; a white feather, a small white plastic human skeleton, a white plastic spoon, a black spotted purse, and a replica human tibia, are some of the recycled objects that hang from the top of an apron skirt that is suspended across the wearer's thighs and groin. The tibia hangs, perhaps provocatively, between the wearer's legs. A purple humanoid mask covers the wearer's face. It has yellow holographic eyes and an orange goatee. The large headdress is attached by means of two shoulder straps, which are covered in pink fur, and a concealed aluminium frame. An assortment of coloured shapes and materials are used to decorate the headdresses. Affixed directly above the wearer's head are a pair of pink circular 'Mickey Mouse' ears and a small silver human skull. Whilst the costume uses a variety of materials and objects, many are red, orange, yellow, green, blue and purple, which are the same as those featured in the Rainbow Flag after 1979. However, no overt symbols or text connects the costume to Sydney's Mardi Gras, and the only accessory supplied with the costume, at least in its preserved state, is an unmarked yellow polyester handbag. Consequently, Tully's creation appears simultaneously noisy and voiceless. Subversion is hinted at by the strangeness of the costume and by its rainbow colour scheme, but not articulated.

The inversion of social and political assumptions through fancy dress costume and floats had been a notable theme within early Mardi Gras parades. In 1983, AngGays, a group of Anglican homosexuals, created a float that depicted the Madonna as homosexual.[87] In 1986, Sisters of Perpetual Indulgence included a parade of ecclesiastical vestments along with tooth picks from the Last Supper and Joan of Arc's sword.[88] In many cases, the subversive nature of participants' outfits was clear and spectators would have been able to comprehend wearer's intentions, but this was not always so. Tully's costume appears to rely on an in-joke or insular narrative that may have been comprehensible to members of his workshop but this was unlikely to have been clear to parade spectators. Comments from contemporaries who worked with Tully tend to confirm what his costume suggests; namely, that he was adept at designing costumes to gain attention but conceived of them to create an atmosphere, rather than to convey pointed messages. Ron Smith, who succeeded Tully as artist director, was interviewed as part of Sydney's Pride History Group's '100 Voices Collection' and explained how his predecessor created costumes and displays that actively encouraged interaction between participants and spectators. His 'great skills' came from a background as a jewellery student and window dresser.

> Peter was already aware of the need to, for the parade to have height, so the people could be seen and things [could] be [of] brilliant colour or metallic so that … you could see them. And we were also very aware from [participating in other demonstrations] of the failings of the soggy banner and the anonymity of the T-Shirt and jeans, and so we were really going to push; particularly Peter as the boss of the watch. He was very, very pushy on there being as many people in costume as possible, and as much décor on floats as possible, and if possible, as much music as possible, so that there could be dancing. And remember, the parade wasn't marshalled at all – so no barricades – so people from the crowd were welcome to come and join the parade, as it went along.[89]

Smith's account implies Tully was aiming at a *gesamtkunstwerk*, where the costumed participants and floats were supplemented by music, choreography and a buoyant crowd to produce a complete aesthetic harmony. He wanted his costumes to be about participation rather than representation. Familiar with America's homosexual culture and protests from a previous visit, Tully apparently aimed to create a similar festive atmosphere in Sydney. The penurious circumstances in which Mardi Gras was organized facilitated this outlook. Smith explains that many participants wore their parade costumes to the Sleaze Ball where they served as decoration because funds were inadequate to renovate the venue.[90]

If Tully's work highlights the potential of fancy dress to fulfil the aims of a social movement, it also draws attention to its limitations. Tully recognized this quandary himself and understood that fancy dress costume did not convey messages unambiguously. Speaking of his involvement in the first parade of 1978, he reflected, 'I was [a] Red Indian costume with wall paint and feathers, [but] there weren't many people in costume at that stage because it was too – the accent was more on the political than on the fun side and suddenly we found ourselves in a riot.'[91]

The communicative ambivalence of Tully's work reflected his artistic process. When designing for Mardi Gras he pursued his long-standing interest in 'urban tribalwear'. In this unique sartorial form he drew inspiration from Australian culture and the dress of traditional societies he had visited within Africa, India and New Guinea. Through the reuse of modern and synthetic materials, he created contemporary interpretations of primeval ceremonial clothing. Whilst this ensured Tully's creations had a visual consistency, it meant his work had no specific connection with Sydney's homosexual community. In this sense Tully's costumes are similar to those worn in contemporary West Africa, because their bricolage construction defies symbolic dissection.[92] This point is apparent from another of Tully's costumes that survives in the collection of the Museum of Applied Arts and Sciences.[93] Designed in 1984 as the centrepiece for a solo exhibition at Sydney's Roslyn Oxley9 Gallery, 'Primitive Futures', the costume is constructed from the same process of recycled bricolage that was used for the 1990 costume. It is constructed from a near identical palette of bright colour. The inclusion of fluffy slippers and prosaic objects to adorn the costume creates a strong visual parity with his later Mardi Gras garment. As with the parade costume, there is also hint at sexual subversion. The exhibition garment is titled 'Don't Ask About Mary', which is presumably an allusion to the biblical couple Mary and Joseph. The inference is that Joseph, ostensibly the wearer of this technicolour coat, is homosexual; hence why we are urged not to ask about his supposed wife. However, it is only through the title, which the parade costume lacks, that Tully's intention becomes clear. Viewed together, the outfits suggest Tully's desire to create an aesthetic harmony through his urban tribalwear motif led to the creation of ambivalent designs in the frame of the Mardi Gras parade. This may have exacerbated long-standing tensions between his workshop and the parade's organizing committee and contributed to his decision to resign in 1986.[94]

If Tully's costumes show how fancy dress could be a problematic champion of homosexual rights, they nonetheless reveal one of the distinct benefits of wearing costumes for public demonstrations. For participants, the effect of Tully's design process was analogous to world making. The collaborative act of collecting garbage and working it into a costume created a sense of empowerment. Artist David McDiarmid observed 'the passion and the intensity and commitment of everyone involved meant that it was from the heart; everything was strong'.[95] The strength of feeling was no less pronounced when the outfits were worn in the parade, as the remarks from Ron Smith above attest. The costumes that were produced by Tully were crucial in motivating participants and, like a *gesamtkunstwerk*, could be galvanizing. Smith suggests Tully wanted to use his tribalwear to create an actual tribe at Mardi Gras. He indicates that Tully may have been cognizant of the philosophy of Ros Bower, founder of the Community Arts Board of Australia, who had visited community art groups across the country and extolled the importance of fostering 'identity and bonding' through the sharing of skills and collaborative working.[96] March participant Clive Faro observed that costume was helpful in encouraging people who were 'frightened' to get involved. To 'dress up in disguise [was to] have a good night with lots of other gay people'.[97] Attendees of the Sleaze Ball felt similarly liberated. For Kimberly O'Sullivan they provided

a chance to express that darker side of your sexuality; [gave] you a chance to dress up in fetish gear and bondage gear and S[ado] M[asochism] gear, or whatever, and to do it very publicly in an environment that's very safe and that's very liberating. It's very sexually powerful and there are very few places where women [could] publicly live out fantasy stuff in a safe environment in the way that men [could] and [to be] able to so is enormously important.[98]

These remarks help to explain why the role of fancy dress costume in Mardi Gras increased. In this frame, dressing up came to be recognized and appreciated more for how it made participants feel and think, rather than how – even if – it worked to convey what they meant. The challenge of incorporating fancy dress costume into Sydney's Mardi Gras remains today. It is shared by similar events around the world. In May 2018, Sheffield Pride in the United Kingdom was criticized for its application form that stated the event was 'a march of celebration not protest'. 'Colourful clothing' that was respectful was permitted, but banners and placards were to be checked by the Parade Manager before they could carried.[99]

Pushing back - Women's marches, Global, 2017

On 21 January 2017, millions of people appeared on the streets of cities around the world to champion the rights of women. The largest simultaneous protest of its kind, the Women's March followed the inauguration of Donald Trump as the United States of America's forty-fifth president, which had occurred in Washington D.C. the previous day. The timing of the March was intentional. Allegations of Trump's disparagement and harassment of women had surfaced during the presidential campaign, along with a video in which he can be heard remarking, 'You know I'm automatically attracted to beautiful [women] – I just start kissing them. It's like a magnet. Just kiss. I don't even wait. And when you're a star they let you do it. You can do anything … Grab them by the pussy. You can do anything.'[100] The majority of people who marched wore conventional clothing and carried expressive placards to express anger and disillusionment about the implication for women's rights following Trump's unexpected victory over the country's first female presidential candidate, Hillary Clinton. A smaller number of marchers wore conceptual and synecdochic costumes, which included Abraham Lincoln, a Founding Father, nineteenth-century suffragettes and vulvas.[101] Many costumes used white, a colour symbolic of purity within the suffragette movement, and pink, a colour representative of female 'caring, compassion, and love'.[102] Pink 'pussyhats' – 'knitted, crocheted, or sewn caps' with distinctive catlike ears – were ubiquitous.[103] Fancy dress costumes were worn again on 8 March 2017, when marches around the world celebrated International Women's Day. Alongside suffragettes, a Darth Vader costume was worn in Jakarta. In New South Wales, Australia, artist Alli Sebastian Wolf, walked the streets with 'Glittoris', a '100:1 scale anatomical model of a clitoris covered in gold sequins', accompanied by The Clitorati, four friends in corresponding costumes of blue and gold.[104] The challenge of incorporating fancy dress costume purposefully within the women's marches was different in both degree and kind to those encountered by the organizers of Sydney's Mardi Gras. As a social movement that was simultaneously pan-national and pan-global, the conveyance of specific ideas and messages was more complex because questions about the efficacy, legality and morality of costumes were more numerous and the agency of individuals, influenced by the cultural norms of the communities in which they marched, was greater.

Many of the people who participated in the January and March events were reacting to a sense of disbelief and paralysis; artist Marilyn Minter likened America's situation to that of Weimar

Germany during the 1930s and the ascendancy of Adolf Hitler.[105] New Yorker Marcia D.B. Levy, who participated in the Washington March with her 'very pregnant daughter', explained: 'We attended as there was no way not to attend. We are women and it was a women's march. A woman just lost an election primarily due to her gender. And to a foul sexist racist creep. We had to go. Period. The end. No way out.'[106] The need to do something to express the mix of feelings stirred by the election campaign was shared by many marchers. *Vogue* correspondent Sarah Brown, who also attended the Washington March, called her mother when the 'first whispers' of a march 'started popping up' on social media after the election. She 'didn't know what the march would be about exactly (neither did the organisers at the time) … [but] wanted to be there, and … wanted to be there with her [mother]'.[107]

The speed with which the January March was coordinated, and the use of word of mouth and social media to disseminate information, explains why many participants wore conventional clothing. Shayne Kopec, a twenty-five-year-old Canadian who participated in the Tokyo March on 21 January, did not appear costumed or carry a sign because of a lack of time, even though a friend had been one of the organizers.[108] Kopec did wear a pussyhat, an uncommon sight in Tokyo, although this had become a conventional part of her winter wardrobe. Levy and her daughter also marched without costume and signage. She recalls, 'At the [train] station, we noticed the first signs and the pussy hats but honestly, we'd been both so … [pre]occupied, we never thought to bring much of anything but a pair of pinkish hats I'd found rummaging around the closet as I ran out the apartment door.'[109] In part, Levy was surprised by the role of costume in the March. She had participated in protests against the Vietnam War in the 1970s and observed that 'this was the first march I attended where costuming played such a role. And signage and HATS.'[110]

Whilst time may have been short, some marchers were determined to wear fancy dress costume. Thirty-five-year-old Lindsay Schober, who participated in the New Orleans March, had worn T-shirts to previous political and social marches, but, inspired by Russia's Pussy Riot and a friend who was planning to wear a 'Guy Fawkes mask with black clothes and a hoodie', she wanted to attend this march as 'a symbol. I wanted a message, a movement, to be translatable in a glance or photograph' (Figure 41).[111] She wore a customized beanie hat in 'hot-pink' wool and a light brown military-style jacket obtained from a thrift store. Schober added a pink pompom to the hat and cut three holes for her eyes and mouth, to turn it into a balaclava. Schober had been unaware that face coverings in New Orleans are illegal beyond Mardi Gras and was unable to wear the hat during the march. Her jacket was decorated with 'a collection of feminist pins, patches, and buttons'. A large, chain-stitched Pussy Riot patch depicting the pink balaclava, which had been made by an artist friend, was affixed to the back.[112] The costume took a couple of hours to complete; the longest time was spent searching for badges to decorate the jacket. Her costume cost approximately $275 (the jacket cost $250).[113]

In London, twenty-five-year-old Amy Cartwright and two of her colleagues, Hannah Monkley and Amy Towl, dressed as suffragettes. Cartwright had no experience of being involved in a costumed march. In part, the decision to dress up was governed by practicality; 'heavy woollen fabrics' would keep her warm.[114] A more pressing reason to attend in costume was to challenge 'online negativity' about the suffrage movement, 'mainly with regards to how elitist a lot of the front runners of the campaign were'. In the week prior to the march, Amy and her colleagues, 'researched as much as we could about the working-class suffragettes, and designed our costumes to look like we were Sylvia Pankhurst and her East London federation of suffragettes'.[115] On Instagram, she explained, 'We wanted to honour the pioneering women before us who fought hard, not just for the vote, but for equality and the rights that we have today. While at the same time to also show that we still have a long, long way to go before true equality is seen the world over.'[116]

FIGURE 41 *Lindsay Schober wearing her Pussy Riot-inspired jacket, 2017. © Lindsay Schober.*

The group's dresses were lent by a costume supplier and based on original designs. Cartwright added an 'authentic Edwardian trim' to her dress. The women wore their own footwear, for comfort, and 'modern thermals under our outfits, as it was a freezing day and we felt covering everything up with an overcoat would have ruined our message. [Our] "Votes for Women" sashes had been made for the opening ceremony of London's Olympic Games in 2012.'[117]

Vivian Vassar attended the New York March with her women's group, 'Bitchin' Palooza', and two sisters-in-law, without a costume, although she frequently attends events in fancy dress.[118] Her decision to dress as a suffragette at follow-up protests in Staten Island was inspired by the imagination of the people marching in Manhattan: 'I saw how people were so creative in their signage and clothing … that I decided to dress as a Suffragette (Figure 42). I wanted to remind people how hard women worked in the past to achieve their goals and going forward if we work together our voices will be heard.'[119] At the Staten Island protests, Vassar wore a white suffragette costume with a plain sash.[120] The textless sash was a deliberate choice: 'I like to ask people what they think I should write on my sash. Because I've gotten so many interesting answers I decided to leave the sash blank'. The outfit, which cost approximately $70 to assemble, consisted of an

> off-white rayon skirt from a costume company; white cotton blouse, from a thrift store; lace trimmed jacket from TJ Maxx; polyester white lace trimmed scarf from a 99-cent store; vintage pin from [her personal] collection; boots and white cotton pantaloons from a clothing swap; white hat from a free box; nylon netting and ribbons from Michaels Craft Store, and white gloves and purse from a thrift store.[121]

The intentions of Alli Sebastian Wolf were different to other women considered here because her Glitoris model had already been conceived at the time of Sydney's Women's March (Figure 43). The project had been inspired by 'the women's marches [that had] formed in protest of the new/now more visible … climate'.[122] Consequently, when new marches were announced, Wolf felt '[i]t would have been criminal not to bring it along'.[123] Her use of the march was also unique, for two reasons. First, she conceived the Glitoris to be an edifying tool to challenge school-based sexual education that had 'created a sexual culture that is so much less rich, pleasure filled and interesting than it could be for all genders and sexualities'.[124] In particular, she wanted to provide women with greater knowledge so they could enjoy their bodies:

> So many people I've talked to didn't know about the shape of the clitoris until they read about my art project. Even highly educated women, who'd participated in the women's rights movements of the 60s and 70s and now work in management and academia didn't have access to this knowledge – it just wasn't available or treated as a priority. One woman I spoke to when performing at the All About Women Festival had studied anatomy for seven years and didn't know. But an eight-year old knows the function and shape of a womb and fallopian tubes. That makes me so sad.

Second, Wolf is experienced in 'roving performances' and the Glitoris was displayed as part of a choreographed performance involving four friends that took approximately three weeks to coordinate.[125]

In these examples, the women who marched in costume make it clear that fancy dress was integral to the personal and political messages they wanted to convey. Amy Cartwright and her colleagues carried a placard with the text 'Same Shit, Different Century', but felt this alone

FIGURE 42 *Vivian Vassar wearing her Suffragette costume, 2017. © Vivian Vassar.*

FIGURE 43 *Inga Ting, Alli Sebastian Wolf and Ellie Downing with The Glitoris, 2017. © Tim da Rin.*

would have been insufficient to make the point that 'brave women went through so much to fight for equal rights (prison and force feeding, alongside physical and mental abuse). We wanted to remember what they had done for us, but also that we had so far to go still to finish the job they started.'[126] The perception that costumes could enable messages to be expressed with greater clarity and resonance reflects a broader, and long-standing, problem besetting social movements; namely, a lack of media attention. Jan Cohen-Cruz notes that the Rally for a Nuclear Freeze, which had been the largest demonstration in American history at the time it was held in June 1981, 'received less coverage than an annual Rose Bowl Parade'. Her point is that media networks have been disinclined to spotlight causes that have 'less compelling presentation or unpopular messages'.[127] Gaining the attention of news networks has proved difficult for women's movements in the United States of America, which have had to develop strategies to secure television coverage.[128] In the case of the Women's March, the wearing of pussyhats, white and pink clothing has helped to emphasize the unity of the diverse people marching. This creates 'a message that resonates with a wide array of communities' and, potentially, attracts more media traction.[129] Suzanne Lacy and Leslie Labowitz suggest that street performance has been most effective in gaining (media) attention when it has used parody and humour.[130]

The efficacy of ludic behaviour was widely considered during and after the January Women's March. For Marcia D.B. Levy, humour was inappropriate. She regretted not having a costume but said that she would have been unable to dress up even if there had been more time to prepare. She argues that 'costuming requires a bit of *joie de vivre* to carry it off and for me, and at the moment of the march, that boat had sailed'.[131] Levy's remark about the appropriateness of humour at a moment of social tension recalls Bakhtin's work on the disruptive and invigorating power of carnival laughter and how ill-suited carnival is within a modern environment. More specifically, Levy's opinion engages with contemporary discussions about the role of comedy within social movements. Writing in *The New Yorker*, Alexandra Schwartz suggested the humorous responses to Trump's shock victory, wherever they appeared, were multifaceted and cathartic. She observed that the humour was 'not as the default mode, a smug substitute for sincerity, but as its accent note, a way of speaking the kind of truth you can't with a straight face'.[132]

During the January Women's March, humour appears to have served two interrelated purposes. First, to make the reality of Trump's election victory and the possible consequences for women's rights comprehensible, and therefore resistible. Second, to give people the confidence to oppose to the authority of their government. As Richard Schechner observes, 'revolutions in their incipient period are carnivalesque', so as to insulate the people involved from the risks and challenges they are likely to confront.[133] Actor and puppeteer, Pamela Mitchell, participated in the Los Angeles March wearing a hand puppet of her own design and construction (Figure 44). Mitchell had conceived of her vagina puppet for a comedy sketch: 'when I thought about a costume I immediately thought of Trump's "Pussy grabbing" comments and my costume was a done deal'.[134] The puppet, which Mitchell wore with a pink woollen beanie and T-shirt, had an accompanying sign that read 'Not Yours to Grab!'. Made of felt, foam, cardboard 'and a lot of hot glue', the puppet cost approximately $20 and took roughly five hours to make.[135] Wearing the puppet made Mitchell feel nervous, because she didn't want it to be taken as 'a vulgarity', but it was 'really well received' during the march. In part, Mitchell suspects this was because it provided 'a bit of comedic relief in a way – super blunt but also a bit abstract, and not sexualized so people liked it as an art piece. By the end of the march I felt like I had really made a (funny) point'. If Mitchell's concerns about her puppet appearing vulgar were not realized during the march, she did receive 'a few extremely negative (and strangely violent and vicious) online reactions – mostly from older white men who felt like I was attacking them and that if I was willing to walk around with a vagina puppet that I must be a "slut" or "couldn't get a real man acting like that". It was really interesting.'[136] Similarly negative comments were also received by Amy Cartwright, who posted images of her costume on Instagram.[137]

During a period when many people felt in need of a 'collective hug' and laughed, according to Sarah Larson, as though at a funeral, the costumes worn by Mitchell and Cartwright were generally comprehensible to spectators, although Lindsay Schober needed to explain parts of her costume to marchers unfamiliar with Pussy Riot.[138] On social media, when the costumes were removed from this supportive environment and seen by a larger number of people, they were interpreted in isolation, and evidently with some misunderstanding and misapprehension. The importance of framing in understanding fancy dress costume that seeks to convey a particular message became apparent when Cartwright and her colleagues were asked to wear their costumes at the Port Eliot Festival, Cornwall, in June 2017. The Festival was themed around the question, 'Can fashion be utilized as a valid form of protest?' In this arena, which drew 'a whole host of creative rebels', the reception offered to Cartwright and her costume was largely positive.[139]

In Jakarta, where a march was organized to coincide with International Women's Day on 8 March 2017, twenty-three-year-old Margianta Surahman Juhanda Dinata recognized the importance of framing and interpretation when he wore a custom-made Darth Vader suit. The black polyester bodysuit was adorned with EVA foam and faux leather to form the chest armour, as was the helmet. A cape and long shawl were made of a black sunwashed chambray

FIGURE 44 *Pamela Mitchell with her vagina hand puppet, 2017. © Pamela Mitchell.*

fabric. Boots were made of faux leather and rubber. The suit cost approximately $110 and took six months to make at a costume supplier.[140] Dinata has long been a *Star Wars* fan, but chose Darth Vader because of the message he thinks the character represents:

> Vader was a good person who got corrupted by power, only to find himself to be good again. I think he really represents all of us, on how we can be bad but we can always redeem ourselves to be good. For me, that is essentially the point of every social movement, to convince people that there is still good in this world.[141]

Dinata's choice of costume is perhaps the opposite of the 'total confidence' and 'absolute moral certainty' that Barbara Brownie and Danny Graydon observe in most superhero costumes.[142]

Instead, the power of his costume resides in its 'dual identity' – Vader's struggle for good and evil – that creates 'a vivid spectacle of otherness'.[143] In selecting this costume, which has been worn widely, 'from a social charity event to a mass theatrical street campaign for tobacco control', Dinata was also keen to make 'a point that sometimes what matters is not only what we say, but how we say it. The theatricality of my costume might be unnecessary for some, but actually it breaks through the "rigid" images of "serious" social rallies, and encouraged people to also enjoy expressing themselves.' He plans to wear the costume in more 'social rallies' and wants 'to keep spreading my touch of theatricality, and hopefully it will encourage more people to find more hopes amongst fantasy'.[144]

In many of the American marches Carrie Fisher's *Star Wars* character Princess Leia was invoked as a symbol of female resistance. Dinata connected with this when he carried a placard that read, 'A Woman's Place is in the Resistance.' However, the wearing of such a polyvalent costume, which has been worn to champion multiple causes, raises questions about the successful reception of Dinata's chosen character.[145] His costume emphasizes how the choice of fancy dress for a protest involves a balance – however perceptible this is to the wearer – between an outfit that makes a clear statement to a spectator, and an outfit that empowers the participant, who is often standing against 'authority, stability, sobriety, immutability, and immortality'.[146] Lindsay Schober, for example, was aware of the compromises that her costume represented: 'My friend and I were both wishing that our costumes could have been complete. [On the] one hand, we wanted to rebel and put them on. On the other hand, we did not want to draw negative attention or do anything that could escalate an already tense situation.'[147] Dinata clarified his choice of Darth Vader costume by explaining that when wearing it he felt like he had 'empowered' himself

> and the other March participants around me. And unlike many other people would assume, there was no alter ego. I even felt more myself than ever within the costume. Moreover, my experience on the March itself has brought more memorable meanings to my costume. I can probably say that my costume is the armour that I have worn to many battlefields in the quest for justice.[148]

For Alli Sebastian Wolf, wearing her costume was a 'special feeling'. It enabled her, first, to quiet misgivings about her physical appearance and, second, to present her artwork more clearly because her role as creator was anonymized. She reflected that:

> I love the anonymity of it – like many women I've been taught to be uncomfortable with my appearance and with getting attention, but in the costume I'm able to be in the spotlight without the spotlight being on me – it's on the artwork and the ideas surrounding it. Getting to be invisible while making the clitoris highly visible is quite empowering.[149]

Wolf and Dinata believe their costumes were successful because their conventional identities were effaced; their costumes were of greater importance than themselves. The character of the wearer needed to recede in order for them to be successfully interpreted. These thoughts elide with discussions in earlier chapters, notably concerning Western African fancy dress and Ku-Klux Klan costumes, where the perceived effectiveness of fancy dress, both for its wearer and immediate audience, is predicated on a temporary attainment of complete anonymity. This is not to suggest the wearers sought to disguise themselves, for their costumes were highly conspicuous, but that the messages conveyed by the costume were more likely to be unambiguous if they were not simultaneously conflated with the character traits of the wearer.

In 2017, people the world over participated in women's marches for different reasons. For some, fancy dress costume elucidated personal feelings. For others, it was deemed inappropriate. For a few people who dressed up, the costumes they wore temporarily effaced their conventional identity, and this was welcome and heightened their self-esteem. Many others rejected wearing any form of fancy dress costume. The reflections of participants emphasize that fancy dress is polyvalent. This makes it powerful and problematic communicator to spectators. The commentaries also make it clear that a primary function of the costumes was to reassure the wearer that their public performance, which manifested their grievances, would act as catalyst for dialogue and change.

Fancy dress - To champion

The imagination and incongruity of fancy dress costume heightens the place of the individual within social and political relationships and has long been used to champion social and political causes. Ostensibly, fancy dress enables concerned citizens and social movements to secure people's attention and to convey their messages with greater ease. The reality is more complex and costume can hinder as much as help the championing of causes. Five points emerge.

First, people who desire to convey a message whilst being part of a social movement consider fancy dress costume to be an integral component in making their communication effective. This is chiefly because its creativity garners attention and is thought to render complex ideas clear.

Second, an important function, and consequence, of fancy dress costume is the empowerment of its wearer and, perhaps, those around them because strangers are united when conventional symbols of status are anonymized.

Third, dressing up helps individuals to situate themselves within a social movement through the communal adoption of identical symbols – like the pussy hat – or use of similar motifs and colours – like those from the Rainbow Flag and Suffragette banner. Whilst this can be invigorating, it provides opportunities for individual narratives to be championed that may differ to the movement's purpose. This observation chimes with Graham Willett's remark about social movements,

> which are not lobby groups or political parties – indeed, they are not organisations at all. Rather they are processes of activity, and networks of those who undertake it. The plurals here (networks, processes) are important: social movements are irreducibly composed of a multitude of networks, groups and organisations, a diversity of ideas, strategies and beliefs, a variety of forms of action.[150]

Fourth, despite acting as a conduit to clarify and communicate personal feelings, fancy dress is widely considered to be comic and irreverent. Consequently, the presence of costumed participants can jeopardize and obfuscate messages of social movements.

Fifth, the anonymization or emphasis that fancy dress costume provides to its wearer's (sexual) identity underscores Alison Bancroft's observation that the body has become an impossible site of gendered authority. It 'contradicts the tendency towards anatomical and biological determinism that underpins many social attitudes towards men and women'.[151] This may go some way to explain the use of fancy dress costume by social movements seeking to challenge social and political marginalization on the basis of malevolence and misunderstandings related to gender, sex and sexual orientation.

Epilogue - ... To Catwalk

In the final months of writing this book, the global prevalence of fancy dress costume seemed hard to dispute. On 28 November 2017, Sotheby's in London, auctioned three oil paintings by twentieth-century Russian artist Alexandra Exter that depict imagined scenes of the Venetian carnival. The combined lot sold for £780,500.[1] Between September 2017 and February 2018, fashion designer Walter Van Beirendonck curated 'PowerMask – The Power of Masks' in Rotterdam's Wereld Museum.[2] Returning to London, the Victoria & Albert Museum's 'The Future Starts Here' exhibition, which ran between May and November 2018, featured its newly acquired Pussy Power Hat, 'a knitting pattern that defied a president'.[3] Antanas Mockus's Super Citizen Suit also featured. This red and yellow lyrca costume, in the style of Superman's outfit, is emblazoned with a red 'C' – for 'Citizen' – across the torso. Mockus wore the ensemble when major of Bogotá, Mexico, to undertake work within local communities to 'set an example of what responsible citizenship might entail'.[4] In April 2018, Limerick-based artist Rachel Fallon used her Power Aprons to champion the repeal of the Eighth Amendment from Ireland's constitution, which criminalized abortion. Drawing on the cultural history of the apron, as a symbol of domesticity and a means to ward off evil, Fallon's hand-made garments made a potent statement about a woman's right to choose what happens to her body.[5] In the August issue of Australia's *Harper's Bazaar*, Jamie Huckbody discussed contemporary catwalk collections that conjure with the grotesque, unusual and 'ugly'.[6] My final day of editing, 5 November – Bonfire Night – sees people in Britain don fancy dress and burn costumed guys to commemorate the foiling of the Gunpowder Plot.[7]

Contrasting examples can be cited to show how the ubiquity of fancy dress costume creates unease and triggers a Newtonian response to ensure it can be policed. Three stories that appeared in British newspapers on consecutive days in October 2018 stand out. On 10 October, Hadley Freeman, writing in *The Guardian*, censured Melania Trump's choice of clothing on a visit to Africa. She likened the wardrobe of the United States of America's First Lady to an 'Out of Africa cosplay tour'.[8] In so doing, Freeman denigrated cosplay with the implication that it is inherently comic and trivial. On 11 October, Kashmira Gander in *The Independent* proffered advice about the insensitive Halloween costumes people should avoid. Readers were cautioned not to black up, not to dress as Anne Frank, and not to 'dress as Caitlyn Jenner or any other trans person'.[9] On 12 October, Rosemary Bennett, writing in *The Times*, reported that the University of Kent student union was introducing a fancy dress policy to guide against politically offensive costumes.[10] The remarks of Gander and Bennett implicitly criticize dress up by suggesting it depends on cultural appropriation and stereotyping. Proximity to Halloween frames the three commentaries, but they underscore how fancy dress costume is at once mainstream and marginal.

These global examples, sartorial snapshots from a twelve-month period, exemplify the contemporary prevalence, popularity, and problematic nature of dressing up. Previous chapters have considered the affectiveness of this sartorial form across different chronologies, cultures and geographies and elucidate it how can cohere, challenge, clarify and champion. Advocating a diachronic approach, and consequently prioritizing breadth over depth, I have sought to identify the attitudes and actions that define fancy dress as a distinct form of costume and cultural expression. Whilst this means that fancy dress costume has been considered apart from other forms of dress and some aspects of the sartorial form have been discussed briefly, I consider this a satisfactory compromise if we are closer to understanding the place dressing up occupies within global cultures and are more able, even willing, to comprehend how something long regarded as 'socially peripheral', to recall Barbara Babcock's words, is 'symbolically central'. In this final section, it remains to tackle the disconnect between the perception and practice of fancy dress costume.

Conclusions

The juxtaposition of fancy dress examples in this book has identified themes within chapters, and these have been summarized at the end each. Themes have also emerged between chapters. This is because the performance of fancy dress is motivated by, and will demonstrate, more than one of the four archetypes that I use to define this sartorial form, even if one of them usually predominates. To bring the threads of this book together, and to identify priorities for further research, in which fancy dress costume can be more readily studied alongside other forms of cultural expression and dress, five summary points can be made. First, communities use fancy dress costume to explore contemporary issues – the zeitgeist – and to probe the strength of its interpersonal bonds. The imagination and incongruity of this sartorial form, combined with its accessibility, means that people of different age, sex, status and society can utilize it to express, immediately, feelings that might be difficult to convey through other forms of dress – or other mediums entirely – because of social censure. The cultural prevalence and chronological persistence of harlequin and pierrot is one example that shows how fancy dress costume can assist the urgent exploration of widely held and complex ideas that could be harmful to communicate in a direct manner (Chapter 3). The shifting status of harlequin and pierrot, as much the instance of sailors cross-dressing in the First World War (Chapter 3), also emphasizes how the role and meaning of fancy dress costume becomes critical during periods of social disruption where people perceive their place in society to be threatened (Chapter 4). Sociologist Fred Davis cautions against the deceptive convenience of connecting clothing trends and changes with periods of pronounced social and political turmoil.[11] More fundamentally, Joanne Finkelstein questions the cohesiveness between individual and society. She suggests 'the modern self ... can no longer be regarded as a basis of social and personal stability' because it has become an 'ultimate value'.[12]

> How one looks, feels, presents oneself and how well one understands one's proclivities and idiosyncrasies, have been elevated in importance above one's abilities to act collectively or be engaged by the interests of a community. Thus, the value attributed to the representation

of the self has the subversive effect of weakening the individual's interest in the political and communal activities of the public domain.[13]

Whilst the individual has come to assume greater importance over the community, particularly in the west, the episodes of fancy dress considered in the book indicate that a connection between notions of self and society remains and fancy dress is an important means of conveying this (Chapters 3 and 4). Further research may confirm what this suggests: the growing number of social movements that involve fancy dress costume during the first half of the twenty-first century is symptomatic of a correlative desire to strengthen interpersonal bonds in response to feelings of social and political malaise.

Second, many of the examples considered within the book, from the fancy dress worn by Princess Alexandra and her daughters (Chapter 1), Gustaf III's regicides (Chapter 2), the attendees of Germany's homosexual balls (Chapter 3) and the participants in the women's marches of 2017 (Chapter 4), emphasize the importance of world making in the performance of fancy dress. This suggests that whilst fancy dress can appear loud and confident, sometimes comic, other times aggressive, the role of an audience is largely secondary. Spectators frame, and consequently legitimize, a dialogue the costume wearer is having internally or with a specific group of people that are most likely to sympathize with their views. The paradox of a deeply personal means of expression being performed in public underscores one of the main ambiguities of this sartorial form. The dynamic tension between the personal and public nature of dressing up explains the polyvalence of this costume, its potential to create misunderstanding and the inclination to trivialize it. As many studies of clothing and human performance are influenced by Goffman's belief in an 'interactional *modus vivendi*' to facilitate effective public relationships, this may be why fancy dress has been marginalized in academic discussion.[14] An inability to decipher a fancy dress costume appears greater among people who are not its intended audience – journalists at the Devonshire ball (Chapter 1) – but intended recipients can also need elucidation – victims of the nineteenth-century Ku-Klux Klan (Chapter 2) and spectators at Sydney's Mardi Gras (Chapter 4).

Third, the ambiguities and polyvalence of fancy dress costume are insightful for reflecting the complexity of contemporary attitudes towards the human body. In *The Body in History*, John Robb and Oliver Harris observe how '[t]he body is society made flesh ... it is always as intricate as society'.[15] They argue that human bodies contain 'inherently antithetical possibilities' and that this has caused a 'long-term evolutionary success of confusion' about what they are and can be.[16] Their writing is useful for thinking about the body enclothed in fancy dress costume because the relationship between dressing up and humans is ambivalent, both physically and figuratively. Physically – materially, tangibly – the relationship between fancy dress and the body poses conundrums because costumes can simultaneously amplify and efface their wearer's conventional identity. The juxtaposition between Princess Alexandra and Alli Sebastian Wolf is particularly striking. Both women sought to define their feminine authority through their choice of fancy dress costume, but where Alexandra's gown emphasized her silhouette and sex, Wolf believed the efficacy of her message would be enhanced if her identity was wholly concealed (Chapters 1 and 4). The personal quandary that arises from the effacement of physical identity by dressing up is perhaps greatest for Gustaf III, who tried to maintain his royal presence when his two bodies – one natural, the other political – were threatened by regicides (Chapter 2). Visible or veiled, fancy dress also alters the way human bodies move. The circumstances in which costumes are worn – from the 'great rooms too crowded' at the Devonshire Ball (Chapter 1), to the barricaded streets of Sydney's Mardi Gras (Chapter 4) – interrupt conventional notions of distance between people, bringing them atypically close or keeping them artificially apart. Fancy dress costume can also cause physical discomfort, as per the 'bull' outfit discussed in Chapter 3, which curtailed its wearer's vision. They can also be cumbersome, as in the case of Peter Tully's Mardi Gras costume with its layers of decoration (Chapter 4).

Material factors shape figurative understandings of the costumed body and highlight oddities. For example, members of the nineteenth-century Ku-Klux Klan established a physical and metaphysical distance from their bodies when they wore female attire over their conventional gendered clothing and appeared in the dress of both sexes simultaneously (Chapter 2). The Swedish regicides who attacked Gustaf III enclothed their bodies to anonymize their conventional identity. Doubtless this was to avoid identification, but it also quietened their mental anguish and emboldened them (Chapter 2). Finally, there is the puzzlement that whilst the conception and wearing of fancy dress costume is often expressive of deeply held personal feelings, its creation is typically entrusted to a third party. The reason for this is probably prosaic: wearers lack clothes-making skills. Nevertheless, even when some ability is discernible and a costume is hand-made, there is a tendency for its design to follow trends. This is apparent with the Good Fortune outfit discussed in chapter one.[17] This garment emphasizes how fancy dress costume is, in this regard, no different to conventional articles of clothing that reflect contemporary fashions. From the twentieth century, personal authorship of costumes appears to have waned as fancy dress garments and accessories were increasingly selected from catalogues or hangers in a shop; many were hired, worn and returned, for the process to be repeated by somebody else on another occasion. The acquisition of a fancy dress costume in the west is therefore markedly different to that in Africa where many are still hand-made and are believed to possess a numinous significance that alters the body and bearing of its wearer.[18] Robb and Harris's term 'body world' is useful for contemplating the various issues summarized here. Highlighting the many ways human bodies can be understood, and implicitly encouraging diachronic analysis, body world expresses the full range of physical and figurative, conscious and subconscious, experiences and depictions of the body that exist across different chronologies and cultures.[19]

Fourth, compelling as they have been since at least the eighteenth century, deterministic discussions about the affectiveness of fancy dress costume are overly simplistic. Whilst some empirical studies do suggest that costume impinges upon its wearer, altering their conduct through deinviduation, the examples considered in this book suggest the relationship between wearers and their costumed wardrobes is symbiotic: the affectiveness and communicative potential of a fancy dress performance is shaped by both. Evidence that suggests fancy dress costume exerts a malevolent influence, enunciates its wearer's negative characteristics, and is consequently a form of spectacle, tends to be expressed by critics, and this provenance needs to be recognized (Chapters 3 and 4).

Fifth, fancy dress costume is a medium through which communities express the importance of their youngest members. Some of the earliest recorded examples of fancy dress costume involve children – typically males – masquerading as temporary religious and political leaders. Today, this sentiment is evident in Europe and the United States of America when adults dress juveniles in costume to proclaim and affirm their allegiances (Chapters 1 and 3). The emphasis on the young is similarly apparent in West African fancy dress (Chapter 1). The apparent centrality of children and adolescents within costumed events provides an important indication of the enduring interpersonal bonds that exist in many global communities. Of course, young people who wear fancy dress costume are not always avatars, directed by the significant adults in their lives. Socially and politically dependant, and typically lacking personal agency, examples throughout this book suggest young people are likely to recognize, and seize, the possibilities of a performative and communicative medium that facilitates the expression of non-normative attitudes. In the twenty-first century, it is noteworthy that younger people have appeared preponderant in social movements that involve fancy dress to question the causes and consequences of economic, political and social change. World making that enables people to clarify their personal and public roles may have a particular appeal for the young, who possess limited social authority (Chapter 4). The complex relationship between fancy dress costume and the 'inherently antithetical possibilities' of the body may also be grasped more readily by younger people, who might be better able to intuit how 'innovation after innovation threatens "natural" boundaries such as the differences between humans, animals and machines'.[20] They are at least more likely to be affected by these changes in their lives.

Derived from diachronic and global reflections on four archetypes of fancy dress costume, my contention is that these five observations can elucidate the shifting meaning and place of this sartorial form from the Middle Ages to modernity. They identify those aspects that make fancy dress a distinct form of costume and can guide discussion about its global persistence. The utility of these observations is apparent by considering two contemporary and globally prevalent examples of fancy dress: the simultaneous growth of cosplay and the emergence of 'critical' and 'experimental' fashions on the catwalk. Conceived as final case studies to explicate the conclusions of this near thousand-year study, the ensuing discussion seeks to emphasize how marginalization of fancy dress costume is a consequence of perception rather than practice.

Cosplay

Possibly originating in Japan, cosplay became globally established during the 1980s.[21] It is perhaps conventionally understood as the imitation of dress and behaviour by fans of fictional, often animated, characters. These acts of simulation typically occur within urban-based conventions that involve hundreds, sometimes thousands, of costumed participants, or fans.[22] Since 2003, the World Cosplay Summit has provided an international forum for cosplayers to congregate and compete.[23] The modelling of characters within cosplay to 'explore and articulate' individual identity is experienced differently between the east and west. In Japan, Cathy Sell observes that 'performances are generally limited to emulating the character's signature pose or reciting their motto'. Skits involving the character, 'which allows space for creativity' in masquerades and parades, are more common in the west.[24] Whatever their cultural circumstances, performances of cosplay are as varied as participants' motivations. In her study of the Japanese Lolita, Thèresa Winge draws attention to 'young women and men who dress as anachronistic visual representations of Victorian-era dolls, covered from head to toe in lace, ruffles and bows'.[25] Frenchy Lunning highlights 'the fancy phenomenon' in America, 'an emerging costume-play movement that has its roots in reenactment and character cosplay, but which has exploded into a panoply of costume genres, periods, and styles performed globally in off-beat public places'.[26] Barbara Brownie argues that cosplay has been co-opted by a new generation of males who have turned the feminized performance of dressing up and the domesticated activity of making costumes into a 'rights-of-passage on the path towards masculinity'.[27] More broadly, Craig Norris and Jason Bainbridge suggest that cosplay is similar to drag because of the challenge it poses: 'it is not merely an act of becoming a particular character, or marking out a particular alignment, but of *disruption*. This is the "play" in "cosplay", a play with identity and, more often, a play with *gender* identity.'[28] Joel Gn is equivocal. Acknowledging the complex relationship between dressing up and the human body, he argues that the mimicked outfit and performance is 'not a portrait of anatomical sex' but a synthesis of gender roles.[29] Consequently, he downplays the 'gender politics' of cosplay and argues that its performance is 'an expression of emotional attachment of the animated body'.[30]

Debates about the cultural place and meaning of cosplay problematize academics' discontinuous study of fancy dress. Distinctions that identify cosplay as a specific form of costume requiring scholarly investigation probably stem from the fact that regular conventions provide a focus for comparison. Ostensibly, this makes themes and trends discernible and verifiable. National and international structures, physical and web-based networks that facilitate cosplay performances presumably make these occasions 'serious' and people's participation affective. Whilst these speculations may be accurate, they nonetheless indicate that differing treatment of cosplay and fancy dress is arbitrary. The issues academics raise about cosplay, still more the comments of cosplayers, suggest these performances are analogous to the fancy dress examples considered in this book, particularly those considered in chapter four.

Cosplayers stress the importance of interpersonal bonds and the psychological boost their costume provides. British cosplayer Victoria Johnson, interviewed as part of a BBC Radio 4 documentary about cosplay, opines:

> There's a huge sense of community, there's family. We all support each other; if things are tough, there will always be someone to rally round, in the same way that any community who share a sport or hobby will always be there for one another. For me, it's given me confidence, self-esteem. It's given me a focus to actually do something with my life.[31]

The community Johnson refers to is global and extends beyond the fixed time and span of conventions. Twenty-one-year-old American Andy Bruening meets 'with friends at completely normal places such as the mall, or a restaurant in more casual cosplay: wig, makeup, and contemporary clothing [where they] hang out and have fun.'[32] Eighteen-year-old Austrian Elisabeth Frank wears her costume 'with friends to get coffee.' Sometimes, they take photographs in their costumes, although she concedes this is 'mostly in rather secluded areas'.[33] Frank also acknowledges the appeal of developing an online following, which incentivizes her to create multiple characters and to feel a greater sense of belonging; '[i]t's just nice to be more included in the community, especially if you'd like to form a cosplay group.'[34] Twenty-eight-year-old British cosplayer Basil Waite wears his Tom Holland Spiderman or Newt Scamander costume for charity work. He has 'helped a young boy through an operation, visited children in hospitals and care homes and appeared at disabled childrens' birthdays'.[35]

Academics have been cautious when discussing the emotional and psychological salve that cosplay provides as a form of world making. By contrast, participants are generally open about what they perceive to be one of its main attractions. Waite describes himself as 'a skinny nerd'. He chose to cosplay Spiderman and Newt Scamander because they have a similar build to him. He also thinks they share a deeper personal connection. As 'skinny awkward young men', Waite suggests his characters 'are probably on the spectrum (I have ADHD) and so it doesn't take much for me to relate to or embody those particular people'.[36] Frank says she is an 'extroverted person' but Fenris, from video game *Dragon Age II*, enables her to be 'a bit more brash and sarcastic'. Cecil Palmer, the fictional presenter of podcast *Night Vale*, 'is just way weirder than I'd ever be in public'.[37] Ronnie Marshall, an eighteen-year-old British cosplayer dresses as Joker from Suicide Squad and Dick Grayson from DC Comics' *Batman* series. Grayson is his 'absolute favourite'.[38] He feels he can 'relate emotionally to him as we both have similar personalities'.[39]

Wearing his costume, he 'honestly feel[s] like a new person, and ... gain[s] lots of confidence'.[40] The ability of cosplay to help people articulate feelings and opinions they would otherwise struggle to convey publicly is an important factor in its global prevalence. Why cosplay should facilitate a deeper expression of personality, particularly for the young, is elucidated by Norbert Elias's discussion of 'youth culture'. Elias argues that the preparation for adulthood and gainful employment becomes longer as society becomes more complex, with the implication that biologically mature people can remain socially immature and become frustrated. A prolonged novitiate potentially causes long-term imbalances within people's personality.[41] Cosplay is not a social aberration, but it does seem to be a conduit through which younger people (research by Winge suggests specifically young women[42]), and perhaps those who perceive themselves to be socially peripheral, seek to communicate.[43]

The psychological importance attached to cosplay is evidenced by the time people spend planning, sourcing and constructing their costumes. Frank can spend up to 200 hours making a costume, which is equivalent to the creation of an *haute couture* garment.[44] Bruening spent two years and employed three different methods to make the overcoat of Gundham Tanaka, a character in video game franchise *Danganronpa*.[45] American Becka Noel, who describes herself as a 'full-time cosplayer', spends anywhere from 'a week to a couple of months' making a costume.[46] The investment of time is necessary because cosplayers tend to construct garments in their entirety and use a variety of construction materials, including wonderflex, fosshape 300, worbla, clear vinyl, cotton and linen.[47] Generally, they also have small budgets, in the region of £25 to £45 per costume, although sums closer to £1,000 are not unheard of.[48] Frugality necessitates effort to produce a garment that resembles its exemplar. The process of putting on costumes can also take considerable time, from thirty minutes to two hours. Bruening takes up to one hour to dress as Shouto Todoroki, a character from the anime series *My Hero Academia*: 'I use professional SFX burn techniques in the makeup, and then heavily dull the vibrant color of the burn to make it more contingent [*sic.*] to the character in the series, who has a very light red opaque scar on the left side of his face.'[49] Bruening's thoroughness may arise from his professional role as a costume designer and technician, although Frank suggests her costume can take 'about an hour, sometimes a bit longer', to put on to her satisfaction.[50]

Attention to detail galvanizes cosplayers and confers a sense of control over their performance, but it is also a source of vulnerability. 'Accuracy shame' has blighted recent competitions and affects the confidence and psychological well-being of the wearer.[51] Bruening recalled a negative experience when he first cosplayed Takashi 'Shiro' Shirogane from the cartoon series Voltron *Legendary Defenders*. It stemmed from a remark about the perceived inaccuracy of his costume:

> I had multiple people outwardly express disinterest in how I did his makeup. And the common theme was my lack of doing an "exaggerated winged eyeliner." At the time I shook off the negativity, but I eventually came forward to discuss it in a 'Cosplay Elitism Panel' at an anime convention in early May 2018. Where I explained "Shiro is a canonically Asian character, doing such an elongated winged eyeliner can thin out the look of the eye and can be perceived as racist ... I [also] like to add my own personal touch to my makeup. When you do such an exaggerated winged eyeliner, it can make your features more feminine, which is counter-productive for a very masculine character such as Shiro."[52]

This incident reveals the multiple layers of identity and representation that can exist within cosplaying. It also emphasizes the ambiguity of the body enclothed in costume. Bruening attempted to balance his desire for accuracy against a concern that Shiro's fictional traits would become problematized when imitated in reality. Simultaneously, he tried to establish a compromise between his desire to convey the persona of a fictional character authentically and an urge to express his identity. For other cosplayers accountability means becoming the truest embodiment of their chosen character, and entirely effacing their own identity. Thirty-six-year-old Londoner Lee Self owns 'around ten' different Spider Man suits.[53] When he wears his costume he feels 'empowered' and 'responsible', like Dinata in his Darth Vader suit.[54] He wants people to 'believe they are seeing Spider Man'.[55] When I asked him what he finds most frustrating about his experience of cosplay, he said it was people who 'portray characters but who don't uphold the values those characters represent'.[56]

In the case of thirty-year-old Austrian Deagal Remyr, who cosplays Captain Jack Sparrow from the Disney film franchise *Pirates of the Caribbean*, the negation of his conventional identity expands his personal frame of action and gives him greater self-esteem, much like Ronnie Marshall. Twice-weekly, he hosts 'livestream Jack Sparrow taverns' in which he dresses as the pirate, 'drink[s] rum, babble[s] philosophical stuff and play[s] pirate songs in an online tavern'; Mondays in English, Thursdays in German.[57] Remyr, who has been performing the character for five years after friends said he 'looked and played the part really well', 'enjoys being Jack Sparrow':

> The character is soooo much fun to play and gives me the possibility to do pretty much anything … From quite a lot of occasions I have learned that many people value their Jack Sparrow encounter with me far more than I would have guessed beforehand. That adds a great deal to my self worth and keeps me going.[58]

Remyr's experience underscores how the affectiveness of fancy dress costume is predicated on a symbiotic relationship between wearer and their wardrobe.

In sum, cosplay appears culturally prevalent and symbolically central because of its ability to reflect a community's concerns and interpersonal bonds, to facilitate personal reflection, and to mediate contemporary attitudes towards the body and the young. It is analogous to the examples of fancy dress costume considered in this book. By studying cosplay in conjunction with other forms of dressing up, rather than in isolation to them, its contemporary relevance and growth also becomes clearer. A similar observation can be made of the work of modern and contemporary fashion designers who conjure with what Jamie Huckbody has recently labelled 'ugly' fashion.

Catwalk

To suggest a connection between fancy dress costume and fashion is not contentious. In the eighteenth century popular vogues, from hussar uniforms to women's hairstyles, were adapted and parodied by people dressing up.[59] During the eighteenth and nineteenth centuries, historic clothing became fancy dress as people wore reimagined aristocratic garments, civil and official uniforms to costumed entertainments. They still do. Unusual outfits also drew comparisons with dressing up. The elaborate coronation robes worn by Britain's George IV in 1821 were likened to 'fancy dress' by Sir Walter Scott.[60] Similar observations are made in the present. In 1997, Lee Alexander McQueen reflected that the pony skin jacket with impala horn shoulders from his autumn/winter collection, 'It's a Jungle Out There' could be considered costume, 'but it's costume with a deadly meaning'.[61] In the twentieth and twenty-first centuries, the influence of fancy dress on modern and contemporary fashions looks to be apparent in the collections of many of the world's leading designers, from the incongruous shapes envisaged by Rei Kawakubo to the bold colours of Walter Van Beirendonck and the playful presentations of Thom Browne (Figure 45). Commentaries often describe the appearance and affect of contemporary fashions in similar terms to fancy dress. Sibling's knitted clothing has been characterized as a 'gaudy orgasmic overload of decorative abandon' that is 'fun and moving' and 'transcends fashion'.[62] Craig Green's clothes are 'notorious for their dramatic and deeply emotive qualities' and possess an 'otherworldly aesthetic'.[63] The prevalence of what has been variously described as 'ugly' and 'deconstructivist' fashion has encouraged scholars to consider the role of the 'carnivalesque' and 'grotesque' in modern and contemporary clothing. In 2017, two terms were presented to frame these enquiries: critical fashion and experimental fashion.

Adam Geczy and Vicki Karaminas use the term critical fashion to explain the genesis of the interrogative and evaluative role they believe fashion now possesses. They contend that the populism of art and art criticism, which increased from the nineteenth century and became more apparent during the 1990s when art's 'collusion with the media, and its gravitational pull to mass appeal, became cornerstones of the art world'.[64] The 'devolution' of art's 'criticality' occurred in direct correlation.[65] The commentative role that art relinquished was taken up by fashion and dress.[66] Critical faculties do not exist within all garments and the authors describe items of clothing characterized by 'usefulness' and 'unobtrusiveness' as 'hermetic fashion', a broad category that includes 'The T-Shirt, the suit, the black dress'.[67] Critical fashion denotes items

FIGURE 45 *Photograph of Thom Browne catwalk show for Spring/Summer 2019 at Paris Fashion Week Womenswear. © Victor Virgile/Getty Images.*

of dress where signification is 'stretched and exaggerated', where it is 'obtrusive and extension, unconventional'.[68] Geczy and Karaminas discuss the work of ten fashion designers to explain how critical fashion manifests itself, including Rei Kawakubo, Gareth Pugh, Viktor & Rolf, Rick Owens, Walter Van Beirendonck and McQueen. Bakhtin's writing superficially informs the analysis of work by Pugh and Van Beirendonck, where reference is made to carnival's inversion of quotidian norms and the existence of polyvalent clowns – 'the human embodiments of carnival' – whose form influences Pugh's silhouettes and Van Beirendonck's interest in avatars.[69]

Granata's concept of experimental fashion evolved parallel to Geczy's and Karaminas's work and consequently makes no reference to critical fashion. Focusing on a short chronological period, from the 1980s to the start of the Millennium, she is specifically concerned to explain the emergence of 'undisciplined' bodies on the catwalk that 'upset gender bodily norms and rules of propriety and beauty'.[70] There is no suggestion that experimental fashion emerged because of critical limitations within the arts. Granata asserts that 'fashion should be interpreted on a par with other aspects of visual and material culture as a constitutive and influential part of culture'.[71] However, in postulating that 'globalisation and the condition of otherness and estrangement developed by living cross-culturally is central to the development of grotesque imagery within fashion', it is implied that the role of the arts, and design in particular, has changed in the twentieth century, perhaps enabling fashion to assume a more important position.[72] Granata suggests that experimental fashions proliferated in the 1980s because they were adept at challenging 'normative discourses', chiefly with regards to 'feminism's desire to open up and question gender and bodily roles'.[73] They could also mediate 'fears of contagion and the obsessive moral policing of bodily borders' in response to the AIDS epidemic.[74] Her analysis includes some of the same designers discussed by Geczy and Karaminas, notably Kawakubo and Beirendonck.

The simultaneous and parallel definition of these terms emphasizes the discontinuous nature of academic engagement with costume (broadly) and fancy dress (specifically). Fundamentally, neither of these concepts refers to fancy dress costume, despite mentioning occasions where it was worn – carnival and the 1980s club scene – and defining critical and experimental fashion in accord with the observations I make above. The marginalization of fancy dress costume exposes the problematic consequences of academics' continued disavowal of this sartorial form. Neither of the two terms is globally applicable and both have serious, if not deleterious, lacunae. It is particularly notable that neither study dwells on the age of people wearing critical and experimental fashions. Contributors to Huckbody's discussion of 'ugly' fashion – a term I consider analogous to 'critical' and 'experimental' – assert how young people – Millennials specifically – adopt incongruous styles of dress to create an authentic identity and to repudiate outdated concepts of beauty. He argues, 'for Millennials exploring fashion's dressing-up box, this means a revival of clothing previously relegated to the naughty step'.[75] Kathleen Burcema, womenswear buyer for *Harrods*, concurs, suggesting, '[t]he shift to the absurd or weird or "ugly" is more relatable to the Millennial generation's idea of street cool. It's a zone they feel comfortable in.'[76] 'Millennial' is an ambiguous term, which Huckbody does not define, but it is interesting that akin to fancy dress costume, 'ugly' fashions – 'critical' and 'experimental', also – appear to enable younger people to articulate personal feelings with acuity.

Specific queries can also be raised. The tendency of fancy dress wearers to critique and lampoon contemporary issues, people and clothing is notable before the popularization of art, which Geczy and Karaminas consider a turning point in the emergence of critical fashion. Moreover, the interrogative qualities of fancy dress costume are apparent in West Africa before the nineteenth century, and here the democratization of art is not a factor. The authors' use of Bakhtin's work on carnival should also be questioned because they make no reference to *The Problems of Dostoevsky's Poetics*. Published five years before *Rabelais and his World*, Bakhtin's second book expresses scepticism about the role of modern carnival. It is dismissive of the 'narrow theatrical-pageantry concept of carnival', which informs elements of Geczy's and Karaminas's argument.[77] These observations do not jeopardize the idea of critical fashion, but they suggest that explicit consideration of fancy dress costume could clarify the development of this term, and the role of the clothing it purports to describe, to make it more robust and globally applicable. Clarification and amplification would also facilitate inclusion of Granata's experimental fashion. Here, too, the omission of fancy dress costume gives rise to several queries. The tendency of disruptive social and political events to 'upset' norms and rules in dress is apparent in fancy dress before the 1980s. Moreover, the connection between upheaval and sartorial disruption is apparent in Africa as much as Europe and the Americas. For example, in Agwa, Nigeria, performers, or 'hunch-backed' 'Diviners', appear costumed with perturbances that resemble 'a large hernia', which is considered amusing (Figure 46).[78] The similitude between this figure, the portly pierrot and the designs of Kawakubo, which Granata, Geczy and Karaminas all consider, is suggestive of the deeper, more complex cultural connections and exchanges than the concept of experimental fashion, or critical fashion, currently allows (Figure 47).[79]

The exclusion of fancy dress costume from these discussions reflects a cultural-cum-sartorial blind spot that pervades writing about the modern and contemporary catwalk. McQueen was unphased when he connected his catwalk collection with fancy dress costume, but his biographers have been more reserved. Major profiles of the designer do not mention his work at fancy dress costumer Angels.[80] Academics and commentators are not alone in downplaying the connection between costume and the catwalk. Some designers forcefully disavow the influence of fancy dress in their work, even when they appear patent. Walter Van Beirendonck, whom Geczy, Karaminas and Granata all reference, denies any association with dressing up.[81] This seems surprising following his curation of 'PowerMask', which included James Ensor's painting, *Skeleton Arresting Masquerade* of 1891, now in a private collection. The image unambiguously depicts seven costumed revellers from a masked ball.[82] African masquerade costumes, western carnival costumes and a series of head coverings associated with contemporary fancy dress entertainments, including that worn by Darth Vader in the *Star Wars* franchise and Ghostface from the *Scream* quartet, were also included in the exhibition. These objects were presented in an accompanying book that concluded European masquerades 'have been undergoing a renewal process for the past 30 years'.[83] The exhibition and book highlighted Charles Fréger's recent work photographing long-standing carnival traditions.[84] In view of the connections that exist between Beirendonck's work and fancy dress costume, the marginalization of the latter appears deliberate. In an interview with *Vestoj* journal, in which he discusses his 2003–4 collection 'Gender?', Beirendonck repudiates fancy dress costume because he considers it unserious:

> There's a thin line between being masculine and dressing up in women's clothes, which isn't what I wanted to end up with. I had to watch out for that line – otherwise you end up with something that's more like dressing up. I don't want to put that on the catwalk or even consider it; my work is a serious preposition for what men should wear.[85]

The aversion designers have towards fancy dress costume was recently underscored by a disruptive riposte staged by Luke Brooks and James Theseus Buck of Rottingdean Bazaar. In June 2018, the duo organized a catwalk show as part of London Fashion Week Men's that consisted solely of conceptual fancy dress costumes (Figure 48).[86] Models carried placards in

FIGURE 46 *Photograph of masker a* Nwa Dibia *Diviner or Diviner child from an Ekeleke masquerade,* *1983. © Herbert M. Cole.*

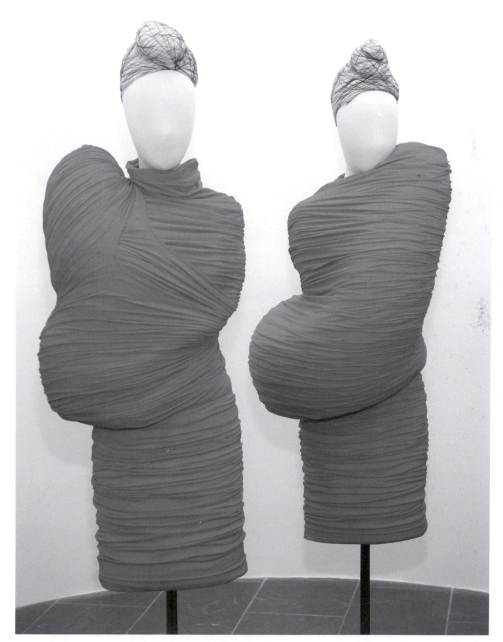

FIGURE 47 *Photograph of Rei Kawakubo/Comme des Garcons, 'Art of the In-Between' Costume Institute Gala, 2017. © Andrew Toth/FilmMagic/Getty Images.*

FIGURE 48 *Photograph of Rottingdean Bazaar MAN catwalk show for Spring/Summer 2019, 2018. © Jemal/Getty images.*

their right hands with the name and internet address of the regional suppliers from which the costume had been hired. The show, which included an anthropomorphic Christmas tree, corn cob, carrot and chicken, was conceived to 'twist' the concept of a fashion show and to exploit the fact that Brooks and Buck were without a public relations team and unable to loan the collection after the show, 'so if stylists want to borrow looks, they'll have to get in touch with the stores we hired them from. We found that quite funny'.[87] Relishing the incongruity of fancy dress costume, Brooks and Buck appeared to emphasize the unsuitably of dress up and fashion. More fundamentally, however, their show confirmed Babcock's premise that the socially peripheral is symbolically central; no longer was the elephant merely in the room, it was centre stage and spotlighted. In a less confrontational, but no less emphatic presentation, artist Bruce Asbestos makes a similar point in his autumn/winter 2018 collection, which does acknowledge the influence of dressing up.

In Asbestos's show, two looks were 'directly lifted from fancy dress'.[88] First, the 'carry me', which he describes as 'a cheap visual trick where you appear to be being carried by something else' (Figure 49). Second, 'traditional dress in the Black Forest, and the hats with the red pompoms'.[89] Asbestos conceived of his collection as an 'artist', which, he suggests, gave him a 'different set of hang ups' to a fashion designer:

> [Consequently], being associated with fancy-dress isn't a problem for me, I just needed enough variation in looks/quality so that I didn't feel it was only from the culture of fancy dress, I didn't want to limit it to that, or only talk about the status of fancy dress – I was trying to keep the reading of the work more open, more uncertain.[90]

Asbestos's approach to clothing design embraces fancy dress costume because of its 'lack of fashion feel, its intentional silliness'.[91] The perceived incongruity and polyvalence of this sartorial form attracted him, as it did Rottingdean Bazaar, for the reasons it deters most clothing designers.

Ostensibly, Asbestos's use of the catwalk is unconventional, chiefly because his presentation does not show clothes to augment a brand, to convey a lifestyle, or even really to sell. His online shop includes only two items from the autumn/winter presentation, an embroidered sweatshirt and T-shirt. Instead, Asbestos says he conceives of the catwalk as a 'strategy to make artwork ... that allows [a] merging of different contexts; street wear, high fashion, performance, theatre, art ... fancy dress'.[92] His models are 'performers wearing an artwork'.[93] They conform to his intentions as creator, express limited personal agency and are not necessarily comfortable in what they wear. Asbestos reflects that 'the[ir] outfit only needed to be comfortable enough to last the two minutes or so on the catwalk ... [W]hat the audience imagines or takes away was more interesting to me than the experience of the model'.[94] This was apparent when men and women walked with cardboard houses, complete with smoking chimneys, affixed to the vamp of their shoes, or had their feet encased within loaves of French-style bread.

Superficially, Asbestos's remarks are antithetical to those of Beirendonck, but the practices they describe are similar. It is their perceptions that differ: Asbestos is prepared to acknowledge the symbolic centrality of fancy dress costume, Beirendonck, whilst apparently interested in the sartorial form, is not. Asbestos's attitude towards the catwalk and the models who walk it, as much as Beirendonck's, reflect the theatricalization of the fashion show, championed most notably by McQueen in shows like Voss, but continued by many designers since, whom Geczy, Karaminas and Granata include in their discussions of critical fashion and experimental

FIGURE 49 *Photograph of 'Carry Me' for Bruce Asbestos Autumn/Winter 2018. Stylist: Helen McGuckin; MUA: Fyza; hand-painted backdrops: Rory Mullen; model: Kofi © Lucie Crewdson, photographer.*

fashion, respectively. All of the designs grouped under these terms seek to elucidate the concerns of their designer's community and to enquire about the strength of interpersonal bonds, to provide space for introspection, and to mediate contemporary attitudes towards the body and the young. The material and metaphysical gap between fancy dress costume and the catwalk is consequently diminished.

The perception that fancy dress is unserious jeopardies a deeper understanding of this sartorial form. The twelve examples of dressing up considered in this book, still more discussion of the global prevalence of cosplay and the emergence of what might be called catwalk subcultures or strategies in the twentieth and twenty-first centuries, show how this marginalization is problematic, perhaps even untenable. In the spirit of an investigative essay and recent endeavours to reappraise aspects of popular culture, to wrest them from obscurity and to query the appropriateness of socialized assumptions based on pre-twentieth-century scholarship, notably through exhibitions – a medium well suited to eschew academic equivocation – notably, the Barbican's 'The Vulgar: Fashion Redefined', the Met Breuer's 'Like Life: Sculpture, Color and the Body', and the Met's exhibition, Camp: Notes on Fashion – I hope sufficient evidence has been presented to substantiate my opening remarks that dressing up is compelling and never solely a laughing matter.[95]

NOTES

Introduction

1   Geoff W. Adams, *The Emperor Commodus: Gladiator, Hercules or Tyrant?* (Boca Raton: Brown Walker Press, 2013), 203–204.

2   See below, 129–136.

3   My understanding of 'dress' is informed by Joanne B. Eicher and Sandra Lee Evenson, *The Visible Self: Global Perspectives on Dress, Culture, and Society*, Fourth Edition (London and New York: Fairchild Books, 2015), 3–4. See also note 8.

4   I start this study in the Middle Ages because of a greater availability and variety of sources. Costumes in antiquity appear to have been worn predominantly for disguise. For example, Callipateria 'disguised herself exactly like a gymnastic trainer' at the Olympic Games (Pausanias, *Description of Greece*, tr. W.H.S. Jones and H.A. Ormerod (Loeb Classical Library, Cambridge, MA: Harvard University Press, 1918–1935), 5.6.8ff). In Aristophanes's play *Lysistrata*, women overthrow the male-dominated assembly by wearing men's clothing. The description of Emperor Nero dressing as a woman when he married a Greek male could constitute fancy dress costume (Tacitus, *The Annals*, tr. Alfred Jacob Church and William Jackson Brodribb (London: E. Clay, Sons and Taylor, 1876), 15.37). The same is true of the account of Alcibiades attending symposia dressed as a woman (Libanius fr.50.2.12–13). He was also buried in women's clothing (Plutarch, *Lives: Alcibiades*, tr. Bernadotte Perrin (Loeb Classical Library, Cambridge, MA: Harvard University Press, 1916), 39.7). In these cases, it is hard to establish the accuracy of the accounts.

5   Barbara A. Babcock, 'Introduction', *The Reversible World: Symbolic Inversion in Art and Society*, ed. Barbara A. Babcock (Ithaca and London: Cornell University Press, 1978), 32.

6   Rachel Hann, 'Debating Critical Costume: Negotiating Ideologies of Appearance, Performance and Disciplinarity', *Studies in Theatre and Performance*, 37:2 (2017), 1–17.

7   For example, Deborah Nadoolman Landis, *Filmcraft: Costume Design* (Lewes: Ilnex Press, 2017), 8.

8   In defining fancy dress costume, the following texts have been informative. Anthea Jarvis, 'Fancy Dress', *The Berg Companion to Fashion*, ed. Valerie Steele (Oxford: Bloomsbury Academic, 2010), 270–272'; Joanne B. Eicher, 'Clothing, Costume and Dress', ibid., 151–152; Thomas Hecht, 'Dance Costume', ibid., 195–199'; Frenchy Lunning, 'Cosplay', *Berg Encyclopedia of World Dress and Fashion: Global Perspectives*, ed. Joanne B. Eicher and Phyllis G. Tortora (Oxford: Berg, 2010), 185–190; Sandra Lee Evenson, 'Dress as Costume in Theater and Performing Arts', ibid., 136–145; Courtney Micots, "Fancy Dress: African Masquerade in Coastal Ghana." In Berg Encyclopedia of World Dress and Fashion: Africa, edited by Joanne B. Eicher and Doran H. Ross. Oxford: Berg Publishers, 2010. Accessed: June 2016. http://dx.doi.org/10.2752/BEWDF/EDch1511. Herbert M. Cole, 'Masquerade, Theater, Dance Costumes', ibid., 120–130; Susan Elizabeth Tselos, 'Creolised Costumes for Rara, Haiti', *Berg Encyclopedia of World Dress and Fashion: Latin America and the Caribbean*, ed. Margot Blum Schevill (Oxford: Bloomsbury Academic, 2005), 257–263; Alexandra B. Bonds, Dongshin Chang and Elizabeth Johnson, 'Performance Dress in China and Taiwan', *Berg Encyclopedia of World Dress and Fashion: East Asia*, ed. John E. Vollmer (Oxford: Berg Publishers, 2010), 153–161; Monica Bethe, 'Performance Dress in Japan', ibid., 404–410; Richard Schechner, *Performance Studies: An Introduction*. Second Edition (London: Routledge, 2006), 28–51, 123–169.

9   Enid Welsford, *The Court Masque: A Study in the Relationship between Poetry & The Revels* (Cambridge: Cambridge University Press, 1927), 126.

10 Aileen Ribeiro, *The Dress Worn at Masquerades in England, 1730 to 1790, and Its Relation to Fancy Dress in Portraiture* (New York & London: Garland Publishing, 1984), 275–278.

11 For example, one article in *The Gentleman's Magazine* of September 1897 refers to 'a fancy dress' to describe one garment at a dress-up ball (vol. 283, 231).

12 The Metropolitan Museum of Art designates items as 'fancy dress' in its catalogue. 'Fancy dress' is used in Donald Albrecht and Jeannie, ed., *Gilded New York: Design, Fashion, and Society* (New York: The Monacelli Press, 2013). There is a degree of fluidity. In recent years, Angels, the UK's largest supplier of fancy dress has noted an increase use of the term 'costume' by customers. The company's marketing director suggests that whilst 'fancy dress' remains widely understood, it is increasingly used to refer to patently comical characters like clowns. Themed dress-up inspired by films and long-standing cultural traditions tends to be described as 'costume' (personal communication, 12 December 2016).

13 The distinction between fancy dress costume and disguise is blurry; many accounts of fancy dress costume refer to 'disguise'. As Efrat Tseëlon notes, 'disguise' appears in the *Oxford English Dictionary*'s definition of mask, disguise and masquerade. 'Introduction: Masquerade and Identities', *Masquerade and Identities: Essays on Gender, Sexuality and Marginality*, ed. Efrat Tseëlon (London: Routledge, 2001), 2.

14 Gaius Suetonious Tranquillus, *The Twelve Caesars*, tr. Robert Graves (London: Penguin, [1957] 2007), 221–222; Richard Abels, *Alfred the Great: War, Kingship and Culture in Anglo-Saxon England* (London and New York: Longman, 1998), 158–159; Peter Longerich, *Heinrich Himmler: A Life*, tr. Jeremy Noakes and Lesley Sharpe (Oxford: Oxford University Press, 2012), 1–2.

15 Pat Poppy, 'Fancy Dress? Costume for Re-enactment', *Costume*, 31 (1997), 100–104. The author does consider re-enactment fancy dress.

16 Therèsa M. Winge, *Body Style* (London and New York: Berg, 2012), 15.

17 For example, James Laver, ed., *Memorable Balls* (London: Derek Verschoyle, 1954); Hadley Freeman, 'You Shall Go to the Ball', *The Guardian*, 18 July 2006. www.theguardian.com/lifeandstyle/2006/jul/18/fashion.shopping?CMP=share_btn_link. Accessed: September 2016.

18 Lawrence Langner, *The Importance of Wearing Clothes* (Los Angeles: Elysium Growth Press, 1991), 149.

19 Ibid.

20 Ibid., 147; Ramzi Fawaz, *The New Mutants: Superheroes and the Radical Imagination of American Comics* (New York and London: New York University Press, 2016), 68, 83.

21 Anon., 'Priest Sorry for Dressing as Hugh Heffner and Simulating Sex with Male Playboy Bunnies in Public Carnival', *iNews*, 15 March 2017. http://inews.co.uk/essentials/news/priest-sorry-dressing-hugh-heffner-simulating-sex-male-playboy-bunnies-public-display/. Accessed: March 2017.

22 For example, Valerie Steele, ed., *A Queer History of Fashion: From the Closet to the Catwalk* (New Haven & London: Yale University Press, 2013); Gert Jonkers and Jop van Bennekom, *Buttoned-Up* (London: Penguin, 2013); *Elegance in an Age of Crisis: Fashions of the 1930s*, ed. Patricia Mears and G. Bruce Boyer (New Haven and London: Yale University Press, 2014). The study of individual designers and design houses has also increased. For example, Amy de la Haye and Valerie D. Mendes, *The House of Worth: Portrait of an Archive* (London: V&A Publishing, 2014); Alexander Fury and Adélia Sabatini, *Dior Catwalk* (London: Thames and Hudson, 2017).

23 Krystyna Pomorska, 'Forward', Mikhail Bakhtin, *Rabelais and His World*, tr. Hélène Iswolsky (Bloomington & Indianapolis: Indiana University Press, 1965), x–xi; Francesca Granta, *Experimental Fashion: Performance Art, Carnival and the Grotesque Body* (London and New York: I.B. Tauris, 2017), 1–11; Adam Geczy and Vicki Karaminas. *Critical Fashion Practice: From Westwood to Beirendonck* (London: Bloomsbury, 2017), 46–47.

24 Michael D. Bristol, *Carnival and Theater: Plebian Culture and the Structure of Authority in Renaissance England* (New York & London: Methuen, 1985); Terry Castle, *Masquerade and Civilization: The Carnivalesque in Eighteenth-Century English Culture and Fiction* (Stanford: Stanford University Press, 1986); Catherine Craft-Fairchild, *Masquerade and Gender: Disguise and Female Identify in Eighteenth-Century Fictions by Women* (Pennsylvania: The Pennsylvania State University Press, 1993).

25 Fancy dress costumes regularly appear in clothing exhibitions although focused displays are rarer. Sara Stevenson and Helen Bennett, *Van Dyck in Check Trousers: Fancy Dress in Art and Life 1700–1900* (Edinburgh: HMSO, 1978); Aileen Ribeiro, *Masquerade* (London: Museum of London, 1983). An exhibition

of garments associated with the Romanov tercentenary ball of 1913 was organized by the Tsaritsyno Museum, but I am unaware of a related catalogue.

26   Bristol, *Carnival and Theater*, 27.

27   Castle, *Masquerade and Civilization*, 72.

28   Mona Ozouf, 'Space and Time in the Festivals of the French Revolution', *Comparative Studies in Society and History*, 17:3 (July, 1975), 372.

29   See notes below. Kinser identifies five phases in the development of carnival. *Carnival American Style: Mardi Gras at New Orleans and Mobile* (Chicago and London: The University of Chicago Press, 1990), 1–7.

30   James C. Scott, *Domination and the Arts of Resistance: Hidden Transcripts* (New Haven and London: Yale University Press, 1990), 178.

31   Charles J. Dunn, *Everyday Life in Traditional Japan* (Rutland, Vermont: Tuttle Publishing, 1969), 6.

32   Kinser, *Carnival*, 5.

33   Victor Turner, *From Ritual to Theatre: The Human Seriousness of Play* (New York: PAJ Publications, 1982), 32.

34   Ingvild S. Gilhus, 'Carnival in Religion: The Feast of Fools in France', *Numen*, 37:1 (June, 1990), 24–52.

35   Kinser, *Carnival*, 114.

36   Keith Thomas, *Religion and the Decline of Magic: Studies in Popular Belief in Sixteenth- and Seventeenth-Century England* (London: Penguin Books, 1971), 1–24.

37   Scott, *Domination*, 178–179, and see Emmanuel Le Roy Ladurie, *Le Carnaval de Romans* (Paris: Editions Gallimard, 1979).

38   See below, 57.

39   Natalie Zemon Davis, 'The Reasons of Misrule: Youth Groups and Charivaris in Sixteenth-Century France', *Past & Present*, 50 (1971), 55.

40   Dunn, *Traditional Japan*, 71.

41   Anu Mänd, *Urban Carnival: Festive Culture in the Hanseatic Cities of the Eastern Baltic, 1350–1550* (Brepols: Turhnout, 2005), 201–207.

42   Samuel C. Kinser, 'The Combats of Carnival and Lent: A Medieval Genre Transformed (Giulio Cesare Croce, ca.1550–1614', *Medieval Folklore*, iii (Fall, 1994), 168.

43   Larry Silver, *Pieter Bruegel* (New York & London: Abbeville Press Publishers, 2011), 209.

44   Bristol, *Carnival and Theater*, 78–87.

45   Silver, *Pieter Bruegel*, 212–213.

46   Peter Baehr and Gordon C. Wells, 'introduction', Max Weber, *The Protestant Work Ethic and the 'Spirit' of Capitalism and Other Writings*, ed. and tr. Peter Baehr and Gordon C. Wells (London: Penguin Books, 2002), ix–xxxii.

47   For example, Peter Burke, *Popular Culture in Early Modern Europe*. Third Edition (Farnham: Ashgate, 2009), 366–380; Grant McCracken, *Culture and Consumption: New Approaches to the Symbolic Character of Consumer Goods and Activities* (Bloomington & Indianapolis: Indiana University Press, 1990), 10–15.

48   Kinser, *Carnival*, 170–171.

49   Ronald Hutton, *The Stations of the Sun: A History of the Ritual Year in Britain* (Oxford: Oxford University Press, 1996).

50   David Underdown, *Revel, Riot and Rebellion: Popular Politics and Culture in England 1603–1660* (Oxford: Oxford University Press, 1985), 73–105.

51   Sydney Anglo, 'An Early Tudor Programme for Plays and Other Demonstrations against the Pope', *Journal of the Warburg and Courtauld Institutes*, 20: 1/2 (January–June, 1957), 179.

52   David Cressy, *Bonfires & Bells: National Memory and the Protestant Calendar in Elizabethan and Stuart England* (Stroud: Sutton Publishing Limited, 2004).

53   Cressy is inclined to stress the achievements of successive royal governments. For useful corollaries, see Hutton, *The Stations of the Sun*, 288–292, 390–392; Geoffrey Parker, 'Success and Failure during the First Century of the Reformation', *Past & Present*, 136 (August, 1992), 43–82.

54   Samuel Kinser, 'Presentation and Representation: Carnival at Nuremberg, 1450–1550', *Representations*, 13 (1986), 23.

55   Ibid., 5–6, 23–24. My emphasis.

56 Ibid., 24–26.
57 Anglo, 'Tudor Programme', 179.
58 Kinser, 'Carnival', 28–29.
59 Yassana Croizat-Glazer, 'The Role of Ancient Egypt in the Masquerades at the Court of François 1ᵉʳ', *Renaissance Quarterly*, 66:4 (2013), 1206–1249; *Ben Jonson: The Complete Masques*, ed. Stephen Orgel (New Haven and London: Yale University Press, 1969), 1–39.
60 Welsford, *Court Masque*, 92–98.
61 Donatella Barbieri, *Costume in Performance: Materiality, Culture, and the Body* (London: Bloomsbury Academic, 2017), 8–10.
62 Welsford, *Court Masque*, 78–79.
63 Dunn, *Traditional Japan*, 6–7; Wolfram Eberhard, *A History of China*, tr. E.W. Dickes. Second Edition (London: Routledge and Kegan Paul Ltd., 1971), 292–293.
64 Anna Beer, *Milton: Poet, Pamphleteer & Patriot* (London and New York: Bloomsbury, 2008), 54–77.
65 Rebecca N. Mitchell, 'The Victorian Fancy Dress Ball, 1870–1900', *Fashion Theory*, 21:3 (2017), 291.
66 Ibid., 291.
67 Quoted in Peter Stallybrass and Allon White, *The Politics and Poetics of Transgression* (Ithaca, NY: Cornell University Press, 1986), 82–86.
68 Christoph Heyl, 'The Metamorphosis of the Mask in Seventeenth- and Eighteenth-Century London', *Masquerade and Identities*, 130.
69 *Gentleman's Magazine* (March 1732), vol. 2, 653.
70 *Gentleman's Magazine* (April, 1880), vol. 246, 469.
71 Mitchell, 'Fancy Dress Ball', 297.
72 Bakhtin, *Rabelais*, 218, 270–271.
73 Jennifer Van Horn, 'The Mask of Civility: Portraits of Colonial Women and the Transatlantic Masquerade', *American Art*, 23:3 (Fall, 2009), 11.
74 Kinser, *Carnival*, 76, 250.
75 Colleen McQuillen, 'Artists' Balls and Conceptual Costumes at the Russian Academy of Arts, 1885–1909', *Fashion Theory*, 16:1 (2012), 30.
76 Colleen McQuillen, *The Modernist Masquerade: Stylising Life, Literature and Costumes in Russia* (Madison: University of Wisconsin Press, 2013), 30, 119.
77 Ibid., 128.
78 Ibid., 134.
79 Ibid., 135.
80 Ibid., 135.
81 In this study, a distinction is made between masque and masquerade, but contemporaries in continental Europe used these terms freely. Welsford, *The Court Masque*, 92–97, 168.
82 For general remarks see Paul Readman, 'The Place of the Past in English Culture c. 1890–1914', *Past & Present*, 186 (2005), 147–199.
83 Welsford, *The Court Masque*, 120, 149.
84 *Van Dyck in Check Trousers*, 45–64.
85 Benjamin L. Wild, 'Romantic Recreations: Remembering Stuart Monarchy in Nineteenth-Century Fancy Dress Entertainments', *Remembering Queens and Kings in Early Modern England and France: Reputation, Reinterpretation, Reincarnation*, ed. Estelle Paranque (New York: Palgrave Macmillan, 2019).
86 Ribeiro, *Masquerade*, 4–6.
87 Ribeiro, *The Dress Worn at Masquerades*, 28.
88 Craft-Fairchild, *Masquerade and Gender*, 172–173; Ann Ilan-Alter, 'Masked and Unmasked at the Opera Balls: Parisian Women Celebrate Carnival', *Masquerade and Identities*, 135–152.
89 Clayton J. Whisnaut, *Queer Identities and Politics in Germany: A History 1880–1945* (New York and York: Harrington Park Press, 2016), 88, 96–97, 101.
90 Ribeiro, *The Dress Worn at Masquerades*, 33–35.
91 Ibid., 217–249, 420–431, 445–452.

92 Ibid., 136–204.

93 Whisnaut, *Queer Identities*, 132–133.

94 *Gentleman's Magazine* (June 1732), vol. xvii, 811.

95 *Gentleman's Magazine* (May 1750), vol., xx, 196.

96 *Gentleman's Magazine* (April 1750), vol. xx, 169; Castle, *Masquerade and Civilization*, 84–85.

97 Ribeiro, *The Dress Worn at Masquerades*, 14–15.

98 Aileen Ribeiro, 'The King of Denmark's Masquerade', *History Today*, 27:6 (June 1977), 385–389.

99 Castle, *Masquerade and Civilization*, 107.

100 Bridget J. Elliott, 'Covent Garden Follies: Beardsley's Masquerade Images of Posers and Voyeurs', *Oxford Art Journal*, 9:1 (1986), 38–48.

101 McQuillen, *Modernist Masquerade*, 121–122; Tom Cross, *Artists and Bohemians: 100 years with the Chelsea Arts Club* (London: Quiller Press, 1992), 59, 63–64, 67, 110–123.

102 Castle, *Masquerade and Civilization*, 110–129.

103 Alan Young, *Tudor and Jacobean Tournaments* (London: George Philip, 1987).

104 Ian Anstruther, *The Knight and the Umbrella: An Account of the Eglinton Tournament 1839* (Gloucester: Alan Sutton, 1986), 246–248.

105 Peter Buchan, *The Eglinton Tournament, And Gentleman Unmasked* (London: Simpkin Marshall & Co., 1840).

106 Benjamin L. Wild, 'Clothing Royal Bodies: Changing Attitudes to Royal Dress and Appearance from the Middle Ages to Modernity', *The Routledge History of Monarchy*, ed. Elena Woodacre, Lucinda H.S. Dean, Chris Jones, Russell E. Martin and Zita Eva Rohr (London: Basingstoke, 2019), 390–408.

107 Mark Girouard, *The Return to Camelot: Chivalry and the English Gentleman* (New Haven & London: Yale University Press, 1991).

108 Eric Hobsbawm, 'Mass-Producing Traditions: Europe, 1870–1914', *The Invention of Tradition*, ed. Eric Hobsbawm and Terence Ranger (Cambridge: Cambridge University Press, 1983), 263–308. In the same volume, see David Cannadine, 'The Context, Performance and Meaning of Ritual: The British Monarchy and the "Invention of Tradition", *c.* 1820–1977', 101–164.

109 Comus, *Grand Fancy Dress Ball, Royal Pavillion Brighton* (Brighton: Tucknott, 1871), 27–28.

110 Ribeiro, *The Dress Worn at Masquerades*, 205–216.

111 Van Horn, 'The Mask of Civility', 11–12.

112 Daniel Thomas Cook, *The Commodification of Childhood: The Children's Clothing Industry and the Rise of the Child Consumer* (Durham & London: Duke University Press, 1994), 28–30.

113 Ibid., 30–31.

114 A.N. Wilson, *The Victorians* (London: Arrow Books, 2002), 330.

115 Museum of London, 77.248i.

116 Museum of London, 51.70. The dress was apparently worn at a children's party in 1906.

117 Wilson, *Victorians*, 330.

118 Quoted in Girouard, *The Return to Camelot*, 34.

119 Ibid.

120 Bradley Shope, 'Masquerading Sophistication: Fancy Dress Balls of Britain's Raj', *The Journal of Imperial and Commonwealth Studies*, 39:3 (2011), 375–392.

121 Celia Marshik, *At The Mercy of Their Clothes: Modernism, the Middlebrow, and British Garment Culture* (New York: Columbia University Press, 2017), 126–127.

122 The Women's Library, 9/27/B/103 (21 December 1892).

123 The Women's Library, 9/27/B/235 (25 January 1899).

124 The Women's Library, 9/27/B/264 (3 January 1900).

125 A. Creighton, 'Masquerade and Christmas', *Stabroek News* (31 December 1988), 14.

126 Dunn, *Traditional Japan*, 74.

127 Anthea Jarvis and Patricia Raine, *Fancy Dress* (Aylesbury: Shire, 1984), 23.

128 Bishopsgate Institute, GDP/51/12.

129 Bishopsgate Institute, GDP/51/14.

130 Walter Moser, ed., *Helen Levitt* (Berlin: Kehrer Heidelberg, 2018), 82–89.

131 Ribeiro, *The Dress Worn at Masquerades*, 39–42; Frank Trentmann, *Empire of Things: How We Became a World of Consumers, from the Fifteenth Century to the Twenty First* (London: Allen Lane, 2016), 210 & 199–200.

132 Marshik, *At The Mercy of Their Clothes*, 104–105.

133 George J. Nicholls, *Bacon and Hams* (London: Richard & Sons Ltd., 1917), ix.

134 Ardern Holt, *Fancy Dresses Described; or What to Wear at Fancy Dress Balls* (London: Wyman & Sons, 1887).

135 Ibid., no pagination.

136 Anon., *Fancy Dress for Children* (London & Edinburgh: Ballantyne & Hanson, 1884); Anon., *Fancy Dress: A Short Chronological Series of Costumes* (London & Edinburgh: Ballantyne & Hanson, 1898); Anon., *Evolution in Costume* (London & Paris: Liberty & Co., 1893); Anon., *Dress and Decoration* (London & Paris: Liberty & Co., 1905).

137 Anon., *Fancy Dress*, no pagination.

138 Holt, *Fancy Dresses Described*, 1–9.

139 Anon., *Fancy Dress for Children*, no pagination.

140 Anon., *Fancy Dress*, no pagination.

141 Readman, 'The Place of the Past', 156.

142 Anon., *Fancy Dress*, no pagination. Costume no. 3.

143 Ibid., Costume no. 16.

144 R.C. Allen, 'Real Incomes in the English-Speaking World, 1879–1913', *Labour Market Evolution: The Economic History of Market Integration, Wage Flexibility and the Employment Relation*, ed. G. Grantham and M. MacKinnon (London: Routledge, 1994), 131.

145 Susan Gail Johnson, 'Like a Glimpse of Gay Old Versailles: Three Gilded Age Balls' *Gilded New York*, 89.

146 Ibid., 112–115.

147 de la Haye and Mendes, *The House of Worth*, 33.

148 Gail Johnson, 'Gay Old Versailles', 93–98.

149 Anon., 'Fancy Dress', *The Sydney Mail* (8 June 1910), 40.

150 Holly Bruce, 'On Dreamlands and Dress: The Role of Women at the Chelsea Arts Club Ball' (Unpublished Central Saint Martins BA thesis, 2013), 28–29.

151 Ribeiro, *The Dress Worn at Masquerades*, 38.

152 Comparison between contemporary photographs and surviving garments in Beaton's wardrobe indicates that he recycled decorative elements from his clothing. Benjamin L. Wild, *A Life in Fashion: The Wardrobe of Cecil Beaton* (London: Thames & Hudson, 2016), 42–45, 50–51.

153 Cecil Beaton, *The Years between: Diaries 1939–44* (London: Weidenfeld and Nicolson, 1965), 129.

154 Sophia Murphy, *The Duchess of Devonshire's Ball* (London: Sidgwick & Jackson, 1984); Cynthia Cooper, *Magnificent Entertainments: Fancy Dress Balls of Canada's Governors General 1876–1898* (New Brunswick: Goose Lane Editions, 1997), 138.

155 Amy Fine Collins, 'A Taste for Living', *Vanity Fair*, 18 August 2014. http://www.vanityfair.com/style/2014/09/niki-de-gunzburg-profile. Accessed: December 2016.

156 Deborah Davis, *Party of The Century: The Fabulous Story of Truman Capote and His Black and White Ball* (Hoboken: John Wiley & Sons, Inc., 2006).

157 Nicholas Foulkes, *Bals: Legendary Costume Balls of the Twentieth Century* (New York; Assouline Publishing, 2011), 272–298.

158 See D.J. Taylor, *Bright Young People: The Rise and Fall of a Generation, 1918–1940* (London: Vintage Books, 2008).

159 Anon., 'Styles Change in Masquerade Costumes: Movie Actors and Actresses and Figures in the Day's News Are Characters Most Popular with New Crop of Maskers', *The Milwaukee Journal* (23 April 1933), 6.

160 Ben Beaumont-Thomas, 'How We Made Cult Cartoon Mr Benn', *The Guardian* (7 March 2017), www.theguardian.com/culture/2017/07/how-we-made-mr-benn-david-mckee-ray-brooks-interview. Accessed: July 2017; Phyllis Galembo, *Dressed for Thrills: 100 Years of Halloween Costume & Masquerade* (New York: Harry N. Abrams, Inc., 2002).

161 David J. Skal, *Death Makes a Holiday: A Cultural History of Halloween* (London and New York: Bloomsbury, 2002), 17–57.

162 Anon., *Fancy Dress: Digital Insights Report*, InsideOnline, September 2016, 16.

163 Ibid.

164 Matt Payton, 'Mexico City Hosts First Ever Day of the Dead Parade Thanks to James Bond', *The Independent*, 31 October 2016, www.indepedent.co.uk/news/world/americas/mexico-city-day-of-the-dead-parade-james-bond-halloween-pictures-a7388191.html. Accessed: November 2016.

165 Anne Thomas, 'Fancy Dress Escapism is Big Business', *Sydney Morning Herald*, 18 June 1982, 15.

166 Personal communication with James Coulbault, December 2017.

167 Rob Crilly, 'Sinister Clown Sightings Spread Across the US', *The Independent*, 16 September 2016, www.independent.co.uk/news/world/americas/clown-sightings-us-spread-woods-luring-children-georgia-north-carolina-south-carolina-a7311606.html. Accessed: September 2016; Esther Addley, 'Killer Clown Sightings in the UK Trigger Police Warning', *The Guardian*, 11 October 2016, www.theguardian.com/uk-news/2016/oct/11/killer-clown-craze-uk-sightings-police-warning?CMP=oth_b-alpnews_d-2. Accessed: October 2016; Anon., 'Man in Clown Mask "Stabs Teen in Sweden"', *BBC News,* 14 October 2016. www.bbc.co.uk/news/world-europe-37657072. Accessed: October 2016.

168 Helena Horton, 'Man Dressed as Batman Chases "Killer Clowns" in Cumbria', 14 October 2016, www.msn.com/en-us/news/offbeat/man-dressed-as-batman-chases-killer-clowns-in-cumbria/ar-AAiTkoB?ocid=se. Accessed: October 2016.

169 Steven Pole, 'Insane Clown Pose', *The Guardian: G2*, 1 November 2016, 6–9.

170 James M. Brophy, 'Carnival and Citizenship: The Politics of Carnival Culture in the Prussian Rhineland, 1823–1848', *Journal of Social History*, 30:4 (1997), 873–904.

171 Kiera Vaclavik, 'World Book Day and Its Discontents: The Cultural Politics of Book-Based Fancy Dress', *The Journal of Popular Culture*, 52:3 (July, 2019), 582–605.

172 Tyga, Twitter Post, 9 April 2016, 10.42am. https://twitter.com/tygashadow26703/status/718856609271820288.

173 Christopher Tyerman, *God's War: A New History of the Crusades* (London: Allen Lane, 2006), 908.

174 Harrison Palmer, Instagram Post, 2 July 2016. www.instagram.com/p/BHXJpI4hdv3/?taken-by=hpx93.

175 Helen June Taylor, Instagram Post, 3 July 2016. No longer available.

176 India Ross, 'Has Gay Pride Sold Out?' *FT Weekend Magazine,* 13/14 August 2016, 15.

177 Marie-Pascale Mallé, 'Du carnaval au carnivalesque. «Le Monde à l'Envers»', *Fêtes, mascarades et carnavals: Circulations, transformations et contemporanéité*, ed. Nathalie Gauthard (Lavérune: éditions L'Entretemps, 2014), 27–56.

178 Abner Cohen, *Masquerade Politics: Explorations in the Structure of Urban Carnival Movements* (Berkeley & Los Angeles: University of California Press, 1993), 11.

179 Ibid., 128.

180 James Gill, *Lords of Misrule: Mardi Gras and the Politics of Race in New Orleans* (Jackson: University Press of Mississippi, 1997), 3–26; 279–282.

181 Lizzie Dearden, 'German Police Spark Outrage for Telling Authorities to Keep Refugees Away from Carnival Celebrations', *The Independent*, 7 February 2017, www.independent.co.uk/news/world/europe/germany-police-email-authorities-refugees-keep-away-carnival-celebrations-north-rhine-westphalia-a7567401.html. Accessed: February 2017.

182 Jamie Huckbody, 'The Ugly Truth', *Harper's BAZAAR Australia*, August 2018, 120–123.

183 www.belltoons.co.uk.

184 Elena Fadeeva, 'Mythologies and Metamorphoses', *Georgina Clapham: Mythologies and Metamorphoses* (Moscow: Triumph Gallery, 2018), 11.

185 Harrison Jacobs, 'Gamers Are Spending Thousands of Dollars a Year on This "Free" Video Game', *Business Insider UK,* 20 March 2015. http://uk.businessinsider.com/redditors-explain-how-they-spent-thousands-of-dollars-league-of-legends-2015-3. Accessed: August 2018.

186 Ashley Clarke, 'genderless kei: harajuku's online fashion revival', *i-D*, 23 February 2016. https://i-d.vice.com/en_uk/article/8xn7pp/genderless-kei-harajukus-online-fashion-revival. Accessed: March 2016.

187 Donald Ritchie, *The Image Factory: Fads and Fashions in Japan* (London: Reaktion Books Ltd, 2003), 8, 12.
188 Heejung Kim and Hazel Rose Markus, 'Deviance or Uniqueness, Harmony or Conformity? A Cultural Analysis', *Journal of Personality and Social Psychology*, 77:4 (1999), 785–800; Shinobu Kitayama, Hazel Rose Markus and Masaru Kurokawa, 'Culture, Emotion, and Well-Being: Good Feelings in Japan and the United States', *Cognition & Emotion*, 14:1 (2000), 93–124; Chie Kanagawa, Susan E. Cross and Hazel Rose Markus, '"Who Am I?" The Cultural Psychology of the Conceptual Self', *Personality and Social Psychology Bulletin*, 27 (2001), 90–103.
189 Hann, 'Critical Costume', 11.
190 Ibid., 12–13.
191 Hajo Adam and Adam D. Galinsky, 'Enclothed Cognition', *Journal of Experimental Social Psychology*, 48:4 (2012), 918–925.
192 A useful summary of Bakhtin's work and its reception is provided by Stallybrass and White, *Politics and Poetics of Transgression*, 6–26.
193 Bakhtin, *Rabelais*, 1–58.
194 Mikhail Bakhtin, *Problems of Dostoevsky's Poetics*, ed. and tr. Caryl Emerson (Minneapolis: University of Minnesota Press, 1984) 160.
195 Victor Turner, *The Anthropology of Performance* (New York: PAJ Publications, 1987), 34–35, 74–75.
196 Ibid., 42.
197 Ibid., 34, 42, 90, 102.
198 Victor Turner, *The Ritual Process: Structure and Anti-Structure* (New Brunswick & London: Aldine Transaction, 2008), 176.
199 Roger Caillois, *Man, Play and Games*, tr. Meyer Barash (Urbana and Chicago: University of Illinois Press, 1958), 9–10.
200 Ibid., 55.
201 Ibid., 75–76.
202 Ibid., 97, 129.
203 Turner, *From Ritual to Theatre*, 41–42.
204 Fawaz, *The New Mutants*, 14.
205 Ibid.
206 Norbert Elias, *The Civilizing Process: Sociogenetic and Pscyhogenetic Investigations*. Revised Edition, tr. Edmund Jephcott, eds. Eric Dunning, Johan Goudsblom and Stephen Mennell (London: Basil Blackwell, 1939). For the use of Elias's work in studies of dress, see Benjamin L. Wild, 'The Civilizing Process and Sartorial Studies', *Clothing Cultures*, 1:3 (2014), 213–224.
207 Bruce, 'On Dreamlands and Dress', 21–23.
208 Babcock, 'Introduction', 14.
209 Geczy and Karaminas, *Critical Fashion Practice*, 4; Granta, *Experimental Fashion*, 1–3.
210 Winge, *Body Style*, 5.

Chapter 1

1 Bakhtin, *Problems*, 160.
2 www.teenvogue.com/story-cultural/appropriation-halloween-costume-video. Accessed: September 2018.
3 Bonnie Wertheim, 'All the Good Pups at the Halloween Dog Parade', *The New York Times*, 23 October 2017. www.nytimes.com/2017/10/23/style/halloween-dog-parade.html. Accessed: October 2017.
4 Vaclavik, 'World Book Day and Its Discontents'.
5 Turner, *Ritual Process*, 176.
6 *Weldon's Fancy Dress for Ladies and Gentleman* (London: Weldon's Ltd., c. 1926–1930), 43.

Demonstrating social order - The Devonshire House Ball

7   The dress is 939 mm long, 533 mm across the shoulders and 457 mm around the low-cut waist.

8   Duchess of Devonshire wore a Worth gown as the Queen of Palmyra and led the 'Orientals' (Chatsworth House); Lady Isobel Stanley wore an eighteenth-century style 'hunting dress' from Worth and likely participated in one of the French courts (Victoria & Albert Museum, T.55:1, 2–2014). Her husband, the Honourable Francis Gathorne-Hardy, dressed in an eighteenth-century style frock coat from L. & H. Nathan and presumably accompanied her in the same group (Victoria & Albert Museum, T.58:1–3-2104); The Duchess of Portland participated in a seventeenth-century group as the Duchess of Savoy in a gown whose maker is unknown (Victoria & Albert Museum, T.464&A-1974). The Marchioness of Tweeddale impersonated the Empress Josephine in the French group (Museum of London, A14552a-b). She was accompanied by page boys William George Montagu Hay and Arthur Vincent Hay who wore costumes by Parisian costumier Auguste (Museum of London, A14553a-c). Princess Maud and her husband Prince Carl of Norway dressed in sixteenth-century costumes (National Museum, Oslo, OK-1991–0256 (Princess Maud of Wales), OK-1991–0251 (Prince Carl of Norway)). The Princess of Wales, appeared as Marguerite of Valois (Museum of London, but belonging to the Royal Collection, RC74862). See Kate Strasdin, *Inside the Royal Wardrobe: A Dress History of Queen Alexandra* (London: Bloomsbury Academic, 2017), 87; the Duke of Sutherland may have participated in the Elizabethan group (Museum of London, 78.19b). In December 2018, the costume worn by William Montagu Hay as Huguenot Comte de St Bris was sold through Kerry Taylor Auctions for £3000.

9   Murphy, *The Duchess of Devonshire's Ball*, 78, 125.

10   Ibid., 125–131.

11   Sophia Topley, 'The Devonshire House Ball', *House Style: Five Centuries of Fashion at Chatsworth*, ed. Laura Burlington and Hamish Bowles (New York: Skira Rizzoli, 2017), 125.

12   Emilia Müller, 'Fashion & Fancy in New York: The American Monarchs', Paper presented at Fashion: Exploring Critical Issues, Oxford, September 2011. www.inter-disciplinary.net/wp-content/uploads/2011/08/muellerfapaper.pdf. Accessed: November 2017, 5.

13   Murphy, *The Duchess of Devonshire's Ball*, 47–48.

14   Ibid., 131, 149.

15   Ibid., 162.

16   Ibid., 166.

17   Emily Soldene, Untitled article, *The Age* (4 September 1897), 13.

18   This is known to have occurred in February 1876 at the Earl of Dufferin's Ball in Ottawa. Cooper, *Magnificent Entertainments*, 62.

19   Anon., *Boston Evening Transcript* (21 July 1897), 6.

20   Terence Pepper, *High Society: Photographs 1897–1914* (London: The National Portrait Gallery Publications, 1998), 20.

21   Strasdin, *Queen Alexandra*, 87

22   I have been unable to identify the colour of Princess Victoria's costume.

23   Strasdin, *Queen Alexandra*, 87.

24   Murphy, *The Duchess of Devonshire's Ball*, 56.

25   Anon., 'Royalty in Fancy Dress', *Munsey's Magazine,* unknown date. http://layfayette.org.uk/munsey.html. Accessed: September 2014.

26   Anne Kjellberg and Susan North, *Style & Splendour: The Wardrobe of Queen Maud of Norway* (London: V&A Publications, 2005), 106–107.

27   Anon., 'Royalty in Fancy Dress'.

28   Anon., 'Ball at Devonshire House', *The Times*, 3 July 1897, 12.

29   Strasdin, *Queen Alexandra*, 88.

30   Anon., 'Ball at Devonshire House', 12.

31   Mitchell, 'Fancy Dress Ball', 301.

32   Rosemary and Donald Crawford, *Michael and Natasha* (London: Weidenfeld & Nicolson, 1977), 148.

33 Arturo Beéche, Janet Ashton and Marlene Koenig, *The Other Grand Dukes – Sons and Grandsons of Russia's Grand Dukes* (Eurohistory, 2013), 184; Jamie H. Cockfield, *White Crow: The Life and Times of Grand Duke Nicholas Mikhailovich Romanov: 1859–1919* (Santa Barbara: Praeger, 2002), 32.

34 Craft-Fairchild, *Masquerade and Gender*, 172–173.

35 Diana Crane, 'Clothing Behavior as Non-Verbal Resistance: Marginal Women and Alternative Dress in the Nineteenth Century', *Fashion Theory*, 3:2 (1999), 241–268.

36 G.J. Barker-Benfield, *The Culture of Sensibility: Sex and Society in Eighteenth-Century Britain* (Chicago: The University of Chicago Press, 1992), 198–199.

37 Beverly Gordon, *The Saturated World: Aesthetic Meaning, Intimate Objects, Women's Lives, 1840–1940* (Knoxville: The University of Tennessee Press, 2006), 1.

38 Murphy, *The Duchess of Devonshire's Ball*, 63.

39 Anon., 'Royalty in Fancy Dress'.

40 Victoria & Albert Museum, T.55:1, 2–2014; Victoria & Albert Museum, T.58:1–3-2104.

41 Amy de la Haye, 'The House of Worth 1858–1914', *Worth*, 14–15.

42 *Boston Evening Transcript*, 6.

43 Conversion using The National Archives currency converter (www.nationalarchives.gov.uk/currency). Accessed: October 2016.

44 *Boston Evening Transcript*, 6.

45 Ibid.

46 Consuelo Vanderbilt Balsan, *The Glitter and the Gold: The American Duchess – in Her Own Words* (London: Hodder & Stoughton [1953] 2012), 102–103.

47 Murphy, *The Duchess of Devonshire's Ball*, 118.

Instilling loyalty - The Co-Operative Wholesale Society

48 John F. Wilson, Anthony Webster and Rachel Vorberg-Rugh, *Building Co-operation: A Business History of The Co-operative Group, 1863–2013* (Oxford: Oxford University Press, 2013), 2.

49 Ibid., 100.

50 Ibid., 126–131.

51 Ibid., 108–109.

52 Jakub Kastl and Lyndon Moore, 'Wily Welfare Capitalist: Werner von Siemens and the Pension Plan', *Cliometrica*, 4:3 (2010), 321.

53 Anon., 'A Bold Advertising Scheme to Reach the Millions', *The Producer*, i (December 1923), 41; Anon., 'Points of View' section, *The Producer* (June 1930), 186; Anon., News Items, *The Producer* (August 1924), 320.

54 Wilson, et al., *Building Co-operation*, 121. See also, Harold W. Atkins, *Advertising for Co-operative Societies*. Second Edition (Leicester: Leicester Co-Operative Printing Society, 1963).

55 *The Producer* (September 1924), 337.

56 *The Producer* (October 1924), 56.

57 Steven Lea Crewe, 'Sport, Recreation and the Workplace in England, *c*. 1918–*c*.1970', Unpublished PhD thesis (Leicester: De Montfort University, 2014), 74–75, 301.

58 Anon., '"Middlesbrough's Recovery": The Value of Cooperative Practices', *The Producer*, xiv (April 1930), 114–115.

59 Ibid., 114.

60 Ibid., 115.

61 Ibid., 114.

62 Anon., 'Northern Lights' article, *The Producer*, viii (February 1928), 216.

63 Anon., 'News Item' article, *The Producer*, xiv (January 1930), 28.

64 Quoted in John Altfield, *With Light of Knowledge: A Hundred Years of Education in the Royal Arsenal Co-operative Society, 1877–1977* (London: Royal Arsenal Cooperative Society, 1981), 31.

65 'Children's Gala, 1923' (National Cooperative Film Catalogue: 007). 05.55–05.57 minutes.

66 Crystal Palace Exhibition, NCFC 033. 07.18–07.20 minutes.

67   Bishopsgate Institute, LCS/E/6/1/C.

68   Patrik Alac, *Bikini Story* (New York: Parkstone International, 2012), 52.

69   Bishopsgate Institute, LCS/E/6/1/C.

70   Lowell J. Satre, 'After the Match Girls' Strike: Bryant and May in the 1890s', *Victorian Studies*, 26:1 (1982), 7–8, 11–12.

71   Museum of London, 85.106/1. Anon., *Weldon's Fancy Dress*, colour supplement, viii.

Unifying nations - West African fancy dress and masquerade

72   Bolaji Campbell, 'Eedun Ogun: War Masquerades in Ibadan in the Era of Modernisation', *African Arts*, 48:1(Spring, 2015), 48.

73   Henry John Drewal, 'Gelede Masquerade: Imagery and Motif', *African Arts*, 7:4 (1979), 63.

74   Norma H. Wolff, 'Egungun Costuming in Abeokuta', *African Arts*, 15:3 (1982), 67.

75   Herbert M. Cole, 'Introduction: The Mask, Masking, and Masquerade Arts in Africa', *I Am Not Myself: The Art of African Masquerade*, ed. Herbert M. Cole (Los Angeles: Museum of Cultural History, 1985), 7–19.

76   I substitute for 'players'.

77   Caillois, *Man, Play and Games*, 83.

78   Courtnay Micots, 'Performing Ferocity: Fancy Dress, Asafo, and Red Indians in Ghana', *African Arts*, 45:2 (Summer, 2012), 34.

79   'Micots, Courtnay. "Masquefest 2012." In Berg Encyclopedia of World Dress and Fashion: Africa, edited by Joanne B. Eicher and Doran H. Ross. Oxford: Berg Publishers, 2010. Accessed: June 2016. http://dx.doi. org/10.2752/BEWDF/EDch1512.'

80   Drewal, 'Gelede Masquerade', 14.

81   Cole, 'Introduction', 20; Picton, 'What's in a Mask?' 50–57; Marian Charles Jedrej, 'A Comparison of Some Masks from North America, Africa, and Melanesia', *Journal of Anthropological Research*, 36:2 (1980), 220–221.

82   Fancy dress and masquerade parades are not unique to West Africa, but much of the current scholarship has focused on the countries in this region.

83   Catherine M. Cole, *Ghana's Concert Party Theatre* (Bloomington and Indianapolis: Indiana University Press, 2001), 106.

84   Margaret Thompson Drewal, 'The State of Research on Performance in Africa', *African Studies Review*, 34:3 (1991), 1. (Quoted by Cole, *Concert Party Theatre*, 106).

85   Cole, *Concert Party Theatre*, 106.

86   Cole, 'Introduction', 19.

87   Micots, 'Performing Ferocity', 33.

88   Ibid., 24.

89   Ibid.

90   Drewal, 'Gelede Masquerade', 39.

91   John W. Nunley, *Moving with the Face of the Devil: Art and Politics in Urban West Africa* (Urbana and Chicago: University of Illinois Press, 1987), 17, 37.

92   Mary Ann Fitzgerald, Henry J. Drewal and Moyo Okediji, 'Transformation through Cloth: An Egungun Costume of the Yoruba', *African Arts*, 28:2 (1995), 56.

93   John Nunley, 'The Fancy and the Fierce', *African Arts*, 14:2 (1981), 54–55.

94   Nunley, *Face of the Devil*, 103, 120–132; ibid., 52–58, 87–88.

95   Hakeem Adam, 'Ghana's Winneba Fancy Dress Festival is a Living Museum', 16 January 2018. www. okayafrica.com/photos-winneba-fancy-dress-festival-living-museum. Accessed: March 2018.

96   Ibid.

97   Ibid.

98   McQuillen, *Modernist Masquerade*, 144.

99   Ibid.

100 Maud Diver, *Far to Seek: A Romance of England and India* (Edinburgh and London: William Blackwood and Sons, 1921), 252.

101 Cole, *Concert Party Theatre*, 20; 74–75; Micots, 'Performing Ferocity', 26, 27; Nunley, *Face of the Devil*, 52, 87.

102 Cole, *Concert Party Theatre*, 53, 104–105.

103 See above, 7–8.

104 Micots, 'Performing Ferocity', 30–32.

105 Toyne V. Erekosima and Joanne B. Eicher, 'The Aesthetics of Men's Dress of the Kalabari of Nigeria', *The Visible Self*, 350.

106 Micots, 'Performing Ferocity', 27.

107 Ibid., 28.

108 Ibid.,17, 24.

109 Cole, 'Introduction', 25.

110 Nunley, *Face of the Devil*, 35.

111 Ibid., 231.

112 Ibid., 55, 203–215.

113 Frances Harding, 'Introduction', *Performance Arts in Africa*, 1–2.

114 Campbell, 'Eedun Ogun', 44.

115 Micots, 'Performing Ferocity', 34.

116 Ibid., 34.

117 Bakhtin, *Problems*, 160.

118 Bristol, *Carnival and Theater*, 27.

Chapter 2

1 Maximilian Josef Rudwin, *The Origin of the German Carnival Comedy* (New York: G.E. Stechert & Co., 1920), 6.

2 Hutton, *Stations of the Sun*, 11, 12, 21, 26, 27, 33, 88–89; Gilhus, 'Carnival in Religion', 24; Elaine Glovka Spencer, 'Custom, Commerce, and Contention: Rhenish Carnival Celebrations, 1890–1914', *German Studies Review*, 20:3 (1997), 332–333.

3 Norma Claire Moruzzi, *Speaking Through the Mask: Hannah Arendt and the Politics of Social Identity* (Ithaca and London: Cornell University Press, 2000), 36.

4 Ibid.

5 Ibid., 37–39.

6 Erving Goffman, *The Presentation of Self in Everyday Life* (London: Penguin [Anchor Books, 1959], 1969), 21.

7 William Shakespeare, 'Twelfth Night', *William Shakespeare's Complete Works*, ed. Jonathan Bate and Eric Rasmussen (Basingstoke: Macmillan, 2007), Act 1, Scene 3, lns. 83–84, 654.

8 See below, 130.

9 Barbara Brownie and Danny Graydon, *The Superhero Costume: Identity and Disguise in Fact and Fiction* (London: Bloomsbury Academic, 2016), 128.

10 For an overview, see John Mack, 'Introduction: About Face', *Masks: Art of Expression*, ed. John Mack (London: British Museum Press, 1994), 9–31.

Defying royal authority - The Siege of Kenilworth Castle

11 Two other chronicles mention the Legate's excommunication but do not allude to any reprisal. 'Annales Monasterii de Waverleia, A.D. 1–1291', *Annales Monastici*, ii, ed. Henry Richards Luard (London: Longman,

1864), 371; 'Chronicon Willelmi de Duobus Bellis apud Lewes et Evehsam Commissis', *Ypodigma Neustriae, a Thoma Walsingham, quondam monachi monasterio S. Albani conscriptum*, ed. Henry T. Riley (London: Longman, 1876), 555–556.

12   Bakhtin, *Rabelais*, 6.

13   Ibid., 17.

14   Gerd Althoff, 'Zur Bedeutung Symbolischer Kommunikation für das Verständnis des Mittelalters', *Frühmittelalterliche Studien*, 31 (1997), 370–389; Gerd Althoff, *Spielregeln der Politik im Mittelalter: Kommunikation in Frieden und Fehde* (Darmstadt: Wissenschaftliche Buchgesellschaft, 1997). See also Barbara Stollberg-Rilinger, 'Symbolische Kommunikation in der Vormoderne: Begriffe-Thesen Forschungsperpetiven', *Zeitschrift für Historiche Forschung*, 31 (2004), 489–527.

15   Bakhtin, Rabelais 84.

16   *The Metrical Chronicle of Robert of Gloucester*, II, ed. William Aldis Wright (London: Eyre & Spottiswoode, 1887), 772.

17   *The Church Historians of England*, vol. V. pt. I, tr. Joseph Stevenson (London: Beeleys, 1858), 378–379.

18   John H. Munro, 'The Medieval Scarlet and the Economics of Sartorial Splendour', *Cloth and Clothing in Medieval Europe: Essays in Memory of Professor E. M. Carus-Wilson*, ed. Negley B. Harte and Kenneth G. Ponting (London: Heinemann Educational, 1983), 13–70.

19   Francis Henry Stratmann and Henry Bradley, *A Middle English Dictionary: Containing Words Used by English Writers from the Twelfth to the Fifteenth Century* (Oxford: Clarendon Press, 1963), 519. I am grateful to Marilyn Corrie for her comments.

20   Michel Pastoreau, *Figures et Couleurs: Étude sur la symbolique et la sensibilité médiévales* (Paris: Le Léopard d'or, 1986), 40.

21   Bakhtin, *Rabelais*, 7; Caillois, *Man, Play and Games*, 43–55.

22   Benjamin L. Wild, 'The Siege of Kenilworth Castle', *English Heritage Historical Review*, 5 (2010), 13.

23   John R. Maddicott, *Simon de Montfort* (Cambridge: Cambridge University Press, 1994), 225–345.

24   *The Chronicle of William of Rishanger of the Barons' Wars*, ed. James Orchard Halliwell (London: John Bowyer Nicols and Son, 1840), 43; 'Chronicon Willelmi de Doubus Bellis apud Lewes et Evesham Commissis', in Ypodigma Neustriae, a Thoma Walsingham, quondam monachi monasterio S. Albani conscriptum, ed. Henry T. Riley (London: Longman, 1876), 552.

25   'Chronicon … de Duobus Bellis', 549.

26   Daniel Williams, 'Simon de Montfort and his Adherents', *England in the Thirteenth Century*, ed. W.M. Ormrod (Woodbridge: The Boydell Press, 1985), 166–177.

27   Benjamin L. Wild, 'A Captive King: Henry III between the Battles of Lewes and Evesham, 1264–1265', *Thirteenth Century England XIII*, ed. Janet Burton et al. (Woodbridge: The Boydell Press, 2011), 41–56.

28   'Annales de Prioratus de Dunstaplia, A.D. 1–1297', *Annales Monastici*, iii., 242; 'Chronicon vulgo dictum Chronicon Thomae Wykes, 1066–1288', *Annales Monastici*, iv., 191.

29   'Chronicon … de Duobus Bellis', 554.

30   Wild, 'Kenilworth', 20.

31   Ibid.

32   Ibid.

33   David A. Carpenter, 'The Household Rolls of King Henry III of England 1216–72', *Historical Research*, 80 (2007), 40.

34   Ibid., 41.

35   *Calendar of the Liberate Rolls, 1260–67*, vol. 5 (London: HMSO, 1961), 225.

36   Paul Edward Dutton, *Charlemagne's Mustache and Other Cultural Clusters of a Dark Age* (Basingstoke and New York: Palgrave Macmillan, 2004), 49.

37   Richard Cassidy and Mike Clasby, 'Matthew Paris and Henry III's Elephant'. https://finerollshenry3.org.uk/redist/pdf/fm-06-2012.pdf. Accessed: August 2017.

38   Rose Graham, 'Letters of Cardinal Ottoboni', *English Historical Review*, 57 (1900), XIII. 102–103.

39   'Chronicle of Hailes Abbey', British Library, Cotton Cleopatra D.iii. ff. 45v–46.

40   *Rishanger*, 43; Chronicon de … Duobus Bellis, 552.

41   'Chronicle of Hailes Abbey', ff. 45v–46.
42   Claire Valente, *The Theory and Practice of Revolt in Medieval England* (London: Routledge, 2003), 74–78.
43   David A. Carpenter, *The Minority of Henry III* (London: Methuen, 1990), 361–370.
44   David I. Ketzer, *Ritual, Politics, and Power* (New Haven and London: Yale University Press, 1988), 131–132.

King killers - The Assassination of Gustaf III of Sweden

45   Nancy Klein Maguire, 'The Theatrical Mask/Masque of Politics: The Case of Charles I', *Journal of British Studies* 28, no. 1 (1989), 1–22; Garry Wills, *Making Make-Believe Real: Politics as Theater in Shakespeare's Time* (New Haven and London: Yale University Press, 2014).
46   Livrustkammeran, 17157 (06:5464).
47   Livrustkammeran, 3497b, 3497f and 3497d.
48   Ibid., 247.
49   Livrustkammeran, 3497a; Gardar Sahlberg, *Murder at the Masked Ball: The Assassination of Gustaf III of Sweden*, tr. Paul Britten Austin (London: Macdonald, 1974), 104.
50   Artaud de Montor, *Histoire de l'assassinat de Gustave III, roi de Suède. Par un officer Polonais, témoin occulaire* (Paris, 1797), 65.
51   Ibid., 63.
52   Livrustkammeran, 3497i and 3497k; Lena Rangström, *Kläder för tid och evighet: Gustaf III sedd genom sina dräkter* (Helsingborg: AB Boktryck, 1997), 247.
53   Livrustkammeran, 3497b.
54   Quoted in Rangström, *Kläder för tid och evighet*, 245.
55   Quoted in Peter Cassirer, 'Gustaf III – The Theatre King: Librettist and Politician', *Gustavian Opera: An Interdisciplinary Reader in Swedish* Opera, Dance and Theatre 1771–1809, ed. Inger Mattson (Uppsala: Almqvist and Wiksell Tryckeri, 1990), 31.
56   Ibid., 32.
57   John Brown, *Memoirs of the Courts of Sweden and Denmark during the Reigns of Christian VII. of Denmark and Gustavus III. and IV of Sweden*, 2 vols. (London: The Grolier Society, 1818), ii, 157.
58   Sahlberg, *Masked Ball*, 103.
59   Brown, *Memoirs*, 159–161; Montor, *L'assassignat*, 61–66. Anon., *The Times*, 7 April 1792, 3; ibid., 10 April 1792, 2; ibid., 11 April 1792, 2; ibid., 16 April 1792, 2; ibid., 17 April 1792, 3; ibid., 23 April 1792, 3.
60   Livrustkammeran, (18553) 5740/2.
61   Sahlberg, *Masked Ball*, 65, 76.
62   Livrustkammeran, (18553) 5740/2; (18551) 5740/1.
63   Castle, *Masquerade and Civilization*, 77.
64   McQuillen, *Modernist Masquerade*, 80.
65   Ibid.
66   Ibid., 81.
67   Rangström, *Kläder för tid och evighet*, 246.
68   Sahlberg, *Masked Ball*, 75, 81.
69   Arnold D. Harvey, 'Gustav III of Sweden', *History Today*, 53:12 (2003), 9–15.
70   Montor, *L'assassignat*, 173–174.
71   Sahlberg, *Masked Ball*, 54. The ball on 16 March was advertised three times, presumably because of its incongruous timing during Lent and the fact that a previous masked ball, scheduled for 9 March, was cancelled, Ibid., 58–59.
72   Brown, *Memoirs*, 155–156; Sahlberg, *Masked Ball*, 22, 38, 54, 58.
73   Ibid., 54, 70.
74   Cassirer, 'The Theatre King', 38–39.
75   David King and Cathy Porter, *Blood & Laughter: Caricatures from the 1905 Revolution* (London: Jonathan Cape, 1983), 63.

76   Marian C. Donnelly, 'Theaters in the Courts of Denmark and Sweden from Frederik II to Gustav III', *Journal of the Society of Architectural Historians*, 43:4 (1984), 328–340.

77   Stig Fogelmarck, 'Gustav III and His Opera House', *Gustavian Opera*, 47.

78   Birgitta Schyberg, '"*Gustaf Wasa*" as Theatre Propaganda', *Gustavian Opera*, 293–322.

79   Matthew H. Wikander, 'Historical Vision and Dramatic Historiography: Strindberg's "Gustav III" in Light of Shakespeare's "Julius Caesar" and Corneille's "Cinna"', *Scandinavian Studies*, 62:1 (1990), 125–126.

80   Rangström, *Kläder för tid och evighet*, 250.

81   Ibid., 249.

82   Ibid., 249.

83   Ronald D. Gerste, *Der Zauberkönig: Gustav III. und Schwedens Goldene Zeit* (Göttingen: Steidl Verlag, 1996), 84.

84   Montor, *L'assassignat*, 61.

85   Rangström, *Kläder för tid och evighet*, 246.

86   Ibid., 251.

87   Brown, *Memoirs*, 166–167.

88   Maguire, 'The Case of Charles I', 18.

89   Brown, *Memoirs*, 186–187.

90   Ibid., 17.

91   Ibid., 6–7.

92   Kinser, *Carnival*, 65, 93.

93   Ibid., 69, where it is noted that there is some anomaly with the dating of this.

94   Julian Budden, *Verdi*. Revised Edition (London: J. M. Dent, 1993), 76–82.

95   Murphy, *The Duchess of Devonshire's Ball*, 123–124.

Resisting change - The Reconstruction Era Ku-Klux Klan

96   Elaine Frantz Parsons, *Ku-Klux Klan: The Birth of the Klan during Reconstruction* (Chapel Hill: University of North Carolina Press, 2015), 21, 24.

97   Ibid., 13, 21, 86–87.

98   Ibid., 18–20.

99   Ibid., 81.

100   The klan's ambiguous relationship with urbanity given their predominantly rural location is raised in a lecture Parsons presented to the Virginia Historical Society. 'Horns, Masks, and Women's Dress: How the First Klan Used Costume to Build US Terrorism', 8 December 2016. http://vimeo.com/195032653. Accessed: September 2017, at 48.05 to 49.52 minutes.

101   U.S. Congress, *Testimony Taken by the Joint Select Committee on the Condition of Affairs in the Late Insurrectionary States*: Ibid. 5; U.S. Congress, *Testimony … North Carolina*, ii (Washington: Government Printing Office, 1872), 153.

102   U.S. Congress, *Testimony … North Carolina*, ii, 71.

103   *Mississippi*, xi (Washington: Government Printing Office, 1872), 85.

104   Ibid., 113, 418.

105   U.S. Congress, *Testimony … North Carolina*, ii, 132.

106   U.S. Congress, *Testimony … Mississippi*, xi, 18; U.S. Congress, *Testimony … Georgia*, i, 7.

107   U.S. Congress, *Testimony … Mississippi*, xi, 71.

108   U.S. Congress, *Testimony … Mississippi*, xi, 40.

109   U.S. Congress, *Testimony … North Carolina*, ii, 88.

110   Anon. 'Museum Director Defends Exhibit of Ku Klux Klan Robe', 2 June 2005. www.siouxcityjournal.com/news/state-and-regional/museum-director-defends-exhibit-of-the-ku-klux-klan-robe/article_c511004c-0E52-5e69-a9d3-9235a7c14d84.html. Accessed: March 2017.

111   U.S. Congress, *Testimony … Georgia*, i, 6; U.S. Congress, *Testimony … Mississippi*, xi, 94.

112 U.S. Congress, *Testimony … North Carolina*, ii, 182.
113 Ibid., 436.
114 Ibid., 92.
115 U.S. Congress, *Testimony … Georgia*, i, 3.
116 U.S. Congress, *Testimony … North Carolina*, ii, 89–90, 113.
117 U.S. Congress, Testimony … Georgia, i, 3; ibid., 116.
118 Gladys-Marie Fry, *Night Riders in Black Folk History* (Chapel Hill: University of North Carolina Press, 1975), 14–15.
119 Parsons, *Ku-Klux Klan*, 128, 186.
120 Ibid., 127, 132.
121 Ibid., 9.
122 Ibid., 145.
123 U.S. Congress, *Testimony … North Carolina*, ii, 116.
124 Ibid., ii, 471.
125 Ibid., ii 474.
126 U.S. Congress, *Testimony … Mississipi*, xi, 84.
127 Ibid., 32.
128 U.S. Congress, *Testimony … North Carolina*, ii, 153.
129 Ibid., 232.
130 Ibid., 454.
131 Elaine Frantz Parsons, 'Midnight Rangers: Costume and Performance in the Reconstruction-Era Ku Klux Klan', *The Journal of American History*, 92:3 (2005), 811–812.
132 Ibid., 814.
133 Kinser, *Carnival*, 48–54.
134 Ibid., 54.
135 U.S. Congress, *Testimony … North Carolina*, ii, 116.
136 The North Carolina Museum of History, H.1996.102.1.
137 Pastoureau, *Figures et Couleurs*, 40.
138 Jennifer Haley, 'Bamana', *I Am Not Myself*, 29; John Wills, 'Voltaic Peoples', *I Am Not Myself*, 36; Gail Wallace and Jeri B. Williams, 'Bidjogo', *I Am Not Myself*, 41; Sonja Wijs, 'Kavat Mask', *PowerMask: The Power of Masks*, ed. Patrick Lennon (Tielt: Lannoo Publishers, 2017), 70.
139 For the cultural exchanges between Africa and America, see Kinser, *Carnival*, 195–214.
140 Fitzgerald, Drewal and Okediji, 'Transformation through Cloth', 56.
141 Margaret Thompson Drewal and Henry John Drewal, 'More Powerful Than Each Other: An Egbado Classification of Egungun', *African Arts*, 11:3 (April 1978), 28.
142 Ibid.
143 Eric Lott, *Love & Theft: Blackface Minstrelsy & the American Working Class* (Oxford: Oxford University Press [1993], 2013), 53.
144 Parsons, *Ku-Klux Klan*, 87.
145 U.S. Congress, *Testimony … Georgia*, i, 23; Adam I.P. Smith, *The American Civil War* (Basingstoke and New York: Palgrave Macmillan, 2007), 171.
146 Norbert Elias and John L. Scotson, *The Established and the Outsiders: A Sociological Enquiry into Community Problems* (London: Sage, 1965), xxiii; Norbert Elias, *The Society of Individuals*, ed. Michael Schröter, tr. Edmund Jephcott (London: Basil Blackwell, [1987] 1991), 211–214.
147 Parsons, *Ku-Klux Klan*, 9, 37, 44.
148 I paraphrase Eric Lott, who is thinking specifically of blackface minstrelsy, *Love & Theft*, 6.
149 U.S. Congress, *Testimony … North Carolina*, ii, 88.
150 Ibid., 473.
151 Patrick Mauriès, *Androgyne: Fashion and Gender* (London: Thames and Hudson, 2017), 18–19.
152 Lenard R. Berlanstein, 'Breeches and Breaches: Cross-Dress Theater and the Culture of Gender Ambiguity in Modern France', *Comparative Studies in Society and History*, 38:2 (1996), 351–353.

153 Mauriès, *Androgyne*, 18–19. Concerns about cross-dressing may have seemed more urgent in the eighteenth and nineteenth centuries, but they were far from new. See, Mark Stoyle, '"Give Mee a Souldier's Coat": Female Cross-Dressing during the English Civil War', *History*, 103:1 (2018), 5–26.

154 Alison Bancroft, 'When the Chevalier d'Eon met Alexander McQueen: History, Gender and Subjectivity in the Costumes in *Eonnagata*', *Studies in Costume & Performance*, 3:1 (2018), 16–17.

155 Parsons, *Ku-Klux Klan*, 94; Lott, *Love & Theft*, 166.

156 DeAnne Blanton and Lauren M. Cook, *They Fought Like Demons: Women Soldiers in the American Civil War* (Stroud: Sutton Publishing, 2002), 7.

157 Ibid., 30.

158 Ibid., 42.

159 Ibid., 149.

160 Ibid., 151.

161 Norman Simms, 'Ned Ludd's Mummers Play', *Folklore*, 89:2 (1978), 166–168.

162 Quoted in ibid., 171.

163 Ibid., 172.

164 Ibid.

165 U.S. Congress, *Testimony … North Carolina*, ii, 434; U.S. Congress, *Testimony … Georgia*, i, 82.

166 Ibid., 434; U.S. Congress, *Testimony … Mississippi, xi*, 5; U.S. Congress, *Testimony … Georgia*, i, 23.

167 Parsons, *Ku-Klux Klan*, 81, 84, 86.

168 Parsons, 'Midnight Rangers', 821–830.

169 Robert Ross, *Clothing: A Global History, or, the Imperialists' New Clothes* (Cambridge: Polity Press, 2008), 103–104.

170 Alison Kinney, *Hood* (London: Bloomsbury, 2016), 37–39; Nancy MacLean, *Behind the Mask of Chivalry: The Making of the Second Ku Klux Klan* (Oxford: Oxford University Press, 1994), 12–13.

171 Anon., *Catalogue of Official Robes and Banners* (Georgia: Knights of the Ku Klux Klan, 1925), no pagination.

172 *Weldon's Fancy Dress*, 39.

173 Parsons, *Ku-Klux Klan*, 305.

174 Hann, 'Critical Costume', 13.

175 Brian Mullen, Michael J. Migdal and Drew Rozell, 'Self-Awareness, Deindividuation, and Social Identity: Unravelling Theoretical Paradoxes by Filling Empirical Lacunae', *Personality and Social Psychology Bulletin*, 29:9 (2003), 1071–1081.

176 Rachel E. White, Emily O. Prager, Catherine Schaefer, Ethan Kross, Angela L. Duckworth and Stephanie M. Carlson, 'The "Batman Effect": Improving Perseverance in Young Children', *Child Development*, 88:5 (2017), 1563–1573.

177 Brownie and Graydon, *The Superhero Costume*, 3.

178 McQuillen, *Modernist Masquerade*, 158.

179 Yuri Lotman, *Universe of the Mind: A Semiotic Theory of Culture*, tr. Ann Shukman (Bloomington and Indianapolis: Indiana University Press, 1990), 59.

180 Ibid., 60.

181 McQuillen, *Modernist Masquerade*, 158.

182 Ibid.

183 Ibid., 160.

Chapter 3

1   Diana Scarisbrick, *Rings: Jewelry of Power, Love and Loyalty* (London: Thames and Hudson, 2007), 253, 260; Palais Galliera, 1989.184.1; Håkan Groth and Lars Strömbold, *Barock och Rokoko i Sverige 1650–1750* (Stockholm: Bokförlaget Prisma, 2005), 239.

2   Marshik, *At the Mercy of Their Clothes*, 114–126.
3   Ibid., 143.
4   McQuillen, *Modernist Masquerade*, 61.
5   Neil Tweedle and Michael Kallenbach, 'Prince Harry Faces Outcry at Nazi Outfit', *The Telegraph*, 14 January 2005. https://www.telegraph.co.uk/news/uknews/1481148/Prince-Harry-faces-outcry-at-Nazi-outfit.html. Accessed: August 2018.
6   Stoyle, 'Female Cross-Dressing', 7, notes 4–6.
7   Mauriès, *Androgyne*, 18–19.
8   See also, Gerhard H. Gaskin, Deborah Wills and Frank Roberts, *Legendary: Inside the House Ballroom Scene* (Durhem: Duke University Press, 2013).
9   Lucas Hilderbrand, *Paris Is Burning: A Queer Film Classic* (Vancouver: Arsenal Pulp Press, 2013), 31.
10   Ibid., 33.
11   Ibid., 50–51, 60.
12   *Paris Is Burning*, 03.42 to 03.59 minutes.

Artistic avatars - Harlequin and pierrot

13   Stallybrass and White, *Politics and Poetics of Transgression*, 103. Original emphasis.
14   Barbieri, *Costume in Performance*, 65–78.
15   Allardyce Nicoll, *The World of Harlequin: A Critical Study of the Commedia dell' Arte* (Cambridge: Cambridge University Press, 1963), 3–8; Wolgang M. Zucker, 'The Image of the Clown', *The Journal of Aesthetics and Art Criticism*, 12:3 (1954), 311.
16   M.A. Katritzky, 'Harlequin in Renaissance Pictures', *Renaissance Studies*, 11:4 (1997), 382, 383–384.
17   Jean Starobinski, *Portrait de l'artist en saltimbanque* (Paris: Gallimard, 1970 [2013]), 101–102.
18   Dante Alighieri, *The Divine Comedy*, tr. Allen Mandelbaum (New York: Alfred A. Knopf, 1995), 148, 153–154.
19   Yve-Alain Bois, 'Picasso the Trickster', *Picasso Harlequin 1917–1937*, ed. Yve-Alain Bois (Milan: SkiraEditore S.p.A., 2009), 31.
20   Helen O. Borowitz, 'Painted Smiles: Sad Clowns in French Art and Literature', *The Bulletin of the Cleveland Museum of Art*, 71:1 (1984), 23–35.
21   Nicoll, *Harlequin*, 83–84; Zucker, 'Clown', 311.
22   Starobinski, *Portrait de l'artist*, 90.
23   Ibid., 108. Original emphasis.
24   Zucker, 'Clown', 314.
25   Zucker begins by discussing the clown although his argument focuses on the portrayal of the harlequin. To provide clarity in the context of my discussion and to avoid distortion of Zucker's words, I occasionally refer to the 'harlequin-clown' in what follows. Ibid., 310–311.
26   Ibid., 314.
27   In England, the development of the clown is conventionally linked to Joseph Grimaldi (1778–1837). My comments apply to Europe generally. Barbieri, *Costume in Performance*, 78–88.
28   Zucker, 'Clown', 314.
29   Ibid., 315.
30   Ibid., 316.
31   Ibid.
32   Ibid.
33   Ibid., 317.
34   Ibid., 312.
35   Milica Banjanin, 'OF HARLEQUINS, DREAMERS, AND POETS: A Study of an Image in the Works of Elena Guro', *Russian Language Journal/Русский язык*, 36:123/124 (1982), 224.
36   Starobinski, *Portrait de l'artiste*, 8.

37 Richard Thomson, *Seurat's Circus Sideshow* (New York: Metropolitan Museum of Art, 2017), 97.

38 Richard Sennett, *The Fall of Public Man* (London: Penguin Books, [Alfred A. Knopf, 1974] 2002).

39 Stallybrass and White, *Politics and Poetics of Transgression*, 103.

40 Starobinski, *Portrait de l'artiste*, 54.

41 Terry Castle, 'The Carnivalization of Eighteenth-Century English Narrative', *PMLA*, 99:5 (1984), 903–916; McQuillen, *Modernist Masquerade*, 12–15, 18–19.

42 State Tretyakov Gallery, Moscow.

43 www.christies.com/lotfinder/konstantin-andreevich-somov-1869-1939-pierrot-and-4618249-details.aspx. Accessed: September 2017.

44 Nancy Olson, *Gavarni: The Carnival Lithographs* (New Haven: Yale University Art Gallery, 1979), 20–21.

45 1955.74.1771.1. Lithograph, 191 × 162 mm, Yale University Art Gallery, New Haven.

46 Maria Peitcheva, *Konstantin Somov Drawings: Colour Plates* (Maria Peitcheva, 2016), 10.

47 Olson, *Gavarni*, 14, 16.

48 1955.74.1621.1. Lithograph, Yale University Art Gallery, New Haven.

49 I am grateful to Philip Rogerson for his help. There is a possibility that Gavarni is making a reference to the oratorical battle between Aeschines and Demosthenes in 330 BCE. In Aeschines speech, 'Against Ctesiphon', which attacks Demosthenes career, the statesman's lack of respect for the rites of Asclepios is mentioned. I suspect this would have been too much for viewers to grasp instantly and I am unsure why Gavarni would choose to reference this verbal duel in the context of a masquerade.

50 It may be relevant that Asclepios also carried a rod, conventionally entwined with a snake. This was occasionally, and mistakenly, linked to the *caduceus* carried by Hermes because of the latter's association with alchemy.

51 Ann Rosalind Jones and Peter Stallybrass, *Renaissance Clothing and the Materials of Memory* (Cambridge: Cambridge University Press, 2000), 4.

52 Pablo Picasso, *At the Lapin Agile,* 1904–1905, oil on canvas, 990 × 1003 mm, private collection; Pablo Picasso, *Family of Saltimbanques,* 1904–1905, oil on canvas, 2128 × 2296 mm, National Gallery of Art, Washington, Chester Dale Collection; Abraham Mintchine, *Portrait of the Artist as a Harlequin,* 1931, 725 × 500 mm, Tate Britain; Banjanin, 'OF HARLEQUINS', 232.

53 Vasily Shukhaev and Alexandre Jacovleff, *Double Self Portrait (Harlequin and Pierrot)* (Russian Museum, St Petersburg, 1914).

54 Pablo Picasso, *Paul as Pierrot,* 1925, 1300 × 970 mm, private collection; Pablo Picasso, *Portrait of Paulo as Pierrot,* 1929, oil on canvas, 970 × 1800 mm, private collection; Pablo Picasso, *Paul in Clown Suit,* 1924; oil on canvas, 500 × 645 mm, Museum of Picasso, Paris; Paul Cézanne, *Mardi Gras,* 1888, oil on canvas, 1020 × 810 mm, The Pushkin Museum of Fine Arts, Moscow.

55 Stephen Moore, 'A Nation of Harlequins'? Politics and Masculinity in Mid-Eighteenth-Century Britain', *Journal of British Studies*, 49:3 (2010), 514.

56 *Vogue*, 37:3 (11 February 1901), 24; *Vogue*, 39:4 (15 February 1912), 22; *Vogue*, 42:11 (1 December 1913), 44; *Vogue*, 42:12 (15 December 1913), 25, 26; *Vogue*, 48:12 (15 December 1916), 42; *Vogue*, 58:13 (1 August 1921), 57.

57 *Weldon's Fancy Dress*, 2.

58 Ibid., 3.

59 Ibid., colour supplement, ii, 40.

60 See above, 65.

61 *Weldon's Fancy Dress*, colour supplement, ii, 40.

62 Oil on canvas mounted on composition board, 9140 × 1016 mm, New York, The Jewish Museum, purchase: Oscar and Regina Gross Memorial Fund, 2001–42.

63 I am grateful to Helen Przibilla for her comments.

64 Rav Yitzchak Sender, *The Commentators' Al Hanissim: Insights on the Sages on Purim and Chanukah* (Israel: Feldheim Publishers, 2000), 244.

65 Elliott Horowitz, *Reckless Rites: Purim and the Legacy of Jewish Violence* (Princeton: Princeton University Press, 2006), 91.

66 Richard C. Green, 'Bloch, Beethoven and Der Blaue Reiter', *Music in Art*, 37:1/2, The Courts in Europe: Music Iconography and Princely Power (2012), 279.
67 Ibid., 289.

Escapism under scrutiny - Homosexual balls during the Wilhelmine and Weimar era

68 (Translations in this section are my own, unless indicated.)
Eric D. Weitz, *Weimar Germany: Promise and Tragedy* (Princeton: Princeton University Press, 2007), 3.
69 Alfred Döblin, *Berlin Alexanderplatz*, tr. Michael Hofmann (London: Penquin, 2018), i.
70 Weitz, *Weimar Germany*, 9.
71 Ibid., 125–126.
72 Ibid., 24.
73 Birgit Schwarz, '"Long Live (occasionally) Tendency in Art!" Dix and the Dialectics of Modernism', *Otto Dix and the New Objectivity*, ed. Ulrike Groos and Nils Büttner (Stuttgart: Kunstmuseum Stuttgart, 2012), 69.
74 James A. van Dyke, 'Otto Dix's Folk Culture', *Otto Dix and the New Objectivity*, 87.
75 Ibid., 90.
76 Wolfgang Theis and Andreas Sternweiler, 'Alltag im Kaiserreich und in der Weimar Republic', *Eldorado: Homosexuelle Frauen und Männer in Berlin 1850–1950: Geschichte, Alltag und Kultur* (Berlin: Frölich und Kaufmann, 1984), 48–73.
77 Wolfgang Theis, 'Anders als die Andern: Geschichte eines Filmskandals', *Eldorado*, 28–30.
78 Robert Beachy, *Gay Berlin: Birthplace of a Modern Identity* (New York: Vintage Books, 2015), 46; Whisnaut, *Queer Identities*, 175, 179–180.
79 *Anders als die Andern*, dir., Richard Oswald, Berlin: Richard Oswald Film Produktion, 1919, 31.40 to 32.25 minutes.
80 Ibid., 37.38 to 37.44 minutes.
81 Ibid., 37.50 to 37.55 minutes.
82 Jens Dobler, *Zwischen Duldungspolitik und Verbrechensbekämpfung: Homosexuellenverfolgung durch die Berliner Polizei von 1848 bis 1933* (Frankfurt: Verlag für Polizeiwissenschaft, 2008), 352.
83 Magnus Hirschfeld, *Homosexualität des Mannes und des Weibes* (Berlin: Louis Marcus, 1914), 686.
84 Ibid.
85 Ibid., 685.
86 Dobler, *Zwischen Duldungspolitik und Verbrechensbekämpfung*, 352.
87 Ibid., 353.
88 Ibid., 352.
89 Ibid., 353. 'Der Leutnant duzt sue und ruft die interessantesten an den Tisch, um vom Schriftsteller besichtigt zu wedern!'.
90 Ibid., 353. 'Manche kommen mit Grabesmienen, unbewusst, trist, und antworten ausweichend; andere schüchtern, mit kleinen kindlichen Gebärden, als spielten sie.'
91 Hirschfeld, *Homosexualität des Mannes und des Weibes*, 686.
92 Ibid. 'Einige erscheinen dicht maskiert in undurchdringlichen Dominos, sie kommen und gehen, ohne daß jemand ahnt, wer sie gewesen sind'.
93 Ibid.
94 Ibid., 685.
95 Ibid., 686.
96 Ibid. 'ein großer Teil in Damenkliedern'.
97 Ibid., 686. '… jetzt tritt ein dicker Kapuziner ein, vor dem sich ehrfurchtsvoll Zigeuner, Pierrots, Matrosen, Clowns, Bäcker, Landsknechte, schmucke Offiziere, Herren und Damen im Reitanzuge, Buren, Japaner und zierliche Gieshas neigen'.

98 Ibid. 'Eine glutäugige Carmen setzt einem Jockey in Brand, ein feuriger Italiener schliesst mit einem Schneemann innigee Freundscaft'.

99 Ibid., 686–687. 'Die in buntesten Farben schillernde fröhliche Schar bietet ein höchst eigenartiges Bild … Kein Mißton trübt die allegmeine Freunde, bis die letzen Teilnehmerinnen beim matten Dämmerlicht des kalten Februarmorgens den Ort verlassen, an dem sie sic unter Mitempfindenden wenige Stunden als das träumen durften, was sie innerlich sind'.

100 Rainer Herrn, commentary on figure 3.4 'community and refuge', *Not Straight From Germany: Sexual Publics and Sexual Citizenship Since Magnus Hirschfeld*, ed. Michael Thomas Taylor, Annette F. Timm and Rainer Herrn (Ann Arbor: University of Michigan Press, 2017), 67.

101 Ibid.

102 Ibid.

103 The costume was sold by the Cotswold Auction Company on 25 August 2015 as lot 491. I have not been able to trace the provenance further (personal communication with Mr Stephen Barlett, April 2018). The costume was sold with another, described as a matador. This is probably incorrect. The accompanying red velvet costume has no maker's label but was clearly sold as a machine-stitched ready-made garment. Consisting of a doublet, hose and short shoulder cape with raised collar. A shirt may be missing. It resembles a 'Red Devil' costume sold by Weldon's. See Figure 7.

104 The attribution is based on the assumption that a red costume to which it became paired at auction is that of a matador, which is unlikely (see note immediately above).

105 Christopher Isherwood, *Christopher and His Kind* (London: Vintage [Methuen, 1977] 2002), 3.

106 Ibid., 29.

107 Stephen Spender, *The Temple* (London: Faber and Faber, 1988), 32–33.

108 Ibid., 156.

109 Quoted and discussed in Sabine Kriebel, 'Sexology's Beholders: The Exhibition POPSEX! in Calgary', *Not Straight From Germany*, 99.

110 Ibid., 98.

111 Ibid., 99.

112 See above, 77–78.

113 Philip Mansel, *Dressed to Rule: Royal and Court Costume from Louis XIV to Elizabeth II* (New Haven and London: Yale University Press, 2005), 18–36; *Wardrobes in Wartime: Fashion and Fashion Images during the First World War 1914–1918*, ed. Adelheid Rasche (Leipzig: E.A. Seemann, 2015).

114 David A. Boxwell, 'The Follies of War: Cross-Dressing and Popular Theatre on the British Front Lines, 1914–18', *MODERNISM/modernity*, 9:9 (2002), 1–20; Alon Rachamimov, 'The Disruptive Comforts of Drag: (Trans) Gender Performances among Prisoners of War in Russia, 1914–1920', *The American Historical Review*, 111:2 (2006), 362–382. See also, Jacob Bloomfield, '*Splinters*: Cross-Dressing Ex-Servicemen on the Interwar Stage', *Twentieth Century British History*, 30:1 (2019), 1–28.

Galvanizing distractions - The Royal Navy

115 Simon J. Bronner, *Crossing the Line: Violence, Play, and Drama in Naval Equator Traditions* (Amsterdam: Amsterdam University Press, 2006), 5; Sophy-Jenny Linon, 'Le passage de la Ligne, ou le carnaval de la mer: Luillier (1705), Léguât (1707)', *Dix-huitième Siècle*, 22 (1990), 185–194.

116 Carie Little Hersch, 'Crossing the Line: Sex, Power, Justice, and the US Navy at the Equator', *Duke Journal of Gender Law and Policy*, 9:277 (2002), 280.

117 Bronner, *Crossing the Line*, 13–14; 'Bunx', *Crossing the Line in H.M.S. Southampton* (London: The Arden Press, 1922).

118 Keith P. Richardson, 'Polliwogs and Shellbacks: An Analysis of the Equator Crossing Ritual', *Western Folklore*, 36:2 (1977), 157.

119 Imperial War Museum (IWM) 8201, 'Joseph Murray'. A similar, but shorter, account of the fancy dress ball appears in Joseph Murray, *Gallipoli As I Saw It* (London: William Kimber, 1965), 51.

120 Murray, *Gallipoli*, 38, 44, 45.

121 IWM 8201.

122 Norman Woodcock and Susan Burnett, *On That Day I Left My Boyhood Behind* (Bromley: Acorn Independent Press, 2014), 42.

123 Bronner, *Crossing the Line*, 8.

124 Ibid., 24.

125 Geoffrey Bennett, *The Battle of Jutland* (Barnsley: Pen and Sword Maritime [B.T. Batsford, 1964], 2015).

126 Steven Zealand, *Sailors and Sexual Identity: Crossing the Line Between 'Straight' and 'Gay' in the U.S. Navy* (New York: Harrington Press, 1995), 61.

127 IWM 06/1271.

128 Boxwell, 'The Follies of War', 16.

129 Ibid., 16–17; Rachamimov, 'The Disruptive Comforts of Drag', 375–376.

130 Boxwell, 'The Follies of War', 16–17; Rachamimov, 'The Disruptive Comforts of Drag', 375–376.

131 Boxwell, 'The Follies of War', 5.

132 IWM 06/1271.

133 Ibid.

134 Ibid.

135 IWM 15715, 'Charles Gordon Stringer', reel 1.

136 Ibid.

137 Ibid.

138 IWM 15715, reel 1.

Chapter 4

1 Sennett, *The Fall of Public Man*, 48, 54.

2 Susan G. Davis, *Parades of Power: Street Theatre in Nineteenth-Century Philadelphia* (Berkeley: University of Los Angeles Press, 1986), 164.

3 Girouard, *The Return to Camelot*, 68–70.

4 Text from www.1000gestalten.de. Accessed: July 2017.

5 Wil Longbottom, 'Spain "Will Act" If Catalan Independence Is Declared on Tuesday', *Sky News*, 9 October 2017. https://news.sky.com/story/spain-will-act-if-catalan-independence-is-declared-on-tuesday-11073647. Accessed: October 2017.

6 Anon., 'Mexico Violence: Clowns Protest over Acapulco Murder Rate', *BBC News*, 8 May 2018. ww.bbc.co.uk/news/world-latin-america-44038976. Accessed: June 2018.

Civic pride - The Sherborne pageant

7 Sherborne School Archive (SS)/Pag/9/1, i, 3.

8 Ibid., 34. *Black & White*, 8 April 1905. Unless indicated, all press cuttings are unpaginated.

9 Ibid., 127. *Western Gazette*, 16 June 1905.

10 Ibid., 3–4; Louis N. Parker, *Several of My Lives* (London: Chapman & Hall Ltd., 1928), 278–279.

11 SS/Pag/9/1, i, 62. *Coventry Standard*, 2 June 1905.

12 Ibid., i, 80. *Nottingham Guardian*, 10 June 1905.

13 Ibid., ii, 5. *Bristol Evening Times*, 17 June 1905.

14 Ibid., i, 106. *Western Press*, 13 June 1905.

15 Ibid., i, 92. *Newcastle Chronicle*, 13 June 1905.

16 Ibid., i, 65. from *Today*, 7 June 1905; ibid., 100. *Star*, 12 June 1905.

17 Ibid., i, 65.

18 Bakhtin, *Problems*, 160.

19 SS/Pag/9/1, i, 6.

20 Ibid.
21 Ibid.
22 SS/Pag/9/1, i, 54. *Coventry Standard*, 2 June 1905; *Westminster Gazette*, 13 June 1905.
23 SS/Pag/9/1, i, 54. *Standard*, 24 April 1905.
24 Ibid.
25 Anon. 'The Ball for the Relief of the Spitalfield Weavers …', *Spectator* (3 June 1837), 4.
26 Gail Johnson, 'Gay Old Versailles', 93–98.
27 For example, stories carried by the *Wiltshire County Mirror,* 14 April 1905 and Toronto's *The Globe,* 29 April 1905 are identical. Ibid., i, 39, 43.
28 SS/Pag/6/5.
29 SS/Pag/9/1, i, 38.
30 SS/Pag/14/1.
31 See above, 40–41.
32 For example, Chalmers Roberts, 'The Sherborne Pageant: A Striking Revival of Old England', *The World's Work and Play*, ed. Henry Norman, vi:31 (*Lady's Pictorial* supplement, June 1905), 7–11. SS/Pag/9/1, i, 60–61; *Queen,* 10 June 1905, ibid., i, 94; *Ladies' Field,* 24 June 1905, ibid., ii, 10.
33 SS/Pag/9/1, ii, 10. *Ladies' Field*, 24 June 1905.
34 Ibid., i, 6.
35 Ibid., i, 48. *Yorkshire Post*, 22 April 1905.
36 SS/Pag/11/5.
37 SS/Pag/9/1, i, 41. *The Queen*, 15 April 1905; ibid., 48. *The Times*, 19 May 1905.
38 Ibid., i, 51. *The Standard,* 24 April 1905 put the number of ladies at 160, ibid., 54.
39 Gordon, *Saturated World*, 110.
40 See also above, 39–42.
41 Bruce, 'On Dreamlands and Dress', 46, 54–55.
42 SS Lib. 11a. *King's School Library Loans Register 1886–1918*. The book was returned on 4 February 1905. Reference owed, with thanks, to Rachel Hassall.
43 Joseph Strutt, *A Complete View of the Dress and Habits of the People of England, From the Establishment of the Saxons in Britain to the Present Time*, 2 vols. (London: J. Nichols, 1796), i, iv.
44 Ibid, Plate LIII.
45 Ibid., ii, Plate CXXII.
46 See above, 37–38.
47 Sherborne Museum, 1968/311.
48 Sherborne Museum, 1995/26/12.
49 SS/Pag/3/6.
50 SS/Pag/6/5.
51 (SS)/Pag/9/1, i, 48. *The Times*, 19 May 1905.
52 Ibid., 104. *Manchester Guardian*, 12 June 1905.
53 Ibid., 124. *Birmingham Post*, 14 June 1905; *Coventry Standard*, 2 June 1905.
54 SS/Pag/11/1/4/2.
55 Readman, 'The Place of the Past', 170.

Finding a voice - Sydney Mardi Gras

56 Graham Carbery, *A History of the Sydney Gay and Lesbian Mardi Gras* (Parkville: Australian Lesbian and Gay Archives Inc., 1995), 7, 242.
57 Nor was this the first gay-themed event in Sydney. For an overview of homosexual campaigning before 1978, see Graham Willett, *Living Out Loud: A History of Gay and Lesbian Activism in Australia* (St Leonards: Allen & Unwin, 2000), 3–127.
58 Ibid., 53.
59 Donn Teal, *The Gay Militants: How Liberation Began in America, 1969–1971* (New York: St Martin's Press, 1971).

60 See below, 126–127.
61 *We'll Dance If We Want To*, SBS (1984), 17.56 to 23.13 minutes.
62 Ibid., 18.36 to 18.39 minutes.
63 Ibid., 20.12 to 20.21 minutes.
64 Ibid., 20.36 to 20.39 minutes.
65 Ibid., 20.57 to 20.59 minutes.
66 Many of Yang's photographs are collected in Gavin Harris, John Witte and Ken Davis, *New Day Dawning: The Early Years of Sydney's Gay & Lesbian Mardi Gras* (Sydney: Pride History Group, 2001), 59,63.
67 Carbery, *Mardi Gras*, 29–30.
68 Ibid., 242.
69 Quoted in ibid., 26.
70 Ibid.
71 Quoted in ibid., 31
72 Ibid., 26.
73 Anonymous male interviewee, 'Feed Them to the Cannibals!', *ABC* (1993), 30.47 to 31.03 minutes.
74 Willett, *Living Out Loud*, 54.
75 Ibid., 77–78.
76 Harris *et al., New Day Dawning*, 16.
77 Kimberly O'Sullivan, 'Feed Them to the Cannibals!', 42.28 to 42.48 minutes.
78 Quoted in Carbery, *Mardi Gras*, 40.
79 Harris *et al., New Day Dawning*, 18.
80 Carbery, *Mardi Gras*, 242.
81 Judith O'Callaghan, 'Glamour on a Shoestring', *Absolutely Mardi Gras: Costume and Design of the Sydney & Lesbian Mardi Gras*, ed. Kirsten Tilgals (Moorebank: Doubleday Books, 1997), 74–103.
82 Ron Smith, File 2, 17:59 to 18:06 minutes.
83 Willett, *Living Out Loud*, 111, 132.
84 Gareth Paull, 'Pre-Sleaze with Ease', *Sydney's Star Observer,* Friday, 4 September 1987, 7.
85 Museum of Applied Arts & Sciences, 95/172/1. For a detailed description of the costume see, https://collection.maas.museum/object/143457.
86 Glynis Jones, 'Peter Tully', *Absolutely Mardi Gras*, 64.
87 Carbery, *Mardi Gras*, 80.
88 Ibid.
89 Ron Smith, file 2, 17:59 to 21:15 minutes.
90 Ron Smith, file 2, 24:49 to 24:59 minutes.
91 Peter Tully, 'Feed Them to the Cannibals!', 06.57 to 07.12 minutes.
92 See above, 51–53.
93 Museum of Applied Arts and Sciences, 86/1189. For a detailed description of the costume see, https://collection.maas.museum/object/55174.
94 Ron Smith, file 2, 32:20 to 33:59 minutes; file 4,05:04 to 13:33 minutes.
95 David McDiarmid, 'Feed Them to the Cannibals!', 39.02 to 39.41 minutes.
96 Ron Smith, file 3, 00:00 to 01:54 minutes.
97 Clive Faro, 'We'll Dance If We Want To', 04.57 to 05.18 minutes.
98 Kimberly O'Sullivan, 'Feed Them to the Cannibals!', 14.49 to 15.18 minutes.
99 Louis Staples, 'Sheffield Pride Criticised for Calling Parade "Celebration, Not Protest"', *Indy100,* 10 May 2018, https://www.indy100.com/article/sheffield-pride-lgbt-rights-protest-celebration-placards-offence-8344621.

Pushing back - Women's marches

100 David A. Fahrenthold, 'Trump Recorded Having Extremely Lewd Conversation about Women in 2005', *The Washington Post,* 8 October 2015. https://www.washingtonpost.com/politics/trump-recorded-having-extremely-lewd-conversation-about-women-in-2005/2016/10/07/3b9ce776-8cb4-11e6-bf8a-3d26847eeed4_story.html?utm_term=.6f4f816134b9. Accessed: October 2017.

101 Sarah Larson, 'Scenes from the March', *Rise Up! The Women's Marches around the World* (New York: Condé Nast, 2017), 34, 39.
102 Erin Reimel and Krystin Arneson, 'A Sea of Pink', *Rise Up!*, 48.
103 Ibid.
104 Personal communication with Alli Sebastian Wolf, November 2017.
105 Quoted in Sarah Brown, 'Why We March', *Rise up!*, 30.
106 Personal communication with Marcia D.B. Levy, September 2017.
107 Brown, 'Why We March', 29.
108 Personal communication with Shayne Kopec, September 2017.
109 Marcia D.B. Levy.
110 Ibid.
111 Personal communication with Lindsay Schober, September 2017.
112 Ibid.
113 Ibid.
114 Personal communication with Amy Cartwright, September 2017.
115 Ibid.
116 Instagram, @flower.in.the.city, 21 January 2017. https://www.instagram.com/p/BPiTjfFhJGM/?taken-by=flower.in.the.city.
117 Amy Cartwright.
118 Personal communication with Vivian Vassar, September 2017.
119 Ibid.
120 Ibid. Vassar's 'second [suffragette] outfit is black and white with a black hat trimmed in purple, white, and green ribbons (for the Suffragette colors – purple symbolizing dignity, white purity, and green hope)'. The sash worn with this costume is green and white.
121 Ibid.
122 Alli Sebastian Wolf.
123 Ibid.
124 Ibid.
125 Ibid. The quoted time includes the making of the Glitoris.
126 Amy Cartwright.
127 Jan Cohen-Cruz, 'General Introduction', *Radical Street Performance: An International Anthology*, ed. Jan Cohen-Cruz (London and New York: Routledge, 1998), 2.
128 Suzanne Lacy and Leslie Labowitz, 'From Feminist Media Strategies for Political Performance', *Radical Street Performance*, 38–41.
129 Julia Felsenthal, 'The Organizers', *Rise Up!*, 17.
130 Lacy and Labowitz, 'From Feminist Media Strategies for Political Performance', 39–41.
131 Marcia D.B. Levy.
132 Alexandra Schwartz, 'Surely They Jest', *Rise Up!*, 81.
133 Richard Schechner, 'From the Street Is the Stage', *Radical Street Performance*, 197.
134 Personal communication with Pamela Mitchell, September 2017.
135 Ibid.
136 Ibid.
137 Amy Cartwright.
138 Brown, 'Why We March', 30; Larson, 'Scenes from the March', 34.
139 Susie Lau, 'Protest Fashion Takes Many Forms at Britain's Port Eliot Festival', 31 July 2017, www.vogue.com/article/protest-fashion-britain-port-eliot-festival?mbid=social_onsite_mail. Accessed: September 2017.
140 Personal communication with Margianta Surahman Juhanda Dinata, October 2017.
141 Ibid.
142 Brownie and Graydon, *The Superhero Costume*, 1.
143 Ibid., 2.
144 Personal communication with Margianta Surahman Juhanda Dinata, October 2017.

145 Joanna Robinson, 'Princess Leia's Legacy', *Rise up!*, 82–85.
146 Schechner, 'from The Street Is the Stage', 197.
147 Lindsay Schober.
148 Margianta Surahman Juhanda Dinata.
149 Alli Sebastian Wolf.
150 Willetts, *Living Out Loud*, 72.
151 Bancroft, 'When the Chevalier d'Eon Met Alexander McQueen', 16.

Epilogue

1   Anon., *Russian Pictures* (London: Sotheby's Auction Catalogue, 2017), Lots 66–68, 74–77.
2   *PowerMask: The Power of Masks*, ed. Patrick Lennon (Tielt: Lannoo Publishers, 2017).
3   Pussy Power Hat, V&A: CD.5–2017.
4   Justin McGuirk, 'Super Citizen Suit', *The Future Starts Here*, ed. Rory Hyde and Mariana Pestana (London: Victoria and Albert Museum, 2018), 56–59.
5   Personal communication with Rachel Fallon, June 2018.
6   Huckbody, 'Ugly Truth', 120–123.
7   Elena Goodinson, 'Lewes Bonfire Night Celebrations – in Pictures'. www.theguardian.com/uk-news/gallery/2017/nov/05/lewes-bonfire-night-celebrations-2017-in-pictures. Accessed: November 2018.
8   Hadley Freeman, 'We Need to Talk about Melania Trump's Out of Africa Wardrobe', *The Guardian*, 10 October 2018. www.theguardian.com/us-news/2018/oct/10/talk-about-Melania-trump-africa-wardrobe-pith-helmet-nazi. Accessed: October 2018.
9   Kashmira Gander, 'How Not to Dress Like an Offensive Idiot on Halloween', *The Independent*, 11 October 2018. www.independent.co.uk/life-style/halloween-costume-how-not-offensive-idiot-fancy-dress-racisim-a8005291.html. Accessed: October 2018.
10 Rosemary Bennett, 'Unforgiven: Now Students Ban Cowboy Outfits', *The Times*, 12 October 2018, 1.
11 Fred Davis, *Fashion, Culture, and Identity* (Chicago and London: The University of Chicago Press, 1992), 123–133.
12 Joanne Finkelstein, *The Fashioned Self* (Cambridge: Polity Press, 1991), 188.
13 Ibid., 189.
14 Goffman, *Presentation of Self*, 21.
15 John Robb and Oliver J.T. Harris, *The Body in History: Europe from the Palaeolithic to the Future* (Cambridge: Cambridge University Press, 2013), 214–215.
16 Ibid.
17 See above, 34–35.
18 *The Body in History*, 12.
19 Ibid., 3, 11.
20 Ibid., 220.
21 On the genesis of cosplay, now see, Thèresa Winge, *Costuming Cosplay: Dressing the Imagination* (London: Bloomsbury, 2019), 2–11. In her book, Winge argues for an American origin to cosplay. Subsequently, she has conceded that there could earlier examples in other continents. See, 'Fandoms and Self-Fashioning: Into the World of Cosplay', Dress: Fancy Podcast (7 June 2019). https://podcasts.apple.com/gb/podcast/episode-22-fandoms-self-fashioning-into-world-cosplay/id1436021370?i=1000440831293. Accessed: June 2019.
22 Lunning, 'Cosplay', 185–190; Thèresa Winge, 'Costuming the Imagination: Origins of Anime and Manga Cosplay', *Mechademia*, 1 (2006), 65–76.
23 www.worldcosplaysummit.jp/en/about/.
24 Cathy Sell, 'Manga Translation and Interculture', *Mechademia*, 6 (2011), 95.
25 Thèresa Winge, 'Undressing and Dressing Loli: A Search for the Identity of the Japanese Lolita', *Mechademia*, 3 (2008), 47–63.

26   Frenchy Lunning, 'Out of the Closet: The Fancy Phenomenon', *Mechademia*, 6 (2011), 139–150.

27   Barbara Brownie, 'The Mascularisation of Dressing Up', *Clothing Cultures*, 2:2 (2015), 145–146. http://uhra.
     herts.ac.uk/bitstream/handle/2299/15884/Accepted_Manuscript.pdf?sequence=10. Accessed: August 2018.

28   Craig Norris and Jason Bainbridge, 'Selling *Otaku*? Mapping the Relationship between Industry and Fandom
     in the Australian Cosplay Science', *Intersections: Gender and Sexuality in Asia and the Pacific*, 20 (2009).
     http://intersections.anu.edu.au/issue20/norris_bainbridge.htm. Accessed: August 2018. Emphasis original.

29   Joel Gn, 'Queer Simulation: The Practice, Performance and Pleasure of Cosplay', *Journal of Media and
     Cultural Studies*, 25:4 (2011), 585.

30   Ibid., 589.

31   Yashmen Kahn, 'Costume Drama: The Wonderful World of Cosplay', *BBC Radio 4*, 31 August, 2017, 20.01 to
     20.24 minutes.

32   Personal communication with Andy Bruening. July 2018.

33   Personal communication with Elisabeth Frank. July 2018.

34   Ibid.

35   Personal communication with Basil Waite. August 2018.

36   Norris and Bainbridge, 'Selling *Otaku*?'

37   Elisabeth Frank.

38   Personal communication with Ronnie Marshall. July 2018.

39   Ibid.

40   Ibid.

41   Wild, 'The Civilizing Process', 215.

42   Winge, *Costuming Cosplay*, 138–164.

43   Ibid., 20, 103.

44   Elisabeth Frank.

45   Andy Bruening.

46   Personal communication with Becka Noel. September 2018.

47   Andy Bruening; Elisabeth Frank.

48   Becka Noel.

49   Andy Bruening.

50   Elisabeth Frank.

51   Vix Tree, 'Bullying in Cosplay', 3 November 2015. www.washingtonpost.co.uk/vix-tree/bullying-in-
     cosplay_b_6841674.html. Accessed: August 2017.

52   Andy Bruening.

53   Personal communication with Lee Self. September 2018.

54   See above, 135–136.

55   Lee Self.

56   Ibid.

57   Personal communication with Deagal Remyr. September 2018. www.twitch.tv/deagal.

58   Ibid.

59   See above, 11.

60   Quoted in E.A. Smith, *George IV* (New Haven and London: Yale University Press, 1999), 188.

61   'Cutting up Rough', *The Works*, season 3, episode 9 (BBC, 20 July 1997), 00.56 to 01.00 minutes.

62   Luke Leitch, 'Sibling', www.vogue.com/fashion-shows/fall-2017-menswear/sibling. Accessed: February 2018;
     Brooke Roberts-Islam, 'SIBLING plunders Lady Di and Babs Windsor for London Fashion Week Show',
     www.huffingtonpost.co.uk/brooke-robertsislam/sibling-plunders-lady-di-_b_14355316.html. Accessed:
     February 2018.

63   http://craig-green.com/pages/about. Accessed: February 2018; Jan Deleon, 'Craig Green on Menswear's
     Future, Fashion Week and Modern Uniforms', 11 May 2017, www.highsnobiety.com/2017/05/11/craig-green-
     mr-porter-collection/. Accessed: February 2018.

64   Geczy and Karaminas, *Critical Fashion Practice*, 3–4.

65   Ibid.

66   Ibid., 4.

67   Ibid.

68   Ibid.

69   Ibid., 46–47, 146–148.

70   Granata, *Experimental Fashion*, 2.

71   Ibid., 3.

72   Ibid., 4.

73   Ibid.

74   Ibid.

75   Huckbody, 'Ugly Truth', 122.

76   Ibid.

77   Bakhtin, *Problems of Dostoevsky's Poetics*, 160; Geczy and Karaminas, *Critical Fashion Practice*, 46–47, 134.

78   Cole, *I Am Not Myself*, 16–17.

79   Granata, *Experimental Fashion*, 36–53.

80   Susannah Frankel, 'Introduction', Andrew Bolton, *Alexander McQueen: Savage Beauty* (New Haven and London: Yale University Press, 2011), 17–20; Dana Thomas, *Gods and Kings: The Rise and Fall of Alexander McQueen and John Galliano* (London: Allen Lane, 2015), 63–73.

81   Anon., 'Walter Van Beirendonck entre couleurs et réflexions', *Intima* (February, 2012), 310–318.

82   *PowerMask*, 172–173.

83   Ibid., 123; Clémence Mathieu, 'Identity and Masked Rituals', *PowerMask*, 150.

84   Charles Fréger, *Wilder Mann* (Berlin: Kehrer Heidelberg, 2012).

85   Anja Aronowsky Cronberg, 'Interviews', *Vestoj*, 7 (2016), 254.

86   Lisa Bowerman, 'Fashion Designers Send Actual Fancy Dress Outfits Down Runway at London's Fashion Week Men's', *Metro* (11 June 2018). https://metro.co.uk/2018/06/11/fashion-designers-send-actual-fancy-dress-outfits-runway-london-fashion-week-mens-7621533. Accessed: June 2018.

87   Emma Elizabeth Davidson, 'Munroe Bergdorf, a Fancy Dress Pumpkin, and Boring Summer Days at MAN SS19', *Dazed*, 10 June 2018. http://www.dazeddigital.com/fashion/article/40312/1/rottingdean-art-school-stefan-cooke-ss19-man-munroe-bergdorf-fancy-dress. Accessed: June 2018.

88   Personal communication with Bruce Asbestos, August 2018.

89   Ibid.

90   Ibid.

91   Ibid.

92   Ibid.

93   Ibid.

94   Ibid.

95   *The Vulgar: Fashion Redefined*, ed. Jane Alison and Sinéad McCarthy (London: Koenig Books, 2016); *Like Life: Sculpture, Color, and the Body*, ed. Luke Syson, Sheena Wagstaff, Emerson Bowyer and Brinda Kumar (New Haven and London: Yale University Press, 2018).

BIBLIOGRAPHY

Abels, Richard, *Alfred the Great: War, Kingship and Culture in Anglo-Saxon England*. London and New York: Longman, 1998.

Adam, Hajo and Adam D. Galinsky. 'Enclothed Cognition'. *Journal of Experimental Social Psychology*, 48:4. 2012, 918–925.

Adam Hakeem. 'Ghana's Winneba Fancy Dress Festival Is a Living Museum', 16 January 2018. www. okayafrica.com/photos-winneba-fancy-dress-festival-living-museum.

Adams, Geoff W. *The Emperor Commodus: Gladiator, Hercules or Tyrant?* Boca Raton: Brown Walker Press, 2013.

Addley, Esther. 'Killer Clown Sightings in the UK Trigger Police Warning', *The Guardian*. 11 October 2016. www.theguardian.com/uk-news/2016/oct/11/killer-clown-craze-uk-sightings-police-warning? CMP=oth_b-alpnews_d-2.

Alac, Patrik. *Bikini Story*. New York: Parkstone International, 2012.

Albrecht, Donald and Jeannine Falino, ed. *Gilded New York: Design, Fashion, and Society*. New York: The Monacelli Press, 2013.

Alighieri, Dante. *The Divine Comedy*. Translated by Allen Mandelbaum. New York: Alfred A. Knopf, 1995.

Alison, Jane and Sinéad McCarthy, ed. *The Vulgar: Fashion Redefined*. London: Koenig Books, 2016.

Allen, R.C. 'Real Incomes in the English-Speaking World, 1879–1913'. *Labour Market Evolution: The Economic History of Market Integration, Wage Flexibility and Employment Relation*. Edited by Graham Grantham and Mary MacKinnon. London: Routledge, 1994, 107–138.

Altfield, John. *With Light of Knowledge: A Hundred Years of Education in the Royal Arsenal Co-operative Society, 1877–1977*. London: Royal Arsenal Cooperative Society, 1981.

Althoff, Gerd. *Spielregeln der Politik im Mittelalter: Kommunikation in Frieden und* Fehde. Darmstadt: Wissenschaftliche Buchgesellschaft, 1997.

Althoff, Gerd. 'Zur Bedeutung Symbolischer Kommunikation für das Verständnis des Mittelalters'. *Frühmittelalterliche Studien*, 31 (1997), 370–389.

Anglo, Sydney. 'An Early Tudor Programme for Plays and Other Demonstrations against the Pope'. *Journal of the Warburg and Courtauld Institutes* 20:1/2 (January–June 1957), 176–179.

'Annales Monasterii de Waverleia, A.D. 1-1291'. *Annales Monastici*, ii. Edited by Henry Richards Luard. London: Longman, 1864.

'Annales de Prioratus de Dunstaplia, A.D. 1-1297'. *Annales Monastici*, iii. Edited by Henry Richards Luard. London: Longman, 1866.

Anon. 'Royalty in Fancy Dress', *Munsey's Magazine*. unknown date.

Anon. 'The Ball for the Relief of the Spitalfield Weavers …', *Spectator*. 3 June 1837, 4.

Anon. *Fancy Dress for Children*. London & Edinburgh, Ballantyne & Hanson, 1884.

Anon. *Evolution in Costume*. London & Paris: Liberty & Co., 1893.

Anon. 'Ball at Devonshire House', *The Times*. 3 July 1897, 12.

Anon. *Boston Evening Transcript*, 21 July 1897, 6.

Anon. *Fancy Dress: A Short Chronological Series of Costumes*. London & Edinburgh: Ballantyne & Hanson, 1898.

Anon. *Dress and Decoration*. London & Paris: Liberty & Co., 1905.

Anon. 'Fancy Dress', *The Sydney Mail*. 8 June 1910, 40.

Anon. *Catalogue of Official Robes and Banners*. Georgia: Knights of the Ku Klux Klan, 1925.

Anon. 'Northern Lights' article. *The Producer*, viii. February 1928, 216.

Anon. *Weldon's Fancy Dress for Ladies and Gentleman*. London: Weldon's Ltd., *c.* 1926–1930.

Anon. 'Middlesbrough's Recovery': The Value of Cooperative Practices'. *The Producer*, xiv. January 1930, 114–115.

Anon. 'News Item' article. *The Producer*, xiv. April 1930, 28.

Anon. 'Styles Change in Masquerade Costumes: Movie Actors and Actresses and Figures in the Day's News Are Characters Most Popular with New Crop of Maskers'. *The Milwaukee Journal* (23 April 1933), 6.

Anon. 'Museum director defends exhibit of Ku Klux Klan Robe'. 2 June 2005. www.siouxcityjournal.com/news/state-and-regional/museum-director-defends-exhibit-of-the-ku-klux-klan-robe/article_c511004c-0E52-5e69-a9d3-9235a7c14d84.html.

Anon. 'Walter Van Beirendonck entre couleurs et réflexions', *Intima* (February 2012), 310–318.

Anon. *Fancy Dress: Digital Insights Report*. insideonline, September 2016.

Anon. 'Man in Clown Mask "stabs Teen in Sweden"', *BBC News*. 14 October 2016. www.bbc.co.uk/news/world-europe-37657072.

Anon. 'Where's Lady Gaga? Singer Hides under Bizarre Floral Hooded Robe at Her Own Perfume Launch Party', *The Daily Mail*. 14 September 2016. www.dailymail.co.uk/tvshowbiz/article-2203062/lady-gaga-dons-bizarre-floral-hooded-robe-perfume-launch-party.html.

Anon. 'Priest Sorry for Dressing as Hugh Heffner and Simulating Sex with Male Playboy Bunnies in Public Carnival', *iNews*. 15 March 2017. http://inews.co.uk/essentials/news/priest-sorry-dressing-hugh-heffner-simulating-sex-male-playboy-bunnies-public-display/.-*RussianPictures*. London: Sotheby's auction catalogue, 2017.

Anon. 'Mexico Violence: Clowns Protest over Acapulco Murder Rate', *BBC News*. 8 May 2018. ww.bbc.co.uk/news/world-latin-america-44038976.

Anstruther, Ian. *The Knight and the Umbrella: An Account of the Eglinton Tournament 1839*. Gloucester: Alan Sutton, 1986.

Atkins, Harold W. *Advertising for Co-operative Societies*, second edition. Leicester: Leicester Co-Operative Printing Society, 1963.

Babcock, Barbara A. 'Introduction'. *The Reversible World: Symbolic Inversion in Art and Society*. Edited by Barbara A. Babcock. Ithaca and London: Cornell University Press, 1978, 13–36.

Baehr, Peter, and Gordon C. Wells. 'Introduction', Max Weber. *The Protestant Work Ethic and the 'Spirit' of Capitalism and Other Writings*. Edited and translated by Peter Baehr and Gordon C. Wells. London: Penguin Books, 2002.

Bakhtin, Mikhail. *Rabelais and His World*. Translated by Hélène Iswolsky. Bloomington & Indianapolis: Indiana University Press, 1965.

Bakhtin, Mikhail. *Problems of Dostoevsky's Poetics*. Edited and translated by Caryl Emerson. Minneapolis: University of Minnesota Press, 1984.

Bancroft, Alison. 'When the Chevalier d'Eon met Alexander McQueen: History, Gender and Subjectivity in the Costumes in *Eonnagata*'. *Studies in Costume & Performance*, 3:1 2018, 11–22.

Barbieri, Donatella. *Costume in Performance: Materiality, Culture, and the Body*. London: Bloomsbury Academic, 2017.

Barker-Benfield, G.J. *The Culture of Sensibility: Sex and Society in Eighteenth-Century Britain*. Chicago: The University of Chicago Press, 1992.

Banjanin, Milica. 'OF HARLEQUINS, DREAMERS, AND POETS: A Study of an Image in the Works of Elena Guro'. *Russian Language Journal/Русский язык*, 36:123/124 (1982), 223–235.

Beachy, Robert. *Gay Berlin: Birthplace of a Modern Identity*. New York: Vintage Books, 2015.

Beaton, Cecil. *The Years Between: Diaries 1939–44*. London: Weidenfeld and Nicolson, 1965.

Beaumont-Thomas, Ben. 'How We Made Cult Cartoon Mr Benn', *The Guardian*. 7 March 2017. www.theguardian.com/culture/2017/07/how-we-made-mr-benn-david-mckee-ray-brooks-interview.

Beéche, Arturo, Janet Ashton and Marlene Koenig. *The Other Grand Dukes – Sons and Grandsons of Russia's Grand Dukes*. Eurohistory, 2013.

Beer, Anna. *Milton: Poet, Pamphleteer & Patriot*. London and New York: Bloomsbury, 2008.

Bennett, Geoffrey. *The Battle of Jutland*. Barnsley: Pen and Sword Maritime [B.T. Batsford, 1964], 2015.

Bennett, Rosemary. 'Unforgiven: Now Students Ban Cowboy Outfits', *The Times*. 12 October 2018, 1.

Berlanstein, Lenard R. 'Breeches and Breaches: Cross-Dress Theater and the Culture of Gender Ambiguity in Modern France'. *Comparative Studies in Society and History*, 38:2 (1996), 338–369.

Bethe, Monica. 'Performance Dress in Japan'. *Berg Encylopedia of World Dress and Fashion: East Asia*. Edited by John E. Vollmer. Oxford: Berg Publishers, 2010, 404–410.

Blanton, DeAnne and Lauren M. Cook. *They Fought Like Demons: Women Soldiers in the American Civil War*. Stroud: Sutton Publishing, 2002.

Bloomfield, Jacob. '*Splinters*: Cross-Dressing Ex-Servicemen on the Interwar Stage'. *Twentieth Century British History*, 30:1 (2019), 1–28.

Bois, Yve-Alain. 'Picasso the Trickster'. *Picasso Harlequin 1917–1937*. Edited by Yve-Alain Bois. Milan: Skira Editore S.p.A., 2009, 19–36.

Bonds, Alexandra B., Dongshin Chang and Elizabeth Johnson, 'Performance Dress in China and Taiwan', *Berg Encylopedia of World Dress and Fashion: East Asia*. Edited by. John E. Vollmer. Oxford: Berg Publishers, 2010, 153–161.

Borowitz, Helen O. 'Painted Smiles: Sad Clowns in French Art and Literature'. *The Bulletin of the Cleveland Museum of Art*, 71:1, 1984, 23–35.

Bowerman, Lisa. 'Fashion Designers Send Actual Fancy Dress Outfits Down Runway at London's Fashion Week Men's', *Metro*. 11 June 2018. https://metro.co.uk/2018/06/11/fashion-designers-send-actual-fancy-dress-outfits-runway-london-fashion-week-mens-7621533.

Boxwell, David A. 'The Follies of War: Cross-Dressing and Popular Theatre on the British Front Lines, 1914–18'. *MODERNISM/modernity*, 9:9 (2002), 1–20.

Bristol, Michael D. *Carnival and Theater: Plebian Culture and the Structure of Authority in Renaissance England*. New York & London: Methuen, 1985.

Bronner, Simon J. *Crossing the Line: Violence, Play, and Drama in Naval Equator Traditions*. Amsterdam: Amsterdam University Press, 2006.

Brophy, James M. 'Carnival and Citizenship: The Politics of Carnival Culture in the Prussian Rhineland, 1823–1848'. *Journal of Social History*, 30:4 (1997), 873–904.

Brown, John. *Memoirs of the Courts of Sweden and Denmark during the Reigns of Christian VII. of Denmark and Gustavus III. and IV of Sweden*, 2 vols. London: The Grolier Society, 1818.

Brown, Sarah. 'Why We March'. *Rise Up! The Women's Marches around the World*. New York: Condé Nast, 2017, 28–33.

Brownie, Barbara. 'The Mascularisation of Dressing Up'. *Clothing Cultures*, 2:2, 2015, 145–146. http://uhra.herts.ac.uk/bitstream/handle/2299/15884/Accepted_Manuscript.pdf?sequence=10-.

Brownie, Barbara and Danny Graydon. *The Superhero Costume: Identity and Disguise in Fact and Fiction*. London: Bloomsbury Academic, 2016.

Bruce, Holly. 'On Dreamlands and Dress: The Role of Women at the Chelsea Arts Club Ball'. Unpublished Central Saint Martins BA thesis, 2013.

Buchan, Peter. *The Eglinton Tournament, and Gentleman Unmasked*. London: Simpkin Marshall & Co., 1840.

Budden, Julian. *Verdi*, revised edition. London: J. M. Dent, 1993.

Burke, Peter. *Popular Culture in Early Modern Europe*, third edition. Farnham: Ashgate, 2009.

Caillois, Roger. *Man, Play and Games*. Translated by M. Barash. Urbana & Chicago: University of Illinois Press, 1961.

Calendar of the Liberate Rolls, 1260–1267, vol. 5. London: HMSO, 1961.

Campbell, Bolaji. 'Eedun Ogun: War Masquerades in Ibadan in the Era of Modernisation'. *African Arts*, 48:1 (Spring 2015), 42–53.

Cannadine, David. 'The Context, Performance and Meaning of Ritual: The British Monarchy and the "Invention of Tradition", *c*. 1820–1977'. *The Invention of Tradition*. Edited by Eric Hobsbawm and Terence Ranger. Cambridge: Cambridge University Press, 1983, 101–164.

Carbery, Graham. *A History of the Sydney Gay and Lesbian Mardi Gras*. Parkville: Australian Lesbian and Gay Archives Inc., 1995.

Carpenter, David A. *The Minority of Henry III*. London: Methuen, 1990.

Carpenter, David A. 'The Household Rolls of King Henry III of England 1216–1272'. *Historical Research*, lxxx (2007), 22–46.

Cassidy, Richard and Mike Clasby. 'Matthew Paris and Henry III's Elephant'. https://finerollshenry3.org.uk/redist/pdf/fm-06-2012.pdf.

Cassirer, Peter. 'Gustaf III – The Theatre King: Librettist and Politician'. *Gustavian Opera: An Interdisciplinary Reader in Swedish Opera, Dance and Theatre 1771–1809*. Edited by Inger Mattson. Uppsala: Almqvist and Wiksell Tryckeri, 1990, 29–44.

Castle, Terry. 'The Carnivalization of Eighteenth-Century English Narrative'. *PMLA*, 99:5. 1984, 903–916.

Castle, Terry. *Masquerade and Civilization: The Carnivalesque in Eighteenth-Century English Culture and Fiction*. Stanford: Stanford University Press, 1986.

'Chronicle of Hailes Abbey', *British Library*, Cotton Cleopatra D.iii.

The Chronicle of William of Rishanger of the Barons' Wars. Edited by James Orchard Halliwell. London: John Bowyer Nicols and Son, 1840.

'*Chronicon vulgo dictum Chronicon Thomae Wykes, 1066–1288*', *Annales Monastici*, iv. Edited by Henry Richards Luard. London: Longman, 1869.

Chronicon Willelmi de Duobus Bellis apud Lewes et Evehsam Commissis', in *Ypodigma Neustriae, a Thoma Walsingham, quondam monachi monasterio S. Albani conscriptum*. Edited by Henry T. Riley. London: Longman, 1876.

The Church Historians of England, vol. V. pt. I. Translated by Joseph Stevenson. London: Beeleys, 1858.

Clarke, Ashley. 'genderless kei: harajuku's online fashion revival', *i-D*. 23 February 2016. https://i-d.vice.com/en_uk/article/8xn7pp/genderless-kei-harajukus-online-fashion-revival.

Cockfield, Jamie H. *White Crow: The Life and Times of Grand Duke Nicholas Mikhailovich Romanov: 1859–1919*. Santa Barbara: Praeger, 2002.

Cohen, Abner. *Masquerade Politics: Explorations in the Structure of Urban Carnival Movements*. Berkeley & Los Angeles: University of California Press, 1993.

Cohen-Cruz, Jan. 'General Introduction'. *Radical Street Performance: An International Anthology*. Edited by Jan Cohen-Cruz. London and New York: Routledge, 1998, 1–6.

Cole, Catherine M. *Ghana's Concert Party Theatre*. Bloomington and Indianapolis: Indiana University Press, 2001.

Cole, Herbert M. 'Introduction: The Mask, Masking, and Masquerade Arts in Africa', *I Am Not Myself: The Art of African Masquerade*, ed. Herbert M. Cole. Los Angeles: Museum of Cultural History, 1985, 15–27.

Cole, Herbert M. 'Masquerade, Theater, Dance Costumes', *Berg Encyclopedia of World Dress and Fashion: Africa*. Edited by Joanna B. Eicher and Doran H. Ross. Oxford: Berg Publishers, 2010, 120–130.

Comus. *Grand Fancy Dress Ball, Royal Pavillion Brighton*. Brighton: Tucknott, 1871.

Cook, Daniel Thomas, *The Commodification of Childhood: The Children's Clothing Industry and the Rise of the Child Consumer*. Durham & London: Duke University Press, 1994.

Cooper, Cynthia. *Magnificent Entertainments: Fancy Dress Balls of Canada's Governors General 1876–1898*. New Brunswick: Goose Lane Editions, 1997.

Craft-Fairchild, Catherine. *Masquerade and Gender: Disguise and Female Identify in Eighteenth-Century Fictions by Women*. Pennsylvania: The Pennsylvannia State University Press, 1993.

Crane, Diana. 'Clothing Behavior as Non-Verbal Resistance: Marginal Women and Alternative Dress in the Nineteenth Century'. *Fashion Theory*, 3:2 (1999), 241–268.

Crawford, Rosemary and Donald. *Michael and Natasha*. London: Weidenfeld & Nicolson, 1977.

Creighton, A. 'Masquerade and Christmas', *Stabroek News*. 31 December 1988, 14.

Cressy, David. *Bonfires & Bells: National Memory and the Protestant Calendar in Elizabethan and Stuart England*. Stroud: Sutton Publishing Limited, 2004.

Crewe, Steven Lea. 'Sport, Recreation and the Workplace in England, *c.* 1918–*c.* 1970'. Unpublished PhD thesis. Leicester: De Montfort University, 2014.

Crilly, Rob. 'Sinister Clown Sightings Spread across the US', *The Independent*. 16 September 2016. www.independent.co.uk/news/world/americas/clown-sightings-us-spread-woods-luring-children-georgia-north-carolina-south-carolina-a7311606.html.

Croizat-Glazer, Yassana. 'The Role of Ancient Egypt in the Masquerades at the Court of François 1er'. *Renaissance Quarterly*, 66:4 (2013), 1206–1249.

Cronberg, Anja Aronowsky. 'Interviews', *Vestoj*. 7, 2016, 226–287.

Davidson, Emma Elizabeth. 'Munroe Bergdorf, a Fancy Dress Pumpkin, and Boring Summer Days at MAN SS19', *Dazed*. 10 June 2018. http://www.dazeddigital.com/fashion/article/40312/1/rottingdean-art-school-stefan-cooke-ss19-man-munroe-bergdorf-fancy-dress.

Davis, Deborah. *Party of the Century: The Fabulous Story of Truman Capote and His Black and White Ball*. Hoboken: John Wiley & Sons, Inc., 2006.

Davis, Fred. *Fashion, Culture, and Identity*. Chicago and London: The University of Chicago Press, 1992.

Davis, Natalie Zemon. 'The Reasons of Misrule: Youth Groups and Charivaris in Sixteenth-Century France'. *Past & Present* 506 (February 1971), 41–75.

Davis, Susan G. *Parades of Power: Street Theatre in Nineteenth-Century Philadelphia* (Berkeley: University of Los Angeles Press, 1986).

Dearden, Lizzie. 'German Police Spark Outrage for Telling Authorities to Keep Refugees away from Carnival Celebrations', *The Independent*. 7 February 2017. www.independent.co.uk/news/world/europe/germany-police-email-authorities-refugees-keep-away-carnival-celebrations-north-rhine-westphalia-a7567401.html.

Deleon, Jan. 'Craig Green on Menswear's Future, Fashion Week and Modern Uniforms', 11 May 2017, www.highsnobiety.com/2017/05/11/craig-green-mr-porter-collection/.

Dobler, Jens. *Zwischen Duldungspolitik und Verbrechensbekämpfung: Homosexuellenverfolgung durch die Berliner Polizei von 1848 bis 1933*. Frankfurt: Verlag für Polizeiwissenschaft, 2008.

Döblin, Alfred. *Berlin Alexanderplatz*. Translated by Michael Hofmann. London: Penquin, 2018.

Donnelly, Marian C. 'Theaters in the Courts of Denmark and Sweden from Frederik II to Gustav III'. *Journal of the Society of Architectural Historians* 43:4 (1984), 328–340.

Drewal, Henry John. 'Gelede Masquerade: Imagery and Motif'. *African Arts*, 7:4 (1979), 8–19, 62–63, 95–96.

Drewal, Margaret Thompson and Henry John Drewal. 'More Powerful than Each Other: An Egbado Classification of Egungun', *African Arts*, 11:3 (April 1978), 28–99.

Drewal, Margaret Thompson and Henry John Drewal. 'The State of Research on Performance in Africa'. *African Studies Review*, 34:3 (1991), 1–64.

Dunn, Charles J. *Everyday Life in Traditional Japan*. Rutland, Vermont: Tuttle Publishing, 1969.

Dutton, Paul Edward. *Charlemagne's Mustache and Other Cultural Clusters of a Dark Age*. Basingstoke and New York: Palgrave Macmillan, 2004.

Eberhard Wolfram. *A History of China*. Translated by E.W. Dickes, second edition. London: Routledge and Kegan Paul Ltd., 1971.

Eicher, Joanne B. 'Clothing, Costume and Dress', *The Berg Companion to Fashion*. Edited by Valerie Steele. Oxford: Bloomsbury Academic, 2010, 151–152.

Eicher, Joanne B. and Sandra Lee Evenson. *The Visible Self: Global Perspectives on Dress, Culture, and Society*, fourth edition. London: Bloomsbury Publishing, 2015.

Elias, Norbert. *The Civilizing Process: Sociogenetic and Pscyhogenetic Investigations*, revised edition. Translated by Edmund Jephcott. Edited by Eric Dunning, Johan Goudsblom and Stephen Mennell. London: Basil Blackwell, 1939.

Elias, Norbert. *The Society of Individuals*. Translated by Edmund Jephcott. Edited by M Schröter. London: Basil Blackwell, [1987] 1991.

Elias, Norbert and John L. Scotson. *The Established and the Outsiders: A Sociological Enquiry into Community Problems*. London: Sage, 1965.

Elliott, Bridget J. 'Covent Garden Follies: Beardsley's Masquerade Images of Posers and Voyeurs'. *Oxford Art Journal*, 9:1 (1986), 38–48.

Erekosima, Toyne V. and Joanne B. Eicher. 'The Aesthetics of Men's Dress of the Kalabari of Nigeria'. *The Visible Self: Global Perspectives on Dress, Culture, and Society*. Edited by Joanne B. Eicher and Sandra Lee Evenson, fourth edition. London: Bloomsbury Publishing, 2015, 349–361.

Evenson, Sandra Lee. 'Dress as Costume in Theater and Performing Arts'. *Berg Encylopedia of World Dress and Fashion: Global Perspectives*. Edited by Joanne B. Eicher and Phyllis G. Tortora. Oxford: Berg, 2010, 136–145.

Fadeeva, Elena. 'Mythologies and Metamorphoses'. *Georgina Clapham: Mythologies and Metamorphoses*. Moscow: Triumph Gallery, 2018.

Fahrenthold, David A. 'Trump Recorded Having Extremely Lewd Conversation about Women in 2005', *The Washington Post*. 8 October 2015. www.washingtonpost.com/politics/trump-recorded-having-extremely-lewd-conversation-about-women-in-2005/2016/10/07/3b9ce776-8cb4-11e6-bf8a-3d26847eeed4_story.html?utm_term=.6f4f816134b9.

Fawaz, Ramzi. *The New Mutants: Superheroes and the Radical Imagination of American Comics*. New York and London: New York University Press, 2016.

Felsenthal, Julia. 'The Organizers'. *Rise Up! The Women's Marches around the World*. New York: Condé Nast, 2017, 14–21.

Fine Collins, Amy. 'A Taste for Living', *Vanity Fair*. 18 August 2014. www.vanityfair.com/style/2014/09/niki-de-gunzburg-profile.

Finkelstein, Joanne. *The Fashioned Self*. Cambridge: Polity Press, 1991.

Fitzgerald, Mary Ann, Henry J. Drewal and Moyo Okediji. 'Transformation through Cloth: An Egungun Costume of the Yoruba'. *African Arts*, 28:2 (1995), 54–57.

Fogelmarck, Stig. 'Gustav III and His Opera House'. *Gustavian Opera: An Interdisciplinary Reader in Swedish Opera, Dance and Theatre 1771–1809*. Edited by Inger Mattson. Uppsala: Almqvist and Wiksell Tryckeri, 1990, 47–63.

Foulkes, Nicholas. *Bals: Legendary Costume Balls of the Twentieth Century*. New York: Assouline Publishing, 2011.

Frankel, Susannah. 'Introduction', Andrew Bolton, *Alexander McQueen: Savage Beauty*. New Haven and London: Yale University Press, 2011, 14–27.

Freeman, Hadley. 'You Shall Go to the Ball', *The Guardian*. 18 July 2006. www.theguardian.com/lifeandstyle/2006/jul/18/fashion.shopping?CMP=share_btn_link.

Freeman, Hadley. 'We Need to Talk about Melania Trump's Out of Africa Wardrobe', *The Guardian*. 10 October 2018. www.theguardian.com/us-news/2018/oct/10/talk-about-Melania-trump-africa-wardrobe-pith-helmet-nazi.

Fréger, Charles. *Wilder Mann*. Berlin: Kehrer Heidelberg, 2012.

Fry, Gladys-Marie. *Night Riders in Black Folk History*. Chapel Hill: University of North Carolina Press, 1975.

Fury, Alexander and Adélia Sabatini. *Dior Catwalk*. London: Thames and Hudson, 2017.

Gail Johnson, Susan. 'Like a Glimpse of Gay Old Versailles: Three Gilded Age Balls'. *Gilded New York: Design, Fashion, and Society*. Edited by Donald Albrecht and Jeannine Falino. New York: The Monacelli Press, 2013, 83–106.

Gaius Suetonius Tranquillus. *The Twelve Caesars*. Translated by Robert Graves. London: Penguin, [1957] 2007.

Galembo, Phyllis. *Dressed for Thrills: 100 Years of Halloween Costume & Masquerade*. New York: Harry N. Abrams, Inc., 2002.

Galembo, Phyllis. *Maske*. New York: Aperture Foundation, 2016.

Gander, Kashmira. 'How Not to Dress Like an Offensive Idiot on Halloween', *The Independent*. 11 October 2018. www.independent.co.uk/life-style/halloween-costume-how-not-offensive-idiot-fancy-dress-racisim-a8005291.html.

Gaskin, Gerhard H., Deborah Wills and Frank Roberts. *Legendary: Inside the House Ballroom Scene*. Durhem: Duke University Press, 2013.

Geczy, Adam and Vicki Karaminas. *Critical Fashion Practice: From Westwood to Beirendonck*. London: Bloomsbury, 2017.

Gerste, Ronald D. *Der Zauberkönig: Gustav III. und Schwedens Goldene Zeit*. Göttingen: Steidl Verlag, 1996.

Gilhus, Ingvild S. 'Carnival in Religion: The Feast of Fools in France'. *Numen*, 37:1 (June, 1990), 24–52.

Gill, James. *Lords of Misrule: Mardi Gras and the Politics of Race in New Orleans*. Jackson: University Press of Mississippi, 1997.

Girouard, Mark. *The Return to Camelot: Chivalry and the English Gentleman*. New Haven & London: Yale University Press, 1991.

Gn, Joel. 'Queer Simulation: The Practice, Performance and Pleasure of Cosplay'. *Journal of Media and Cultural Studies*, 25:4 (2011), 583–593.

Godden, Cecil P. *The Story of the Sherborne Pageant*. Sherborne: F. Bennett, 1905.

Goffman, Erving. *The Presentation of Self in Everyday Life*. London: Penguin [Anchor Books, 1959], 1969.

Goodinson, Elena. 'Lewes Bonfire Night Celebrations – in Pictures'. www.theguardian.com/uk-news/gallery/2017/nov/05/lewes-bonfire-night-celebrations-2017-in-pictures.

Gordon, Beverley. *The Saturated World: Aesthetic Meanings, Intimate Objects, Women's Lives, 1890–1940*. Knoxville: The University of Tennessee Press, 2006.

Graham, Rose. 'Letters of Cardinal Ottoboni'. *English Historical Review*, lvii (1900), 87–120.

Granta, Francesca. *Experimental Fashion: Performance Art, Carnival and the Grotesque Body*. London and New York: I.B. Tauris, 2017.

Green, Richard C. 'Bloch, Beethoven and Der Blaue Reiter'. *Music in Art*, 37:1/2, The Courts in Europe: Music Iconography and Princely Power (2012), 275–290.

Groth, Håkan and Lars Strömbold. *Barock och Rokoko i Sverige 1650–1750*. Stockholm: Bokförlaget Prisma, 2005.

Haley, Jennifer. 'Bamana'. *I Am Not Myself: The Art of African Masquerade*. Edited by Herbert M. Cole. Los Angeles: Museum of Cultural History, 1985, 28.

Hann, Rachel. 'Debating Critical Costume: Negotiating Ideologies of Appearance, Performance and Disciplinarity'. *Studies in Theatre and Performance*, 37:2 (2017), 1–17.

Harding, Frances. 'Introduction'. *The Performance Arts in Africa: A Reader*. Edited by Frances Harding. London and New York: Routledge, 2002, 1–26.

Harris, Gavin, John Witte and Ken Davis. *New Day Dawning: The Early Years of Sydney's Gay & Lesbian Mardi Gras*. Sydney: Pride History Group, 2001.

Harvey, Arnold D. 'Gustav III of Sweden'. *History Today*, 53:12 (2003), 9–15.

de la Haye, Amy and Valerie D. Mendes, eds. *The House of Worth: Portrait of an Archive*. London: V&A Publishing, 2014.

Hecht, Thomas. 'Dance Costume'. *The Berg Companion to Fashion*. Edited by Valerie Steele. Oxford: Bloomsbury Academic, 2010, 195–199.

Hersch, Carie Little. 'Crossing the Line: Sex, Power, Justice, and the US Navy at the Equator'. *Duke Journal of Gender Law and Policy*, 9:277 (2002), 277–324.

Heyl, Christoph. 'The Metamorphosis of the Mask in Seventeenth- and Eighteenth-Century London'. *Masquerade and Identities: Essays on Gender, Sexuality and Marginality*. Edited by Efrat Tseëlon. London: Routledge, 2001, 114–134.

Hilberbrand, Lucas. *Paris Is Burning: A Queer Film Classic*. Vancouver: Arsenal Pulp Press, 2013.

Hirschfeld, Magnus. *Homosexualität des Mannes und des Weibes*. Berlin: Louis Marcus, 1914.

Hobsbawm, Eric. 'Mass-Producing Traditions: Europe, 1870–1914'. *The Invention of Tradition*. Edited by Eric Hobsbawm and Terence Ranger. Cambridge: Cambridge University Press, 1983, 263–308.

Holt, Ardern. *Fancy Dresses Described; or What to Wear at Fancy Dress Balls*. London: Wyman & Sons, 1887.

Horowitz, Elliott. *Reckless Rites: Purim and the Legacy of Jewish Violence*. Princeton: Princeton University Press, 2006.

Horton, Helena. 'Man Dressed as Batman Chases "Killer Clowns" in Cumbria', 14 October 2016. www.msn.com/en-us/news/offbeat/man-dressed-as-batman-chases-killer-clowns-in-cumbria/ar-AAiTkoB?ocid=se.

Huckbody, Jamie. 'The Ugly Truth'. *Harper's BAZAAR Australia* (August 2018), 120–123.

Hutton, Ronald. *The Stations of the Sun: A History of the Ritual Year in Britain*. Oxford: Oxford University Press, 1996.

Ilan-Alter, Ann. 'Masked and Unmasked at the Opera Balls: Parisian Women Celebrate Carnival', *Masquerade and Identities: Essays on Gender, Sexuality and Marginality*. Edited by Efrat Tseëlon. London: Routledge, 2001, 135–152.

Isherwood, Christopher. *Christopher and His Kind*. London: Vintage [Methuen, 1977] 2002.

Jacobs, Harrison. 'Gamers Are Spending Thousands of Dollars a Year on This 'Free' Video Game', *Business Insider UK*. 20 March 2015. http://uk.businessinsider.com/redditors-explain-how-they-spent-thousands-of-dollars-league-of-legends-2015-3.

Jarvis, Anthea. 'Fancy Dress', *The Berg Companion to Fashion*. Edited by Valerie Steele. Oxford: Bloomsbury Academic, 2010, 270–272.

Jarvis, Anthea and Patricia Raine. *Fancy Dress*. Aylesbury: Shire, 1984.

Jedrej, Marian Charles. 'A Comparison of Some Masks from North America, Africa, and Melanesia', *Journal of Anthropological Research*, 36:2 (1980), 220–230.

Jones, Glynis. 'Peter Tully'. *Absolutely Mardi Gras: Costume and Design of the Sydney & Lesbian Mardi Gras*. Edited by Kirsten Tilgals. Moorebank: Doubleday Books, 1997, 64.

Jonkers, Gert and Jop van Bennekom. *Buttoned-Up*. London: Penguin, 2013.

Kanagawa, Chie, Susan E. Cross and Hazel Rose Markus. '"Who Am I?" The Cultural Psychology of the Conceptual Self'. *Personality and Social Psychology Bulletin*, 27 (2001), 90–103.

Kastl, Jakub and Lyndon Moore. 'Wily Welfare Capitalist: Werner von Siemens and the Pension Plan'. *Cliometrica*, 4:3 (2010), 321–348.

Katritzky, M.A. 'Harlequin in Renaissance Pictures'. *Renaissance Studies*, 11:4 (1997), 381–419.

Ketzer, David I. *Ritual, Politics, and Power*. New Haven and London: Yale University Press, 1988.

Kim, Heejung and Hazel Rose Markus. 'Deviance or Uniqueness, Harmony or Conformity? A Cultural Analysis'. *Journal of Personality and Social Psychology*, 77:4 (1999), 785–800.

King, David and Cathy Porter. *Blood & Laughter: Caricatures from the 1905 Revolution*. London: Jonathan Cape, 1983.

Kinney, Alison. *Hood*. London: Bloomsbury, 2016.

Kinser, Samuel. 'Presentation and Representation: Carnival at Nuremberg, 1450–1550', *Representations* 13 (1986), 1–41.

Kinser, Samuel. *Carnival American Style: Mardi Gras at New Orleans and Mobile*. Chicago and London: The University of Chicago Press, 1990.

Kinser, Samuel. 'The Combats of Carnival and Lent: A Medieval Genre Transformed (Giulio Cesare Croce, ca.1550–1614)'. *Medieval Folklore*, iii (Fall, 1994), 167–185.

Kitayama, Shinobu, Hazel Rose Markus and Masaru Kurokawa. 'Culture, Emotion, and Well-Being: Good Feelings in Japan and the United States'. *Cognition & Emotion*, 14:1 (2000), 93–124.

Kjellberg, Anne and Susan North. *Style & Splendour: The Wardrobe of Queen Maud of Norway*. London: V&A Publications, 2005.

Kriebel, Sabine. 'Sexology's Beholders: The Exhibition POPSEX! in Calgary'. *Not Straight from Germany: Sexual Publics and Sexual Citizenship Since Magnus Hirschfeld*. Edited by Michael Thomas Taylor, Annette F. Timm and Rainer Herrn. Ann Arbor: University of Michigan Press, 2017.

Lacy, Suzanne and Leslie Labowitz. 'From Feminist Media Strategies for Political Performance'. *Radical Street Performance: An International Anthology*. Edited by Jan Cohen-Cruz. London and New York: Routledge, 1998, 38–41.

Landis, Deborah Nadoolman. *Filmcraft: Costume Design*. Lewes: Ilnex Press, 2017.

Langner, Lawrence. *The Importance of Wearing Clothes*. Los Angeles: Elysium Growth Press, 1991.

Larson, Sarah. 'Scenes from the March', *Rise Up! The Women's Marches around the World*. New York: Condé Nast, 2017.

Lau, Susie. 'Protest Fashion Takes Many Forms at Britain's Port Eliot Festival'. 31 July 2017. www.vogue.com/article/protest-fashion-britain-port-eliot-festival?mbid=social_onsite_mail.

Laver, James, ed. *Memorable Balls*. London: Derek Verschoyle, 1954.

Le Roy Ladurie, Emmanuel. *Le Carnaval de Romans*. Paris: Editions Gallimard, 1979.

Leitch. Luke. 'Sibling'. www.vogue.com/fashion-shows/fall-2017-menswear/sibling.

Lennon, Patrick, ed. *PowerMask: The Power of Masks*. Tielt: Lannoo Publishers, 2017.

Linon, Sophy-Jenny. 'Le passage de la Ligne, ou le carnaval de la mer: Luillier (1705), Léguât (1707)'. *Dix-huitième Siècle*, 22 (1990), 185–194.

Longbottom, Wil. 'Spain "Will Act" if Catalan Independence Is Declared on Tuesday', *Sky News*. 9 October 2017. https://news.sky.com/story/spain-will-act-if-catalan-independence-is-declared-on-tuesday-11073647.

Longerich, Peter. *Heinrich Himmler: A Life*. Translated by Jeremy Noakes and Lesley Sharpe. Oxford: Oxford University Press, 2012.

Lotman, Yuri. *Universe of the Mind: A Semiotic Theory of Culture*. Translated by Ann Shukman. Bloomington and Indianapolis: Indiana University Press, 1990.

Lott, Eric. *Love & Theft: Blackface Minstrelsy & the American Working Class*. Oxford: Oxford University Press [1993], 2013.

Lunning, Frenchy. 'Cosplay', *Berg Encyclopedia of World Dress and Fashion: Global Perspectives*. Edited by Joanne B. Eicher and Phyllis G. Tortora. Oxford: Berg, 2010, 185–190.

Lunning, Frenchy. 'Out of the Closet: The Fancy Phenomenon'. *Mechademia*, 6 (2011), 139–150.

Mack, John. 'Introduction: About Face'. *Masks: Art of Expression*. Edited by John Mack. London: British Museum Press, 1994, 9–31.

MacLean, Nancy. *Behind the Mask of Chivalry: The Making of the Second Ku Klux Klan*. Oxford: Oxford University Press, 1994.

Maddicott, John R. *Simon de Montfort*. Cambridge: Cambridge University Press, 1994.

Maguire, Nancy Klein. 'The Theatrical Mask/Masque of Politics: The Case of Charles I'. *Journal of British Studies*, 28:1 (1989), 1–22.

Mallé, Marie-Pascale. 'Du carnaval au carnivalesque. «Le Monde à l'Envers»'. *Fêtes, mascarades et carnavals: Circulations, transformations et contemporanéité*. Edited by Nathalie Gauthard. Lavérune: éditions L'Entretemps, 2014, 27–56.

Mänd, Anu. *Urban Carnival: Festive Culture in the Hanseatic Cities of the Eastern Baltic, 1350–1550*. Turnhout: Brepols Publishers nv, 2005.

Mansel, Philip. *Dressed to Rule: Royal and Court Costume from Louis XIV to Elizabeth II*. New Haven and London: Yale University Press, 2005.

Marshik, Celia. *At The Mercy of Their Clothes: Modernism, the Middlebrow, and British Garment Culture*. New York: Columbia University Press, 2017.

Mathieu, Clémence. 'Identity and Masked Rituals', *PowerMask: The Power of Masks*. Edited by Patrick Lennon. Tielt: Lannoo Publishers, 2017, 139–151.

McCracken, Grant. *Culture and Consumption: New Approaches to the Symbolic Character of Consumer Goods and Activities*. Bloomington & Indianapolis: Indiana University Press, 1990.

McGuirk, Justin. 'Super Citizen Suit', *The Future Starts Here*. Edited by Rory Hyde and Mariana Pestana. London: Victoria and Albert Museum, 2018, 56–59.

McQuillen, Colleen. 'Artists' Balls and Conceptual Costumes at the Russian Academy of Arts, 1885–1909'. *Fashion Theory*, 16:1. 2012, 29–48.

McQuillen, Colleen. *The Modernist Masquerade: Stylising Life, Literature and Costumes in Russia*. Madison: University of Wisconsin Press, 2013.

Mears, Patricia and G. Bruce Boyer, eds. *Elegance in an Age of Crisis: Fashions of the 1930s*. New Haven and London: Yale University Press, 2014.

The Metrical Chronicle of Robert of Gloucester, II. Edited by William Aldis Wright. London: Eyre and Spottiswoode, 1887.

Micots, Courtnay. 'Fancy Dress: African Masquerade in Coastal Ghana', *Berg Encyclopedia of World Dress and Fashion: Africa*. Edited by Joanna B. Eicher and Doran H. Ross. Oxford: Berg Publishers, 2010, Accessed: June 2016. http://dx.doi.org/10.2752/BEWDF/EDch1511.

Micots, Courtnay. 'Performing Ferocity: Fancy Dress, Asafo, and Red Indians in Ghana'. *African Arts*, 45:2 (Summer 2012), 24–35.

Micots, Courtnay. 'Masquefest 2012.' In *Berg Encyclopedia of World Dress and Fashion: Africa*, edited by Joanne B. Eicher and Doran H. Ross. Oxford: Berg Publishers, 2010. Accessed: June 2016. http://dx.doi.org/10.2752/BEWDF/EDch1512.

Mitchell, Rebecca N. 'The Victorian Fancy Dress Ball, 1870–1900'. *Fashion Theory*, 21:3 (2017), 291–315.

Moore, Stephen. '"A Nation of Harlequins"? Politics and Masculinity in Mid-Eighteenth-Century Britain'. *Journal of British Studies*, 49:3 (2010), 514–539.

de Montor, Artaud. *Histoire de l'assassignat de Gustave III, roi de Suède. Par un officer Polonais, témoin occulaire*. Paris, 1797.

Moruzzi, Norma Claire. *Speaking through the Mask: Hannah Arendt and the Politics of Social Identity*. Ithaca and London: Cornell University Press, 2000.

Moser, Walter, ed. *Helen Levitt*. Berlin: Kehrer Heidelberg, 2018.

Mullen, Brian, Michael J. Migdal and Drew Rozell. 'Self-Awareness, Deinviduation, and Social Identity: Unravelling Theoretical Paradoxes by Filling Empirical Lacunae'. *Personality and Social Psychology Bulletin*, 29:9 (2003), 1071–1081.

Müller, Emilia. 'Fashion & Fancy in New York: The American Monarchs'. Paper presented at Fashion: Exploring Critical Issues, Oxford, September 2011. www.inter-disciplinary.net/wp-content/uploads/2011/08/muellerfapaper.pdf.

Munro, John H. 'The Medieval Scarlet and the Economics of Sartorial Splendour'. *Cloth and Clothing in Medieval Europe: Essays in Memory of Professor E. M. Carus-Wilson*. Edited by Negley B. Harte and Kenneth G. Ponting. London: Heinemann Educational, 1983, 13–70.

Murphy, Sophia. *The Duchess of Devonshire's Ball*. London: Sidgwick & Jackson, 1984.

Murray, Joseph. *Gallipoli As I Saw It*. London: William Kimber, 1965.

Nicholls, George J. *Bacon and Hams*. London: Richard & Sons Ltd, 1917.

Nicoll, Allardyce. *The World of Harlequin: A Critical Study of the Commedia dell' Arte*. Cambridge: Cambridge University Press, 1963.

Norris, Craig and Jason Bainbridge. 'Selling *Otaku*? Mapping the Relationship between Industry and Fandom in the Australian Cosplay Science'. *Intersections: Gender and Sexuality in Asia and the Pacific*, 20 (2009). http://intersections.anu.edu.au/issue20/norris_bainbridge.htm.

Nunley, John W. 'The Fancy and the Fierce'. *African Arts*, 14:2 (1981), 52–58,87–88.

Nunley, John W. *Moving with the Face of the Devil: Art and Politics in Urban West Africa*. Urbana and Chicago: University of Illinois Press, 1987.

O'Callaghan, Judith. 'Glamour on a Shoestring'. *Absolutely Mardi Gras: Costume and Design of the Sydney & Lesbian Mardi Gras*. Edited by Kirsten Tilgals. Moorebank: Doubleday Books, 1997, 74–103.

O'Toole, Emer. *Girls Will Be Girls: Dressing Up, Playing Parts and Daring to Act Differently*. London: Orion Books, 2015.

Olson, Nancy. *Gavarni: The Carnival Lithographs*. New Haven: Yale University Art Gallery, 1979.

Orgel, Stephen, ed. *Ben Jonson: The Complete Masques*. New Haven & London: Yale University Press, 1969.

Ozouf, Mona. 'Space and Time in the Festivals of the French Revolution'. *Comparative Studies in Society and History*, 17:3 (1975), 372–384.

Parker, Geoffrey. 'Success and Failure during the First Century of the Reformation'. *Past & Present*, 136 (1992), 43–82.

Parker, Louis N. *Several of My Lives*. London: Chapman & Hall Ltd., 1928.

Parsons, Elaine Frantz. 'Midnight Rangers: Costume and Performance in the Reconstruction-Era Ku Klux Klan'. *The Journal of American History*, 92:3 (2005), 811–836.

Parsons, Elaine Frantz. *Ku-Klux Klan: The Birth of the Klan during Reconstruction*. Chapel Hill: University of North Carolina Press, 2015.

Parsons, Elaine Frantz. 'Horns, Masks, and Women's Dress: How the First Klan Used Costume to Build US Terrorism', 8 December 2016. http://vimeo.com/195032653.

Pastoreau, Michel. *Figures et Couleurs: Étude sur la symbolique et la sensibilité médiévales*. Paris: Le Léopard d'or, 1986.

Paull, Gareth. 'Pre-Sleaze with Ease', *Sydney's Star Observer*. Friday, 4 September 1987, 7.

Pausanias. *Description of Greece* Translated by W.H.S. Jones and H.A. Ormerod. Loeb Classical Library, Cambridge, MA: Harvard University Press, 1955.

Payton, Matt. 'Mexico City Hosts First Ever Day of the Dead Parade Thanks to James Bond', *The Independent*. 31 October 2016. www.indepedent.co.uk/news/world/americas/mexico-city-day-of-the-dead-parade-james-bond-halloween-pictures-a7388191.html.

Peitcheva, Maria. *Konstantin Somov Drawings: Colour Plates*. Maria Peitcheva, 2016.

Pepper, Terence. *High Society: Photographs 1897–1914*. London: The National Portrait Gallery Publications, 1998.

Picton, John. 'What's in a Mask?' *The Performance Arts in Africa: A Reader*. Edited by Frances Harding. London and New York: Routledge, 2002, 49–68.

Plutarch, *Lives: Alcibiades*. Translated by Bernadotte Perrin. Loeb Classical Library, Cambridge, MA: Harvard University Press, 1916.

Pole, Steven. 'Insane Clown Pose', *The Guardian: G2*. 1 November 2016, 6–9.

Poppy, Pat. 'Fancy Dress? Costume for Re-enactment'. *Costume*, 31 (1997), 100–104.

Rachamimov, Alon. 'The Disruptive Comforts of Drag: (Trans)Gender Performances among Prisoners of War in Russia, 1914–1920'. *The American Historical Review*, 111:2 (2006), 362–382.

Rangström, Lena. *Kläder för tid och evighet: Gustaf III sedd genom sina dräkter*. Helsingborg: AB Boktryck, 1997.

Rasche, Adelheid. Editor. *Wardrobes in Wartime: Fashion and Fashion Images during the First World War 1914–1918*. Leipzig: E.A. Seemann, 2015.

Readman, Paul. 'The Place of the Past in English Culture c. 1890–1914'. *Past & Present*, 186 (2005), 147–199.

Reimel, Erin and Krystin Arneson, 'A Sea of Pink'. *Rise Up! The Women's Marches around the World*. New York: Condé Nast, 2017, 46–47.

Ribeiro, Aileen. 'The King of Denmark's Masquerade'. *History Today*, 27:6 (1977), 385–389.

Ribeiro, Aileen. *Masquerade*. London: BAS Printers Limited, 1983.

Ribeiro, Aileen. *The Dress Worn at Masquerades in England, 1730 to 1790, and Its Relation to Fancy Dress in Portraiture*. New York: Garland Publishing, 1984.

Richardson, Keith P. 'Polliwogs and Shellbacks: An Analysis of the Equator Crossing Ritual', *Western Folklore*, 36:2 (1977), 154–159.

Ridley, Jane. *Bertie: A Life of Edward VII*. London: Vintage Books, 2012.

Ritchie, Donald. *The Image Factory: Fads and Fashions in Japan*. London: Reaktion Books Ltd, 2003.

Robb, John and Oliver J.T. Harris. *The Body in History: Europe from the Palaeolithic to the Future*. Cambridge: Cambridge University Press, 2013.

Roberts, Chalmers. 'The Sherborne Pageant: A Striking Revival of Old England', *The World's Work and Play*, ed. Henry Norman, vi:31 (June 1905), 7–11.

Roberts-Islam, Brooke. 'SIBLING Plunders Lady Di and Babs Windsor for London Fashion Week Show'. www.huffingtonpost.co.uk/brooke-robertsislam/sibling-plunders-lady-di-_b_14355316.html.

Robinson, Joanna. 'Princess Leia's Legacy'. *Rise Up! The Women's Marches around the World*. New York: Condé Nast, 2017, 82–87.

Rosalind Jones, Ann and Peter Stallybrass. *Renaissance Clothing and the Materials of Memory*. Cambridge: Cambridge University Press, 2000.

Ross, India. 'Has Gay Pride Sold Out?' *FT Weekend Magazine*. 13/14 August 2016, 15.

Ross, Robert. *Clothing: A Global History, or, the Imperialists' New Clothes*. Cambridge: Polity Press, 2008.

Rudwin, Maximilian Josef. *The Origin of the German Carnival Comedy*. New York: G.E. Stechert & Co., 1920.

Sahlberg, Gardar. *Murder at the Masked Ball: The Assassination of Gustaf III of Sweden*. Translated by Paul Britten Austin. London: Macdonald, 1974.

Satre, Lowell J. 'After the Match Girls' Strike: Bryant and May in the 1890s'. *Victorian Studies*, 26:1 (1982), 7–31.

Scarisbrick, Diana. *Rings: Jewelry of Power, Love and Loyalty*. London: Thames and Hudson, 2007.

Schechner, Richard. *Performance Studies: An Introduction*, second edition. London: Routledge, 2006.

Schwartz, Alexandra. 'Surely They Jest'. *Rise Up! The Women's Marches around the World*. New York: Condé Nast, 2017, 80–81.

Schwarz, Birgit. '"Long Live (Occasionally) Tendency in Art!" Dix and the Dialectics of Modernism'. *Otto Dix and the New Objectivity*. Edited by Ulricke Groos and Nils Büttner. Stuttgart: Kunstmuseum Stuttgart, 2012, 62–71.

Schyberg, Birgitta. '"Gustaf Wasa" as Theatre Propaganda'. *Gustavian Opera: An Interdisciplinary Reader in Swedish Opera, Dance and Theatre 1771–1809*. Edited by Inger Mattson. Uppsala: Almqvist and Wiksell Tryckeri, 1990, 293–322.

Scott, James C. *Domination and the Arts of Resistance: Hidden Transcripts*. New Haven and London: Yale University Press, 1990.

Sender, Rav Yitzchak. *The Commentators' Al Hanissim: Insights on the Sages on Purim and Chanukah*. Israel: Feldheim Publishers, 2000.

Sennett, Richard. *The Fall of Public Man*. London: Penguin Books, [Alfred A. Knopf, 1974] 2002.

Sell, Cathy. 'Manga Translation and Interculture'. *Mechademia*, 6 (2011), 93–108.

Shakespeare, William. 'Twelfth Night'. *William Shakespeare's Complete Works*. Edited by Jonathan Bate and Eric Rasmussen. Basingstoke: Macmillan, 2007.

Shope, Bradley. 'Masquerading Sophistication: Fancy Dress Balls of Britain's Raj'. *The Journal of Imperial and Commonwealth Studies*, 39:3 (2011), 375–392.

Silver, Larry. *Pieter Bruegel*. New York & London: Abbeville Press Publishers, 2011.

Simms, Norman. 'Ned Ludd's Mummers Play'. *Folklore*, 89:2 (1978), 166–178.

Skal, David J. *Death Makes a Holiday: A Cultural History of Halloween*. London and New York: Bloomsbury, 2002.

Smith, E.A. *George IV*. New Haven and London: Yale University Press, 1999.

Soldene, Emily. Untitled article. *The Age*, 4 September 1897, 13.

Spencer, Elaine Glovka. 'Custom, Commerce, and Contention: Rhenish Carnival Celebrations, 1890–1914', *German Studies Review*, 20:3 (1997), 323–341.

Spender, Stephen. *The Temple*. London: Faber and Faber, 1988.

Stallybrass, Peter and Allon White. *The Politics and Poetics of Transgression*. Ithaca, New York: Cornell University Press, 1986.

Staples, Louis. 'Sheffield Pride Criticised for Calling Parade 'Celebration, Not Protest', *Indy100*. 10 May 2018. https://www.indy100.com/article/sheffield-pride-lgbt-rights-protest-celebration-placards-offence-8344621.

Starobinski, Jean. *Portrait de l'artist en saltimbanque*. Paris: Gallimard, 1970 [2013].

Steele, Valerie, ed. *A Queer History of Fashion: From the Closet to the Catwalk*. New Haven & London: Yale University Press, 2013.

Stevenson, Sara and Helen Bennett, eds. *Van Dyck in Check Trousers: Fancy Dress in Art and Life*. Glasgow: Bell & Bain Ltd, 1978.

Stollberg-Rilinger, Barbara. 'Symbolische Kommunikation in der Vormoderne: Begriffe-Thesen Forschungsperpektiven'. *Zeitschrift für Historiche Forschung*, 31 (2004), 489–527.

Stoyle, Mark. 'Give Mee a Souldier's Coat': Female Cross-Dressing during the English Civil War'. *History*, 103:1, 2018, 5–26.

Strasdin, Kate. *Inside the Royal Wardrobe: A Dress History of Queen Alexandra*. London: Bloomsbury Academic, 2017.

Stratmann, Francis Henry and Henry Bradley. *A Middle English Dictionary: Containing Words Used by English Writers from the Twelfth to the Fifteenth Century*. Oxford: Clarendon Press, 1963.

Strutt, Joseph. *A Complete View of the Dress and Habits of the People of England, from the Establishment of the Saxons in Britain to the Present Time*, 2 vols. London: J. Nichols, 1796.

Syson, Luke, Sheena Wagstaff, Emerson Bowyer and Brinda Kumar, eds. *Like Life: Sculpture, Color, and the Body*. New Haven and London: Yale University Press, 2018.

Tacitus, *The Annals*. Translated by Alfred Jacob Church and William Jackson Brodribb. London: E. Clay, Sons and Taylor, 1876.

Taylor, D.J. *Bright Young People: The Rise and Fall of a Generation, 1918–1940*. London: Vintage Books, 2008.

Taylor, Michael Thomas., Annette F. Timm and Rainer Herrn, eds. *Not Straight from Germany: Sexual Publics and Sexual Citizenship since Magnus Hirschfeld*. Ann Arbor: University of Michigan Press, 2017.

Teal, Donn. *The Gay Militants: How Liberation Began in America, 1969–1971*. New York: St Martin's Press, 1971.

Theis, Wolfgang and Andreas Sternweiler, 'Alltag im Kaiserreich und in der Weimar Republic'. *Eldorado: Homosexuelle Frauen und Männer in Berlin 1850–1950: Geschichte, Alltag und Kultur*. Berlin: Frölich und Kaufmann, 1984, 48–73.

Theis, Wolfgang and Andreas Sternweiler. 'Anders als die Andern: Geschichte eines Filmskandals', *Eldorado: Homosexuelle Frauen und Männer in Berlin 1850–1950: Geschichte, Alltag und Kultur*. Berlin: Frölich und Kaufmann, 1984, 28–30.

Thomas, A. 'Fancy Dress Escapism Is Big Business'. *The Sydney Morning Herald*, 18 June 1982, 15.

Thomas, Dana. *Gods and Kings: The Rise and Fall of Alexander McQueen and John Galliano*. London: Allen Lane, 2015.

Thomas, Keith. *Religion and the Decline of Magic: Studies in Popular Belief in Sixteenth- and Seventeenth-Century England*. London: Penguin Books, 1971.

Thomson, Richard. *Seurat's Circus Sideshow*. New York: Metropolitan Museum of Art, 2017.

Topley, Sophia. 'The Devonshire House Ball', *House Style: Five Centuries of Fashion at Chatsworth*. Edited by Laura Burlington and Hamish Bowles. New York: Skira Rizzoli, 2017, 122–139.

Tree, Vix. 'Bullying in Cosplay', 3 November 2015. www.washingtonpost.co.uk/vix-tree/bullying-in-cosplay_b_6841674.html.

Trentmann, Frank. *Empire of Things: How We Became a World of Consumers, from the Fifteenth Century to the Twenty First*. London: Allen Lane, 2016.

Tseëlon, Efrat. Introduction: Masquerade and Identities'. *Masquerade and Identities: Essays on Gender, Sexuality and Marginality*. Edited by Efrat Tseëlon. London: Routledge, 2001, 1–17.

Turner, Victor. *From Ritual to Theatre: The Human Seriousness of Play*. New York: PAJ Publications, 1982.

Turner, Victor. *The Anthropology of Performance*. New York: PAJ Publications, 1987.

Tselos, Susan Elizabeth. 'Creolised Costumes for Rara, Haiti'. *Berg Encyclopedia of World Dress and Fashion: Latin America and the Caribbean*. Edited by Margot Blum Schevill. Oxford: Bloomsbury Academic, 2005, 257–263.

Turner, Victor. *The Ritual Process: Structure and Anti-Structure*. New Brunswick & London: Aldine Transaction, 2008.

Tweedle, Neil and Michael Kallenbach. 'Prince Harry Faces Outcry at Nazi Outfit', *The Telegraph*. 14 January 2005. https://www.telegraph.co.uk/news/uknews/1481148/Prince-Harry-faces-outcry-at-Nazi-outfit.html.

Tyerman, Christopher. *God's War: A New History of the Crusades*. London: Allen Lane, 2006.

U.S. Congress, *Testimony Taken by the Joint Select Committee on the Condition of Affairs in the Late Insurrectionary States …*, 13 vols. Washington: Government Printing Office, 1872.

Underdown, David. *Revel, Riot and Rebellion: Popular Politics and Culture in England 1603–1660*. Oxford: Oxford University Press, 1985.

Vaclavik, Kiera. 'World Book Day and Its Discontents: The Cultural Politics of Book-Based Fancy Dress'. *The Journal of Popular Culture*, 52:3 (July, 2019), 582–605.

Valente, Claire. *The Theory and Practice of Revolt in Medieval England*. London: Routledge, 2003.

Van Dyke, James A. 'Otto Dix's Folk Culture'. *Otto Dix and the New Objectivity*. Edited by Ulricke Groos and Nils Büttner. Stuttgart: Kunstmuseum Stuttgart, 2012, 84–97.

Van Horn, Jennifer. 'The Mask of Civility: Portraits of Colonial Women and the Transatlantic Masquerade'. *American Art*, 23: 3 (2009), 8–35.

Vanderbilt Balsan, Consuelo. *The Glitter and the Gold: The American Duchess – in her Own Words*. London: Hodder & Stoughton [1953] 2012.

Wallace, Gail and Jeri B. Williams. 'Bidjogo'. *I Am Not Myself: The Art of African Masquerade*. Edited by Herbert M. Cole. Los Angeles: Museum of Cultural History, 1985, 40.

Weitz, Eric D. *Weimar Germany: Promise and Tragedy*. Princeton: Princeton University Press, 2007.

Welsford, Enid. *The Court Masque: A Study in the Relationship between Poetry & the Revels*. New York: Russell & Russell Inc., 1962.

Wertheim, Bonnie. 'All the Good Pups at the Halloween Dog Parade', *The New York Times*. 23 October 2017. www.nytimes.com/2017/10/23/style/halloween-dog-parade.html.

Winge, Thérèsa. 'Costuming the Imagination: Origins of Anime and Manga Cosplay'. *Mechademia*, 1 (2006), 65–76.

Winge, Thérèsa. 'Undressing and Dressing Loli: A Search for the Identity of the Japanese Lolita'. *Mechademia*, 3 (2008), 47–63.

Winge, Thérèsa. *Body Style*. London: Berg, 2012.

Winge, Thérèsa. *Costuming Cosplay: Dressing the Imagination*. London: Bloomsbury, 2019.

Whisnaut, Clayton J. *Queer Identities and Politics in Germany: A History 1880–1945*. New York and York: Harrington Park Press, 2016.

White, Rachel E., Emily O. Prager, Catherine Schaefer, Ethan Kross, Angela L. Duckworth and Stephanie M. Carlson. 'The "Batman Effect": Improving Perseverance in Young Children'. *Child Development*, 88:5 (2017), 1563–1573.

Wijs, Sonja. 'Kavat Mask'. *PowerMask: The Power of Masks*. Edited by Patrick Lennon. Tielt: Lannoo Publishers, 2017, 70.

Wikander, Matthew H. 'Historical Vision and Dramatic Historiography: Strindberg's "Gustav III" in Light of Shakespeare's "Julius Caesar" and Corneille's "Cinna"'. *Scandinavian Studies*, 62:1 (1990), 123–129.

Wild, Benjamin L. 'The Siege of Kenilworth Castle, 1266'. *English Heritage Historical Review* 5. 2010, 13–23.

Wild, Benjamin L. 'A Captive King: Henry III between the Battles of Lewes and Evesham, 1264–5'. *Thirteenth Century England XIII: Proceedings of the Paris Conference 2009*. Edited by Janet Burton, Frédérique Lachaud, Phillipp Schofield, Karen Stober, Björn Weiler. Woodbridge: The Boydell Press, 2011, 41–56.

Wild, Benjamin L. 'The Civilizing Process and Sartorial Studies'. *Clothing Cultures*, 1:3 (2014), 213–224.

Wild, Benjamin L. *A Life in Fashion: The Wardrobe of Cecil Beaton*. London: Thames and Hudson, 2016.

Wild, Benjamin L. 'Clothing Royal Bodies: Changing Attitudes to Royal Dress and Appearance from the Middle Ages to Modernity', *The Routledge History of Monarchy*. Edited by Elena Woodacre, Lucinda H.S. Dean, Chris Jones, Russell E. Martin and Zita Eva Rohr. London: Routledge, 2019, 390–408.

Wild, Benjamin L. 'Romantic Recreations: Remembering Stuart Monarchy in Nineteenth-Century Fancy Dress Entertainments'. *Remembering Queens and Kings in Early Modern England and France: Reputation, Reinterpretation, Reincarnation*. Edited by Estelle Paranque. New York: Palgrave Macmillan, 2019.

Willett, Graham. *Living Out Loud: A History of Gay and Lesbian Activism in Australia*. St Leonards: Allen & Unwin, 2000.

Williams, Daniel. 'Simon de Montfort and His Adherents', *England in the Thirteenth Century*. Edited by W.M. Ormrod. Woodbridge: The Boydell Press, 1985, 166–177.

Wills, Garry. *Making Make-Believe Real: Politics as Theater in Shakespeare's Time*. New Haven and London: Yale University Press, 2014.

Wills, John. 'Voltaic Peoples'. *I Am Not Myself: The Art of African Masquerade*. Edited by Herbert M. Cole. Los Angeles: Museum of Cultural History, 1985, 34.

Wilson, A.N. *The Victorians*. London: Arrow Books, 2002.

Wilson, John F., Anthony Webster and Rachel Vorberg-Rugh. *Building Co-operation: A Business History of The Co-operative Group, 1863–2013*. Oxford: Oxford University Press, 2013.

Wolff, Norma H. 'Egungun Costuming in Abeokuta'. *African Arts*, 15:3 (1982), 66–71, 91.

Woodcock, Norman and Susan Burnett. *On That Day I Left My Boyhood Behind*. Bromley: Acorn Independent Press, 2014.

Young, Alan. *Tudor and Jacobean Tournaments*. London: George Philip, 1987.

Zealand, Steven. *Sailors and Sexual Identity: Crossing the Line between "Straight" and "Gay" in the U.S. Navy*. New York: Harrington Press, 1995.

Zemon Davis, Natalie. 'The Reasons of Misrule: Youth Groups and Charivaris in Sixteenth-Century France'. *Past & Present* 50 (1971), 41–75.

Zucker, Wolgang M. 'The Image of the Clown'. *The Journal of Aesthetics and Art Criticism*, 12:3 (1954), 310–317.

INDEX